ook on
hemen

NESSELRODE AND THE RUSSIAN RAPPROCHEMENT
WITH BRITAIN, 1836–1844

Count Karl Robert Nesselrode (1780–1862), by Sir Thomas Lawrence. Copyright reserved. Reproduced by permission of Her Majesty the Queen.

Nesselrode

and the

Russian Rapprochement

with Britain, 1836-1844

Harold N. Ingle

UNIVERSITY OF CALIFORNIA PRESS
BERKELEY · LOS ANGELES · LONDON

University of California Press
Berkeley and Los Angeles, California

University of California Press, Ltd.
London, England

Copyright © 1976, by
The Regents of the University of California

ISBN 0–520–02795–7
Library of Congress Catalog Card Number: 74–79764
Printed in the United States of America
Designed by Dave Comstock

For my parents

Contents

Preface

RARELY HAS Russia reached out to the leading Western power in a spirit of open cooperation comparable with that in which she extended a hand to Britain under Nesselrode's influence. The whole episode contrasted strikingly with an undercurrent of rivalry, keenly felt on both sides—a rivalry that in Russia stimulated strong official and intellectual reactions to Britain as the archetype of modern Western material power and progress. This first book devoted to Nesselrode, and first study of the rapprochement itself, presents a montage of extensively documented evidence accounting for the exceptional character of the episode and placing it among the important events in the history of Russian relations with the West.

It is intended to revitalize some of the provocative questions that Nesselrode and his policy posed for Russians. Together Russia and Britain reopened the European concert by treaties in 1840 and 1841 that placed the straits of the Bosphorus and the Dardanelles under international control, closing them to Russian warships. Was this not the height of folly, Nesselrode's Russian opponents asked? Was it not the key to Russia's vulnerability at Sevastopol? A Russian solution to the Eastern Question would have closed the straits to rivals and given Russia free access to the Mediterranean. The folly was attributed to the prolonged influence of a personality and a policy which, as the poet Tyutchev alleged in "Count K. V. Nesselrode," contradicted the immutable laws of Russia's history and could not conceivably interfere with her universal destiny. The significance of the rapprochement is thus seen in light of its ultimate failure, and of reactions in which romantic ideology supported a realistic rejection of Nesselrode's approach, signaling a shift from classic diplomacy toward modern, nationalistic Realpolitik.

History has not been generous to Nesselrode. Mentioned in numerous works, he is usually subject to a perfunctory condemnation in one of two prominent ways: the Russian interpretation, tsarist and Soviet alike, reveals continuity with the initial, nationalistic reaction under Nicholas I, and faults him for failing to meet the British challenge squarely, to the detriment of real national interests and security. The Western interpretation, common to a wide range of viewpoints, is that far from betraying Russia he spinelessly served the autocrat and a traditional policy truly Russian in its aggressive menace to Europe. A third, somewhat antiquated interpretation, offers greater precision and balance in the treatment of diplomatic events and more sympathetically credits his ideals and principles despite his failure; represented by a mere handful of scholars, for example F. F. Martens, it lapsed early in the present century.

My approach is closer to the third school in some respects. I am more interested in events and circumstances, and in accurately presenting the evidence, than in rationalistic abstractions or sweeping explanations of historical processes. The portrait I offer is sympathetic, although it should be noted that this results from methodology, not commitment. I have attempted to convey a congenial understanding of Nesselrode's outlook and political philosophy, allowing a grasp of his diplomacy in terms of his own values and frame of reference, without demolishing them a priori in terms of our own. While I believe this conduces to a fresh, open-ended awareness of the nettlesome questions raised, I am not playing the devil's advocate. Whatever relevance may be found here belongs to the human effort to understand history.

It is appropriate to mention the generous assistance and many kindnesses received both during the graduate studies in international politics and history that led to this work and in its actual preparation. First, I wish to express my gratitude to my teachers at the Johns Hopkins University and the University of California, and to mention in particular my special debts to Professor Robert M. Slusser and Professor Robert W. Tucker during my stay at Hopkins, and to Professor Nicholas V. Riasanovsky at Berkeley and Professor C. Bickford O'Brien at Davis. The research was greatly facilitated by privileges of access to important collections of private papers, state documents, and rare books, granted by the British Museum and Public Record Office in London, the Ministère des Affaires Étrangères at the Quai d'Orsay, and the Finnish State Archive and the University of Helsinki Library, by the University of California Library at Berkeley and Davis, especially in obtaining materials on loan, and by the considerable advantage of nearly a year's study in Finland made possible by a grant from the University of California. Finally, I would like to say that this book would not exist without the material help and encouragement I have received from members of my family, my friends, and especially from Gundbor—a superb secretary and editor, and indefatigable ally in adventures in various corners of the world. I alone am responsible for the contents of these pages.

H. N. INGLE

November 1974
Creston, British Columbia

A Note on Documentation

DATES ARE GIVEN new style in the text and in original forms (whether old style or new style or both) in footnotes. Extracts from Crown-copyright records in the Public Record Office are reproduced with the permission of the Controller, H. M. Stationary Office. Other extracts from documents are reproduced with the permission of the British Museum and Library, and the Ministère des Affaires Étrangères of France. The following main abbreviations and short titles are used in the notes:

Lettres et papiers: A. D. Nesselrode, ed., K. R. Nesselrode, *Lettres et papiers du Chancelier comte de Nesselrode, 1760–1856* (Paris, 1904–1912), 11 vols.

FO: Foreign Office Archive, Great Britain, Public Record Office, London.

BMAddMSS: Additional Manuscripts, British Museum, London.

MAE: Archives du Ministère des Affaires Étrangères (Quai d'Orsay), Paris.

SIRIO: *Sbornîk Imperatorskogo Russkogo Istoricheskogo Obshchestva* (St. Petersburg, 1867–1917), 148 vols.

Recueil: F. F. Martens, *Recueil des Traités et conventions conclus par la Russie avec les puissances étrangères* (St. Petersburg, 1874–1909), 15 vols.

Nouveau Recueil: G. F. Martens, *Nouveau Recueil des principaux Traités,* etc. (Göttingen, 1817–1842), 17 vols.

I. Preliminary Notes

A German in Russian Service

GERMAN BY BIRTH, raised and educated in Frankfurt and Berlin, Count Karl Robert Nesselrode served Russia for fifty-nine years under five rulers, and in a career marked by consistent success rose from midshipman in 1797 to Chancellor of the Empire in 1845. He retired in 1856 at the age of seventy-five, after forty years at the head of the Ministry of Foreign Affairs. His prominent role in the government and a half-century of diplomacy made him an outstanding statesman.

But he did not win an esteemed place in Russian history. As a foreigner and protagonist of the European orientation that Alexander I imparted in foreign policy, he was a controversial figure, opposed by nationalistic Russians throughout his long tenure in office. Afterward he became a symbol of diplomatic errors held responsible for the weakness and vulnerability demonstrated by Russia's defeat in the Crimean War. Tsarist officials later denounced the "cosmopolitan type of Russian diplomacy practiced during the Nesselrodian epoch,"[1] and patriotic Russians of various convictions—liberal, conservative, romantic and realistic, reactionary and revolutionary—alike rejected the approach that Nesselrode had carried over from Alexander's reign to that of Nicholas I in 1825–1855. The foremost historian specializing in foreign relations under Nicholas I, S. S. Tatishchev, condemned Nesselrode as a spokesman for what he termed the "political system of the Holy Alliance"—denoting not merely the idealistic statement of principles that Russia, Austria, and Prussia signed in 1815, or Alexander's dream of Christian brotherhood and unity, but all of the engagements Russia had entered in pursuit of closer relations with the West, including her participation in the major efforts to institute a classic European system—the congresses and the concert.[2] The worst blunders nationalists associated with Nesselrode's influence were cooperation with Austria, since they regarded Metternich's conservative foreign policy as antithetical to Russian interests, and with Britain, in their estimation Russia's foremost rival. For at least twenty years after the war, the case of Britain, the most liberal, progressive, industrialized, imperialistic Western power, provided the main object-lesson in the folly of impossible ideals.[3] Even

1. A. P. I. (Izvolsky?), "Zametka o D. P. Severine," *Russkii arkhiv* (1899), vol. 2: 447. Severin is credited with loyalty to the traditions of Russian diplomacy, abandoned by Alexander I, while Nesselrode is identified with the predominant "cosmopolitan" approach of a whole "epoch," which, the article asserts, has been condemned by the "final judgment" of history. The term "Nesselrodian epoch" held special significance: "S imenem grafa K. V. Nessel'rode sviazana tselaia epokha v istorii russkoi diplomatii. . . . Nessel'rode iavlialsia po svoemu zvaniiu otvetstvennym rukovoditelem russkoi politiki, vyrazitelem eia chaianii i idealov. . . . Byt mozhet dazhe, i v nastoiashchee vremia nashe ministerstvo inostrannykh del ne vpolne osvobodilos ot nekotorykh perezhitkov Nessel'rodovskoi epokhi." E. S. Shumigorskii, "Odin iz revnostneishikh nasaditelei nemetskago zasil'ia v Rossii. Graf Karl Vasil'evich Nessel'rode," *Russkaia starina* (1915), vol. 161: 160.

2. Cf. S. S. Tatishchev, *Vneshniaia politika Imperatora Nikolaia Pervago: vvedenie v istoriiu vneshnikh snoshenii Rossii v epokhu Sevastopol'skoi voiny* (St. Petersburg, 1887), ch. 1, "The Political System of the Holy Alliance"; *Diplomaticheskiia besedy o vneshnei politike Rossii. 1890* (St. Petersburg, 1898), 71.

3. An important attempt to treat the problems of competition realistically is M. A. Terent'ev, *Rossiia i Angliia v bor'be za rynki* (St. Petersburg, 1876), note "Chto nam delat?" 212–264. For a sharp denunciation of the "world-exalted" policy of the period before the Crimean War for its economic effects, cf. V. A. Pol'etika, "Po

men who had sympathized with Nesselrode's desire for bipartisanship, as an alternative to meeting the British challenge head-on, realized that he had made a mistake. "Great historical lessons have taught us that we cannot count on the friendship of Great Britain, and that she can strike us by means of continental alliances while we cannot reach her anywhere," observed Alexander Meyendorff, who, as Nesselrode had, doubted Russia's capability to surpass Britain, particularly in industrial development.[4] After the Congress of Berlin in 1878 when Germany loomed on the horizon as another contestant for European supremacy interested in containing Russian ambitions in the Balkans and Near East, "Germanism" received additional emphasis as a source of the earlier errors, especially in the increasingly influential Pan-Slav interpretation, although the dangers of naive Anglophilism were recalled, for example, in connection with the rapprochement of the 1830's and 40's, on the "jubilee" of Sevastopol's fall in 1905, when Britain supported Japan in a war that led again to the destruction of Russian naval power.[5] At the beginning of the war in 1914, Nesselrode was remembered as "one of the most zealous propagators of German influence in Russia" —virtually a traitor as the Pan-Slavs had held since the 1840's.[6] The extreme nationalist interpretation made a smooth transition from tsarist to Soviet ideology, amplified more than altered by Russia's convulsive withdrawal from the European paroxysm in 1917.[7] Soviet scholars such as E. V. Tarle and F. I. Kozhevnikov

---

povodu 'Ekonomicheskoi Provalov,'" *Russkii arkhiv* (1887), vol. 8: 535–540.
4. A. F. Meyendorff, ed., *Correspondance diplomatique de M. de Staal* (Paris, 1929), vol. 2: 26.
5. Hence the publication in 1905 of an anonymous poem written during the Crimean War, with notes stating that the following lines refer to the bid for close trade relations with Britain in the early 1840's: "My znaem, tut ne Turkakh delo: / Vam Turki lish odin predlog. / Net, vam Rossiia nadoela, / Ona vam v gorle poperek. / Posmotrim! My dlia vas ne nuzhny-l', / A vy ne nuzhny vovse nam. / . . . / Ne nuzhny nam prozhiny vashi / I vse mashiny . . . Vzdor kakoi!" A. Mozherovskii, ed., "Nastroenie russkago obshchestva vo vremia Sevastopol'skoi . . . ," *Russkii arkhiv* (1905), vol. 2: 537.
6. Shumigorskii, "Nessel'rode," *op. cit.*, 160–161.
7. In R. C. Tucker's words, "Russia's mighty act of secession from the Europe-centered world order of the nineteenth century." "Russia, the West, and World Order," *World Politics* (October 1959), vol. 12, no. 1: 19: Yet in many respects Russia's withdrawal was brought about by the collapse of such order.

have shown remarkable fidelity to Tatishchev's precedent.[8] Nesselrode had long epitomized the rootless, cosmopolitan non-
entity, the foreigner wielding influence dangerous to Russian security. Now, supported by the Marxist-Leninist denunciation of
"cosmopolitanism" that serves as rationale for rebellion against
the "burdensome legacy of tsarist Russia's past, when the ruling
classes bowed down to the West," Soviet history finds him guilty
of having "sacrificed Russia's national interests" in the quest for
peace and harmony with the Western powers, particularly in
relations with Austria and Britain.[9]

To understand Nesselrode's role, then, we begin with the
fact that he was a foreigner, an émigré, a "German Russian." But
in a country in which the Germans comprised one of the important national minorities, this was not an exceptional situation.
Nesselrode took his place in a community that was numerous,
clannish, ethnocentric, and readily stereotyped by its "true Russian" critics and accused of cultural alienation. Yet as a national
minority, the Germans were different: almost synonymous with
the "foreign community" of Westerners, they were a perspica-
cious, even privileged minority that provided the government with
many officials and military officers, and the society at large with
what frequently were looked upon as typical Western tradesmen,
entrepreneurs, capitalists, private farmers, doctors, teachers, engineers, and other professionals. To some Russians, the capital at
St. Petersburg was little more than an artificial, luxurious haven
for a government of foreigners, led by Germans, divorced from
the roots of society, the masses, and the heartland with Moscow
and the Kremlin at its center. Even when the Germans were re-
sented and subjected to repressive "Russification," however, as
they were increasingly under Nicholas I, they also were accepted
as a necessary evil. "And not only in the government, but we
ourselves have grown so accustomed to the notion that Russia
cannot be governed without the Germans that we cannot imagine
the Russian ministries and the Russian army without Nesselrode,
Kankrin, Diebitsch, Benckendorff, Adlerberg—we cannot!" pro-

8. Cf. E. V. Tarle, *Krymskaia voina* (Moscow, 1950), 2 vols.; F. I.
   Kozhevnikov, *Russkoe gosudarstvo i mezhdunarodnoe pravo (do
   XX veka)* (Moscow, 1947).
9. "Kosmopolitizm," *Bol'shaia sovetskaia entsikopediia* (2nd. ed., Moscow, 1949–1958), vol. 13: 113–114; "Nessel'rode, Karl Vasil'evich,"
   ibid., vol. 29: 494.

tested Herzen's journal *Kolokol*, an opponent of "Germanism."[10] The thousands of Germans that had moved to Russia in the *Auswanderung* of the previous century seemed to have been the vanguard of an "invasion."[11] If they had been mere reminders of imitativeness in style and useful reform of the type advanced by Peter the Great, which in the eighteenth century had enhanced national pride and power,[12] in the nineteenth they stood for a willingness to embrace the West in humble backwardness, as if it would be better to be the provincial backyard of Europe than to be independent and truly Russian. Nesselrode, recognized mainstay of the German faction in Nicholas's government, was justly accused of this form of condescension. But nothing in his background and upbringing had prepared him to believe that Russia was superior to the West, or that the walled-in insularity apparently vital to her independence was preferable to lively intercourse with the West.

Nesselrode's mature outlook reflected several outstanding influences in his early years, the more so because he was a conservative given to nostalgic longing for the eighteenth-century world of his childhood. His father Wilhelm—an enlightened, widely-traveled, Catholic Westphalian—was hardly one to instil patriotic feeling for Russia, although he happened to be employed by Catherine as Envoy to Portugal when Karl was born in Lisbon on December 14, 1780; nor was his mother Louise, a Protestant from Frankfurt, or her wealthy banking family— Gontard (the same that employed the poet Hölderlin)—which helped to raise the boy from the age of six when his mother died. His parents, uniting a declining feudal nobility that was in step with the Enlightenment yet traced its title and heritage back to the Holy Roman Empire, with an ambitious, enterprising, capitalistic upper middle-class family, brought together two segments of society that contributed to the introduction of the word "cosmopolitan" into modern usage during the same period. If Nesselrode, like his father, considered himself German even while

10. "Russkie nemtsy i nemetskie russkie," *Kolokol* (15 October 1859), no. 54: 440.
11. Cf. F. F. Vigel, *La Russie envahie par les allemands* (Paris and Leipzig, 1844).
12. Cf. H. Rogger, *National Consciousness in Eighteenth-Century Russia* (Cambridge, Mass., 1960), ch. 1, "The Government of Foreigners."

in Russian service, it was not in the romantic, nationalist sense of the nineteenth century, but in the "universalist" sense, which Srbik also has noted in Metternich (and in both cases may owe something to similar Rhenish Catholic ancestry and values). Wilhelm had looked to the whole of Europe as a field of opportunity when it came time to make his fortune, and had served not only Catherine, but the Elector of the Palatinate, and the Austrian, Dutch, French, and Prussian courts as well. He had been so affected by life at Versailles and Paris, where he mingled with the "encyclopedists and *philosophes*," that when he took up residence at Berlin, Frederick the Great found him "more French than German."[13] Then too, he was Anglophile, in the manner of Voltaire and Montesquieu, and as his son did later, he acquired a knowledge of the English language and read the major English works. When he retired in Frankfurt at the end of the century, he had visited Russia only briefly. Karl's relationship with his father was close, and the paternal influence, which extended to professional matters, undoubtedly was strong. But the unusual character of Nesselrode's background was nowhere more apparent than in his religious beliefs. He was baptized as an Anglican. He later explained this by saying that his mother (Lutheran in a family also having Jewish and Catholic branches), wished him to be Protestant and made use of the only such clergy available in Lisbon. To Russians this seemed an inadequate explanation. What was his father's attitude, with an archbishop of Cologne in his family? And why did Nesselrode continue with this faith, taking communion at the chapel of the British Embassy in Petersburg? His wife Marie was Russian Orthodox, his son Dmitry Greek. "As for me, I am *Anglican*," he proclaimed.[14] In Russia, where the church was an arm of the state, it seemed logical that he should be British too. According to one story, he had been baptized at birth on board a British ship, and "might therfore be claimed by Great Britain, since he was born under her flag."[15] But an explanation not readily seen by official na-

13. Nesselrode, "Autobiographie," *Lettres et papiers*, vol. 2: 17–18.
14. Nesselrode to Meyendorff (13 April 1840), *Lettres et papiers*, vol. 8: 21.
15. I. G. Golovin, *Russia Under the Autocrat Nicholas the First* (London, 1846; reprint, New York, 1970), 312. Golovin was employed by Nesselrode for awhile prior to the publication of this book, and in fact defected after a disagreement with him.

tionalists rests with a tendency to regard the Reformation as superficial, not profoundly divisive—its conflicts mere cracks in the surface of Christendom, as Nesselrode put it—and to reach for a "true catholicism" compatible with various forms of worship, without yielding to the intellectual impulse to resolve inconsistencies. In Russian context, the same fundamental attitude could be applied to the schism and the doctrine of the Third Rome, and it lay behind the spirit of the Holy Alliance. A Jesuit scholar interested in Nesselrode's diplomacy in behalf of relations between Eastern and Western Christians has observed that the "bizarre diversity" in his family background led him to assume that different religions could exist harmoniously in Russia. "To live in peace, that was the ideal; and to achieve it, one must make reciprocal concessions and sacrifices, and not demand the impossible"—the world's conversion to one's own beliefs.[16]

In 1796 Nesselrode graduated from a gymnasium in Berlin. He wanted to be a naval officer, and as a favor to his father Catherine granted him an appointment as midshipman in the Baltic Fleet. Enthusiastic, ambitious, and self-disciplined, he soon advanced to midshipman Flag-Adjutant of the fleet. But his boyhood dreams gave way in the face of chronic seasickness leading to a more serious illness that put him ashore. Six months after his arrival in Russia, Catherine died and was succeeded by her son Paul, whose preference for Germans in the government contributed to his unpopularity among Russians. For Nesselrode, however, the royal bias made it opportune to remain in Russia. In his words, Paul I, "learning that I had been raised in Berlin, and being as he was, asked me if I would like to join the army."[17] He selected the horse guards, and again showed unusual promise. He was chosen to accompany Paul to Moscow for the coronation, and a few months later set out with his regiment to support the Second Coalition against Napoleon. But he was not destined to fight. Paul called him back to serve as an aide. In 1800 he was promoted to Chamberlain, and by the time of the palace revolution and Paul's murder in 1801 he was contemplating a career as a diplomat. His father opposed the decision at first, and by one account remarked: "He wants to be a diplomat but does not

---

16. A. Boudou, S.J., *Le Saint-Siège et la Russie: Leurs relations diplomatiques au XIX siècle 1814–1847* (Paris, 1922), 491.
17. Nesselrode, "Autobiographie," 21–22.

have the necessary qualifications. He does not have the devil in him, and without the devil a diplomat will go nowhere."[18]

Nesselrode took his first post at Berlin soon after the accession of Alexander I. In the following fifty-five years his father's observation was borne out in a sense, because Nesselrode proved that he lacked something, perhaps a Faustian trait, which might have elevated him to true greatness. But he did build a career that was too striking to be written off to chance. He took an active part in nearly all of the major events of European diplomacy from the Treaty of Tilsit to the Crimean War; he held on to his position in the government against heavy opposition; he advanced steadily under two autocrats, Alexander and Nicholas I, whose temperaments were very different; and he influenced foreign policy at crucial moments. But in assessing his influence it must be realized that he worked quietly in the background, always subordinate both to Alexander, who was his own minister to a large extent, and to Nicholas, among the most absolute of nineteenth-century autocrats.[19]

Nesselrode was pragmatic. The qualities that held him in office for fifty years, when others such as Czartoryski and Capodistria passed from the scene too quickly to leave much more than regret for what might have been, were simply the attributes of a good administrator. They were undramatic—the same he brought to bear in his much-loved game of whist—a precise mind, a reliable memory, a ready wit, and a "gift of concentration" that enabled him to "handle large quantities of business."[20] He struck Cobden as "like Metternich" more a master of "finesse and diplomacy, than as a man of genius."[21] Real genius required engagement, devotion to a cause in keeping with the spirit of the time, and while Nesselrode's ideals were noble and humanitarian, they were those of the *ancien régime*. If his "Germanism" infuriated Russians it was not because of any romantic affinity for

18. V. von Enze, "Iz dnevnik," *Russkii arkhiv* (1875), vol. 1: 350.
19. Cf. P. K. Grimsted, *The Foreign Ministers of Alexander I: Political Attitudes and the Conduct of Russian Diplomacy, 1801–1825* (Berkeley and Los Angeles, 1969); and N. V. Riasanovsky, *Nicholas I and Official Nationality in Russia, 1825–1855* (Berkeley and Los Angeles, 1959).
20. K. F. Vitzhum von Eckstädt, *St. Petersburg und London in den Jahren 1852–1864* (Stuttgart, 1886), vol. 1: 5.
21. From Cobden's diary of his journey to Russia, in J. Morley, *The Life of Richard Cobden* (London, 1881), vol. 1: 451.

a German Volksgeist, but because in "his style always sweet and measured" he was the cool, correct, methodical German bureaucrat whose diplomacy lacked panache and patriotic fervor.[22] But to his critics his manner was secondary; what he stood for was more objectionable. The early years of his career followed to some extent the vicissitudes of relations with France. On his first assignments at Berlin, Stuttgart, and in 1805–1806 as Secretary at the Russian Embassy at the Hague, he showed himself to be an enthusiast for alignment against Napoleon, and before long his own friendships and fortunes as well as his political philosophy were committed to it. While nationalistic Russians saw no fault in an accommodation which would have given the French Emperor free reign to settle his score in the West without Russian interference, from a conservative viewpoint it was vital, as Friedrich Gentz later told Nesselrode, to break the French "preponderance that has destroyed European equilibrium and makes it impossible to reestablish."[23] Nesselrode was elated by the formation of the Third Coalition in 1805 when Alexander appointed him as an aide. But the trail of defeats from Ulm to Friedland was discouraging. He stolidly endured the changes of men and policies which he regarded as consequences of retreat, and regretted the loss of Prince Adam Czartoryski, who had shown him kindness. After the Treaty of Tilsit, which he helped to compose but disliked, and the agreement with France in 1808, he was sent to Paris. The appointment, he recalled, "antagonized me more than it flattered me," and his reports "were hardly favorable to the alliance with France."[24] He found himself at odds with other Russians, now openly Francophile, who wanted the alliance because they expected Napoleon to support Russian conquests in the Near East and Asia. It was even said that he used his influence while functioning with Michael Speransky as an intermediary in the exchange between Alexander I and Talleyrand to help drive Russia and France into conflict. In any event, Russia's cooperation with France turned out entirely to his liking in that it demonstrated the value of things Russia lost—including the benefit of friendship and trade

22. Barante to Thiers (n.d. March 1836), *Souvenirs du baron de Barante, de l'Académie française 1782–1866* (Paris, 1890–1901), vol. 5: 326.
23. Gentz to Nesselrode (2 May 1813), *Lettres et papiers*, vol. 5: 86.
24. Nesselrode, "Autobiographie," 63.

with Britain. When he left Paris in 1811 he was convinced that war was as certain as Napoleon's urge to be dictator of Europe. En route to Petersburg he stopped at Vienna to try to convince Metternich of the need for a new alliance, but was sent away without "so much as a reassuring promise."[25] On his return to Russia, Alexander appointed him Secretary of State without portfolio.

It was also in 1811, however, that Nesselrode experienced a major setback for the policies he supported, in "the disgrace of my intimate friend Speransky . . . my principal benefactor with the Emperor." Speransky, with Nesselrode a protégé of Count Victor Kochubey, was disliked in nationalistic circles because as Alexander's main adviser he was advancing reforms that seemed to be carrying Russia away from the traditional pattern of tsarist autocracy, following Western examples in some institutions. Nesselrode regarded his fall as "an event that could only have a bad effect on my future." Some of his letters were found in Speransky's desk and brought to Alexander's attention, and for awhile he worried that he might suffer a similar fate. Speransky was a casualty of factional politics, a "victim of intrigue" by men Nesselrode felt were "acting in behalf of public opinion against the reforms," men who had "impressed His Majesty that on the eve of a war in which patriotism alone would be able to save the country it would be unwise to injure national feeling by keeping near him a man who might be accused of . . . treason." ("The voice of the people is the voice of God," said the chief spokesman against Speransky, the historian N. M. Karamzin in his "Memoir" of 1811 to Alexander. "No one will be able to persuade Russians that in matters of foreign policy the counselors of the Emperor have followed the principles of sincere, wise patriotism."[26]) He believed that Speransky's correspondence with the French government was innocent, and the innuendo of treason nonsense. Speransky had written merely to obtain information about French administration and had done little more as a result than use the Napoleonic Council of State as a model for the Russian Council of Empire, and "the plan

25. *Ibid.*, 74.
26. N. M. Karamzin, "A Memoir on Ancient and Modern Russia," R. Pipes, *Karamzin's Memoir on Ancient and Modern Russia* (Cambridge, Mass., 1959), 147.

Speransky's reforms embraced was far more vast," he said.[27]

The decisive moment in foreign policy came after Napoleon's retreat in 1812. "Russia was rid of her enemies," Nesselrode recalled, and "the next question was: Should we be content with the liberation of the fatherland or should we take the fortuitous opportunity to bring about that of Europe?"[28] Many Russians were not anxious to involve their country in the calamities that befell Western Europe, and Field Marshal M. I. Kutuzov spoke for them when he advised Alexander not to pursue Napoleon but to let the British deal with him as they would. There was no reason why Russia should be concerned with the outcome. "But the Emperor, inspired by great and noble sentiments, rejected this timid advice."[29]

Nesselrode's future was now allied with Russia's new role in Europe as a leader of the alliance, and with Alexander's inclination, unprecedented for a Russian ruler, to identify Russian interests with those of the European community. In 1813 he took part in the negotiations of the Breslau Convention and the treaty with Britain for subsidies, signing both. He also returned to Vienna to try once again to convince Metternich to join the new coalition, and after a difficult negotiation in which he was aided by Gentz's influence and by Metternich's ultimate failure to make a deal with Napoleon, he concluded the desired pact in 1813—the Treaty of Toeplitz. He attended the Council of Chatillon in February 1814, and in March signed the Treaty of Chaumont, by which the allied powers rejected a partition and agreed to restore the territorial status quo ante in France. With Talleyrand he drafted the proclamation issued on the allied entry into Paris, which promised to uphold a constitution if the French people wanted it. He took part in the negotiations for the first Treaty of Paris in May 1814, which anticipated the creation of a new order at a congress to be held in Vienna. In the same year Alexander gave him tentative charge of the ministry, with his former title, Secretary of State, and appointed him Chief Plenipotentiary in the Russian delegation to the Congress of Vienna.

At Vienna Nesselrode's role was auxiliary to that of Alexander I and the older and more experienced statesmen, although

27. Nesselrode, "Autobiographie," 75–76.
28. Nesselrode, "Autobiographie," 89.
29. *Ibid.*

he assumed a definite position on certain issues, and at one point suffered a momentary eclipse as a result of having disagreed with Alexander. A young man of thirty-three when the congress opened in September 1814, he was proud to take part in an event of such great importance—the creation of "the European political system," as Gentz said to him, intended to make possible the "ancient dream of the golden age, that of perpetual peace."[30]

That Nesselrode's conservatism allied him actively with the movement for European unity is well illustrated by his relationship with Gentz. The two met in Berlin soon after Gentz published his work *On the State of Europe Before and After the French Revolution* in 1801.[31] It was this essay which prompted Nesselrode to introduce himself to Gentz and initiated a friendship that endured for many years. "It is truly a masterpiece which can only pass on to posterity and be placed beside the works of Montesquieu, Blackstone, and Burke," Nesselrode commented, "an immense success, and from this moment Gentz became a most courageous defender of good principles." Among other things, he praised Gentz for drawing attention to "the mechanics of English administration" and "the English system of finance," which he considered superior.[32] But the main lesson of Gentz's work, the lesson to be taken to heart, was that the sordid turmoil and suffering caused by the French Revolution had touched all of Europe and revealed the error of regarding revolution in one country as an independent affair. The interests of any state, whatever the form of its political system, must be viewed as subordinate to the interests of the European commonweal. "It especially satisfies me that in each letter I receive new and flattering proof that our ideas about the general course of affairs are in perfect accord," Nesselrode told Gentz, and Gentz for his part affirmed that "There exist very few men to whom I feel as sincerely and profoundly attached as I do to you, and who better justify my existence than you do." It was Nesselrode who brought Gentz into

30. Gentz to Nesselrode (27 January 1818), *Lettres et papiers*, vol. 5: 292, 236.
31. Gentz, *Von dem politischen Zustande von Europa vor und nach der französischen Revolution* (Berlin, 1801). English translation: *On the State of Europe Before and After the French Revolution* (4th ed., London, 1803).
32. Nesselrode to M.-J.-W. Nesselrode (15 November 1801), *Lettres et papiers*, vol. 2: 153–154; Nesselrode, "Autobiographie," 34.

Alexander's counsels before the congress where Gentz played the most important role of his life, as "Secretary of Europe." By the end of 1815, they felt their task had been accomplished. "We have worked hard, and we have worked well," Gentz told Nesselrode; "I hope that by this arrangement, Europe, whatever her opinion of the foundation we have laid, will do us justice."[33] The Congress of Vienna marked the beginning of a new era requiring a new foreign policy for Russia. The renunciation of the foreign policy followed by Catherine the Great, now considered a traditional, imperialistic policy of aggrandizement, had been implicit all along. Nesselrode was not a man to serve such a policy. Mallet du Pan, a federalist he ranked with Burke and Gentz,[34] had warned in a work published in 1790 that it would be impossible to institute a classic system in Europe unless Russia abandoned her aggressive ways. Instead of conquering new territory, she would do better to divert her energy to the search for new markets, following the British example, since "British capitalists and mercantilists provide the main stimulus to Russian commerce and enliven its feeble circulation."[35] Gentz had said that Catherine's policy had acted against the interests of Europe hardly less than the policy Napoleon pursued, because it rested upon "mistaken ideas about the true interests and strength of nations."[36] In later years, one of the trademarks of Nesselrode's circle was the rejection of the foreign policy followed to the end of the eighteenth century, as expressed for example in the tutorial lessons prepared for the Tsarevich Alexander Nikolaevich in 1838.[37]

Nesselrode's Russian critics were correct in their allegations

33. Nesselrode to Gentz (26 March 1813), *Lettres et papiers*, vol. 5: 58; Gentz to Nesselrode (22 November 1815), *Lettres et papiers*, vol. 5: 233.
34. Nesselrode, "Autobiographie," 33.
35. F. Mallet du Pan, *Du péril de la balance politique ou exposé des causes qui l'ont altérée dans le Nord, depuis l'avènement de Catherine II au Trône de Russie* (Stockholm, 1790), 5, 130.
36. Gentz, *State of Europe*, 146.
37. E. P. von Brunnow, "Aperçu des transactions politiques du Cabinet de Russie" (1838), *SIRIO* (1881), vol. 31: 199. Nesselrode and Brunnow applauded Peter I and Catherine II for their Europeanizing domestic policies, but condemned their foreign policies. In this respect it was true that, "if Nesselrode insisted on anything with all of his energy, it was that he wanted to break away from the old tradition followed by Catherine II." Boudou, *Le Saint-Siège*, 412.

that he was closer to Metternich than to most Russian statesmen. The two men cooperated in diplomacy, and shared a similar background and philosophy. But there were obvious differences—for example, Nesselrode wholeheartedly backed the Holy Alliance whereas Metternich did not—that may have placed Nesselrode even closer to the classic principles Gentz espoused.[38] Gentz did not share Metternich's cynical disdain for the Holy Alliance. For good reason he regarded its ideals not merely as expressions of high-flown sentiment, but as political principles; he had provided part of the inspiration for it, and his famous "Project for the Declaration"—virtually the prologue for the Congress of Vienna—which moved Alexander I to tears when Gentz read it to him, has been aptly described as the Holy Alliance "stripped of its specific religious character."[39] The Holy Alliance was intended as a political instrument, as its Russian critics were painfully aware; its purpose was not to align the conservative states, but to provide a foundation for a united Europe, including Britain from the outset and eventually France. Gentz, along with Alexander and Nesselrode, was dismayed when Britain refused to join; Metternich was not, and assured Britain that his own participation was meaningless. In fact, from the alliance of Austria, Britain and France of January 3, 1815, onward, Metternich showed a reluctance to operate on the basis of an inclusive system that did not offer Austria a pivotal role with influence beyond her real power. This was astute statecraft, yet opposed alignments were inconsistent with a classic balance of power. "I am very fond of M. Metternich," Gentz confided to Nesselrode, "but I prefer liberty and a prosperous future for Europe."[40] Metternich, more realistic than Gentz and Nesselrode, probably did not fully share Nesselrode's confidence in "that power of union and concord which in our day has created a new political system."[41]

38. Although Gentz's relationship with Metternich is well known, his association of more than two decades with Nesselrode, which included employment as an adviser to the Russian Ministry of Foreign Affairs, has received close study for only one year. Cf. B. Leffmann, *Gentz und Nesselrode: Ein Beitrag zur diplomatischen Geschichte des Jahres 1813* (Bonn, 1911).

39. P. F. Reiff, *Friedrich Gentz* (Champaign-Urbana, 1912), 151.

40. Gentz to Nesselrode (16 April 1813), *Lettres et papiers*, vol. 5: 78.

41. Nesselrode to Seroskerken, Russian Envoy to the United States (1823), in W. Ford, "Genesis of the Monroe Doctrine," *Massachusetts Historical Society Proceedings*, 2nd. series (March 1901–February 1902, Boston), vol. 15: 402.

Alexander I was pleased with Nesselrode's performance at Vienna, and in 1816 he placed him in charge of the ministry with the title First Secretary of State. (Nesselrode was never Minister of Foreign Affairs.) [42] The ministry itself had been created in 1802 in the expectation that foreign relations would become more important than ever before. It was a larger, more complex institution than the college it replaced. It had its own Advisory Council, Chancellery, Department of Economics and Accounting, and Asiatic Department, and in addition to its own staff and the embassies and consulates abroad, which grew in number, it had charge of the State Archive and the archives of St. Petersburg and Moscow, and some special functions, such as handling communications between Russian Catholics and Uniats and the Vatican, and the publication of its own periodical, the *Journal de St. Pétersbourg*. (The *Journal* was an instrument for quasi-official or "public" diplomacy, noteworthy as an early forum for the Russian free-trade school.) The ministry also subsidized visits by foreigners, who sometimes wrote about Russia, and publications by Russians abroad—two uncommon examples being major sources for social and economic history during the reign of Nicholas I, Baron von Haxthausen who published *The Russian Empire, Its People, Institutions and Resources* after his visit in the 1840's, and Louis Tengoborskii, a professional diplomat who published his *Studies of the Productive Forces of Russia* in Paris in 1852–1854. [43] The expansion of activities and functions also was indicated by formal ties that linked the ministry, unlike the college, with the State Chancellery, the Council of State (or Council of Empire), the Committee of Ministers, and the administrative organs for Caucasia, Finland, and Poland. Significantly, the staff included a high proportion of foreigners. If foreign affairs had "assumed so strange an aspect to a Russian eye that both European enlightenment

42. On the history of the ministry under Nesselrode, cf. the official *Ocherki istorii Ministerstva Inostrannykh del, 1802–1902* (St. Petersburg, 1902); and the tutorial lessons prepared for Alexander Nikolaevich, V. A. Polenov, "Obozrenie prezhniago i nyneshniago sostoianiia Ministerstva Inostrannykh del" (1837), *SIRIO* (1881), vol. 31: 163–195.
43. A. Haxthausen, *Studien über die innern Zustande, das Volksleben und insbesondere die ländlichen Einrichtungen Russlands* (Berlin, 1847–1852), 3 vols.; L. Tengoborskii, *Etudes sur les forces productives de Russie* (Paris, 1852–1854), 4 vols.

and extensive experience were required to comprehend them,"[44] the ministry also became a source of condescension that bred hatred.

"Someone once advised Count Nesselrode to endeavor to place Russians in official stations abroad," wrote Golovin, who had worked for Nesselrode, "to which he replied: 'The Russians have never done anything but make blunders.' "[45] Enlightened education was an advantage: Nesselrode required a good knowledge of geography, politics, European systems of government, economics, and history; fluency in several languages, and by his personal preference additional familiarity with Greek or an Oriental language; and a refined knowledge of the arts and high culture. (Russians complained that he disdained the Russian language, but he did make it a practice to employ a few people who were "geuine connoisseurs of the Russian language.")[46] A remarkably high proportion of his staff had noteworthy interests in the arts, literature, history, and the classics, and a number had studied in Western universities. To whatever extent the British Ambassador, Clanricarde, was correct when he reported in 1841 that "the administration of every department of the Russian government, except the Foreign, is deplorable," Nesselrode's ministry was distinguished by able management.[47]

In his professional conduct, he combined energy and outgoing friendliness with strict self-discipline. His subordinates sometimes found him overly exacting. But if they happened to clash with him, as Golovin did, they might find themselves victim of a sharp impatience and slicing wit that would leave them smouldering. To others who had to deal with him, he was invariably charming, engaging, and almost overly anxious to please. Physically he was small, barely over five feet in height (Napoleon, meeting him at Erfurt, allegedly observed, "There is a little man who one day will be a great man."), and on occasion his opponents alluded to him as "the dwarf." He suffered from gout and poor eyesight, but to the dismay of those who kept hoping he would retire, his excellent health and mental

44. A. T. von Grimm, *Alexandra Feodorowna, Kaiserin von Russland* (Leipzig, 1866), vol. 2: 65–66.
45. Golovin, *Russia*, 315–316.
46. *Sbornik moskovskago glavnago arkhiva Ministerstva Inostrannykh del* (Moscow, 1880), vol. 1: 54.
47. Clanricarde to Palmerston (13 January 1841), *FO* 65/272.

alertness continued into his seventies. He was by nature a social being, he thoroughly enjoyed company, and presided over gatherings in his salon and the banquet hall of the ministry perhaps several times a week on the average. He welcomed female companionship, frequented the circle of the Tsarina Alexandra, and it might be added that it was he who recognized the potential inherent in Princess Lieven's special combination of intellect and allure, and launched her incredible career in diplomacy and intrigue. Among the qualities he admired in others were beauty, refined sensitivity, subtlety, courtliness, worldliness, and nobility. He was convinced that the aristocracy existed to defend the highest values and most civilized institutions, and ambitiously coveted the title "Prince" as a reward for his own service—an honor he never received, but saw bestowed on one of his most powerful opponents, Alexei Orlov, by Alexander II at the end of the Crimean War.

He believed in the pursuit of happiness, and in the possibility of an orderly life, free of serious conflict and discord—an illusion, given the conditions of his day, which was not dispelled by his own existence, however. His marriage to Marie Gur'ev, daughter of Minister of Finance Dmitry Gur'ev, an attractive, lively companion, outspoken critic of the nationalists (and of the Tsar Nicholas for repressive aspects of his rule), gave him a fortune, a touchstone with native Russia, and three children— Marie, Helen, and Dmitry Karlovich. The immediate family also included a niece adopted at an early age, Maria Nesselrode, who to her uncle's joy became a brilliant pianist, his "symphonie en blanc majeur," known throughout Europe by her married name, Kalergis, and for sentiments that were more Polish than Russian. All members of the family traveled extensively in the West, and in fact gravitated westward, so that by the generation of his grandchildren, among whom was the wife of Baron Leon von Moltke, only Helen's branch remained in Russia, her place secured by marriage to M. P. Khreptovich, a nationalist. The many excursions he himself made in Europe, pausing here and there to call on friends and relatives, to take the waters at the fashionable spas, and to indulge his passion for music, alone suggest the orientation that was the earmark of his ministry. He loved the Italian and German opera, and was partial to Rossini, whom he met at Troppau, and to Mozart and Beethoven, whose Fifth

Symphony he held to be a masterpiece without peer. Among his other avocations, which in eighteenth-century aristocratic style included such things as collecting musical instruments, paintings, and books—was a great interest in horticulture. He raised his favorite flowers—camellias, rhododendrons, and azaleas—in gardens and greenhouses where he also cultivated delicacies to surprise guests at his table. His social functions were noted for the entertainment, frequently by artists he patronized on their visits to the Russian capital, and for the excellence of the food and wine. (His reputation as a gourmet has endured in the pudding that was the source of Leskov's pun on his name, "Kisel'-vrode," in his lampoon on Russian relations with Britain—"The Tale of the Squint-Eyed, Left-Handed Smith of Tula and the Steel Flea.")[48]

After half a century in Russia, Nesselrode's style of life was no more indigenous, by and large, than if he had been the British Governor-General of India. But this did not mean that his influence was necessarily superficial. Even outside of his responsibilities as minister, his activities did have an impact on society. He admired Peter the Great as a Westernizer, and although he had little in common with the intellectual Westernizers, he believed that Russia needed nothing as much as massive Europeanization. While he decried materialism as vain, he displayed a great deal of respect for science and technology. He was a member of the Academy of Sciences. He was fascinated by steam power, steamships, railroads, and by agricultural innovations such as new crops and new breeds of livestock. He invested part of his fortune in textile manufacturing; he owned large estates in the Ukraine, and in Livonia and Courland, on which he raised cotton and bred Russia's first large flocks of merino sheep; and with other Germans, prominently Benckendorff, he put money into trade and transport companies in the belief that lively foreign and domestic commerce would stimulate Russian initiative and enterprise.[49]

48. A pun with a double meaning, literally "jelly-like." Cf. N. S. Leskov, "Levsha (skaz o Tul'skom kosom levshe i o stal'noi blokhe)," *Sobranie sochinenii* (Moscow, 1958), vol. 7: 26–59.
49. His private interests are mentioned in numerous contemporary sources and in some more recent works. Cf. M. K. Rozhkova, *Ocherki ekonomicheskoi istorii Rossii pervoi poloviny XIX veka* (Moscow, 1959), 176; his interest in agricultural experimentation

With such investments and official responsibility for negotiating trade agreements and foreign loans (including several with the House of Rothschild based in his familial home, Cologne), he naturally took an interest in economic policy. He served on various committees on tariff policy, monetary reform, and the budget, and on the famous Vasil'chikov committee in 1840–1842. The views he expressed carried weight. For example, Secretary M. A. Korf recorded in a meeting on financial policy that Nesselrode, speaking in Russian no less, clarified an important point "intelligently, cleverly, carefully—showing greater knowledge both of theory and of practical financial affairs than the others."[50]

Nesselrode was a moderate free-trader. His philosophy stemmed from the Western physiocratic tradition taken up by Gentz, Cobden, and Peel, among others, and supported in Russia by the free-trade circle that formed around Heinrich Storch during Alexander's reign. Storch tutored Nikolai Pavlovich, and his following included Nesselrode's father-in-law, Minister of Finance Gur'ev. Free trade found little official support after 1823, although it had an able spokesman in one of Nesselrode's diplomats, Louis Tengoborskii—the foremost Russian economist under Nicholas I. Nesselrode supported Gur'ev's efforts to lower tariffs, but then recognized the necessity to reverse the process in order to redress the balance of trade after 1821. With tongue in cheek, the German apostle of economic nationalism, Friedrich List, who influenced Gur'ev's successor, Count E. F. Kankrin, and attacked English classic economics for "cosmopolitanism," praised Nesselrode for supporting higher tariffs: "The most enlightened and discerning statesman of Russia, Count Nesselrode, did not hesitate to confess . . . 'Russia finds herself compelled by circumstances to take up an independent system of trade; the products of the empire have found no foreign market, the home manufactures are ruined or on the point of being so, all the ready money of the country flows toward foreign lands, and the most

---

is indicated, for example, in P. Kozlov, "Askaniia-Nova v eia proshlom i nastoiashchem. Istorii Anhal'tskoi kolonii v iuzhnoi Rossii," *Russkaia starina* (1914), vol. 158: 359. His merino sheep were renowned, and probably prompted "De l'eleve des moutons et du commerce des laines en Russie," *Journal de St. Pétersbourg* (15 June and 29 June 1843), special supplement.

50. M. A. Korf, "Imperator Nikolai v soveshchatel'nykh sobraniiakh," *SIRIO*, vol. 98: 143.

substantial trading firms are nearly ruined."[51] List did not include Nesselrode's statement that it was "with the most lively feelings of regret" that Gur'ev's policy had been reversed.[52]

Later Nesselrode advocated selective reductions and, as Gur'ev had, positive support such as credit bank loans to help potentially competitive enterprises get started and contend with Western manufactures in Russian as well as foreign markets. But for the most part, freer trade would have to be preceded by specific agreements with other countries to insure a balance. If foreign markets for Russian raw materials, agricultural products, and rudimentary manufactures were thus secured, both in Europe and in Asia, dependence on Western manufactures could be justified. It was in his willingness, even eagerness, to accept dependence on foreign products and markets that he differed with Kankrin and the nationalists, who at this stage were quite ready to embrace economic backwardness as a small price to pay for independence and autonomy. Free trade was an integral part of the classic approach formulated for example by Gentz and Friedrich Ancillon in their concept of "natural alliances," and their belief that the whole world would eventually become economically interdependent.

In yet another area, that of legal philosophy, Nesselrode's conservatism clashed with Russian nationalism. He subscribed to eighteenth-century ideas of natural law, believed in the gradual evolution of positive norms, and held Montesquieu and Blackstone in high esteem—which gave him something in common with the framers of constitutions in many parts of the world, including the United States. On the domestic level, he strongly favored reform as conceived by Speransky, which may be interpreted as a step toward constitutional limitations on autocratic power. He embraced the ideal of equality before the law and bemoaned the inequities of the Russian system. "In achieving justice and equality we unfortunately are behind all of the other nations of Europe," he said. Enlightened legislation could not be carried into effect without extensive reform reaching into administration.

51. F. von List, *The National System of Political Economy* (reprint, New York, 1966), 92.
52. Nesselrode's announcement of the tariff of 1821, in "On the Tariff, and the Effects of the British Policy," *National Magazine* (August 1845), vol. 1: 231.

"In the hands of the censors and idiotic judges the best legislation remains ineffective," he complained. He regarded emancipation as urgent, an issue of immense importance, but it would be pointless without prior guarantees of equality and private rights. "A better system of justice must precede emancipation," he stated in 1843.[53] As did Ancillon, under whom he had studied law in Berlin, he regarded sovereignty as a function of legal order rather than as a mandate for the unlimited exercise of power.[54] He believed in an evolving law of nations and in what might be termed universal civil law. (It is interesting in this respect that Speransky's Legal Code of 1835 contained the category *obshchenarodnoe pravo*—universal public law.) He shared with Alexander I the belief that the Congress of Vienna heralded the codification of a "Public Law of Europe"; it was fundamental that classic diplomacy was a legislative activity, contributing to the definition of the rights and obligations of the state.

Nesselrode's conservatism belonged to the mainstream of Western political philosophy, far removed from the traditions of Official Nationality and the doctrine of "Faith, Tsar, and Fatherland." For him Karamzin and Uvarov were fanatics, their ideology contrary to the texts he held in high regard—Saint Pierre, François Saint Priest, Montesquieu, Blackstone, Adam Müller, Burke, and Gentz. Even the Russians who influenced him most—Alexander I, Kochubey, and Speransky—followed the same European tradition.

As Nesselrode's Russian antagonists pointed out, his policies found few antecedents in Russian history and his political philosophy little support in the traditions of government expressed in Official Nationality, beyond an abstract commitment to defend the existing order. And that raised difficulties. The status quo denoted the balance, the equilibrium within a system that was vital to peace, and peaceful change. It was not synonymous with stasis, although its meaning was transformed by reactionary politics, as Grunwald has said, from the "harmony of an organism" to "a kind of paralysis after convulsion."[55] It

---

53. Nesselrode to Meyendorff (19 March 1842, 13 June 1846, 4 April 1843), *Lettres et papiers*, vol. 8: 170, 325, 206.
54. Cf. J. P. F. Ancillon, *Ueber Souveränität und Staats-Verfassung* (2nd. ed., Berlin, 1816).
55. Grunwald, *Metternich* (London, 1955), 259.

was true that Nesselrode held "socialism, communism, the dis-
ordering passion for democratic institutions, the insane idea of
reconstituting public law on imaginary principles of race, language, and nationality" to be "dangerous heresies"—against the
unity and harmony of the natural order.[56] As ideological justifi-
cations for war and revolution, they pitted "radical extremes"
against "moderation," a word that in his vocabulary denoted
both restraint in the exercise of power and the *juste milieu*.[57] He
also rejected these things on philosophical grounds, as the con-
ceits of "utopians" and "ideologues" who believed man could
be the master of matter, the conqueror of nature, the creator of
his own salvation. Man was mortal. True nobility derived from
a grasp of human limitations, and humbleness in the face of an
infinite universe and God—expressed in the apothegms that he,
along with Burke and Gentz, repeated: "Events march ahead of
human reason," "Man proposes, God disposes," and so forth.
But this student of Montesquieu could accept the existence of
different political systems if they were produced by natural
evolution. Constitutional, representative, and democratic institutions such as those of Britain and the United States were "legiti-
mate," as was the communism of peasant communes on his
estates in Russia. The British government was highly esteemed
by the *philosophes* and conservative writers, among them Gentz,

56. Nesselrode's annual report for 1848, in Grunwald, "Nesselrode et
le 'gendarme de l'Europe,' " *Trois siècles de diplomatie russe* (Paris,
1945), 191.
57. Cf. Ancillon, *Du Juste milieu, ou du rapprochement des extrêmes*
(Brussels, 1837), 2 vols. As expressed in a letter by Nesselrode's
colleague Victor Balabin to Dmitry Nesselrode (7 January 1852):
"In every political situation one may always observe two kinds of
political influences, inherent in the nature of men and things—one
which tends to drive them to extremes, and another which holds
them close to things best conserved." The word "moderation" was
frequently used in connection with Russian alternatives to a policy
of aggression. Alexander I's support for the European system was
attributed to his philosophy of "moderation." Under Nicholas I,
Nesselrode was identified, for example by P. de Bourgoing, French
minister at Petersburg, in *Les guerres d'idiome et de nationalité*
(Paris, 1849), as the mainstay of the "party of moderation." The
contrasting view was that Russian professions of "moderation" were
confessions of weakness. "History shows that Russian moderation
is nothing but a matter of opportunity," wrote J. M. Chopin,
Russie (Paris, 1838), vol. 2: 621.

who believed that the American Revolution had been justified, and praised the government of the United States to Nesselrode as "an enlightened and liberal system."[58] The French Revolution, on the other hand, was condemned. But if Nesselrode favored a restoration, this was not prompted by great confidence in the Bourbons, who in his view had produced "tyrants" little better than Napolean, or by any desire for a return to absolute monarchy.[59] "The French Revolution must complete its course as did the English Revolution of the seventeenth century," Gentz had written to him.[60] Similarly, Burke, Gentz, and others he admired had denounced tsarist autocracy for its excesses. Thus, to classify him as a conservative does not clear up the problem of his role in Russian politics, where the real divisions on large questions did not conform with a liberal-conservative dichotomy at all. Nesselrode probably was more open-minded, and more willingly reconciled with liberal changes than most officials under Nicholas I. We note, for example, his surprisingly mild reaction to the Decembrist Revolution in 1825, which, he said, demonstrated that all order was combustible and could go up in smoke. But the Decembrists were, in his words, "a society that had neither criminal purposes nor tragic effect, although it did no good."[61] He recognized the injustices of the Russian system, its backwardness in comparison with the leading Western countries, he had grieved the "vast" unrealized potential of Speransky's reforms, and he certainly did hope for changes that would do some good.

Russians who were discontented with Alexander's decision to pursue Napoleon and liberate Europe were overshadowed by the excitement of the allied campaign, the victory, and the Congress of Vienna. When it was over, Russia was committed to a

---

58. Gentz to Nesselrode (27 January 1818), *Lettres et papiers*, vol. 5: 294. Cf. Gentz, *The French and American Revolutions Compared*, John Quincy Adams, translator (Chicago, 1959).
59. Nesselrode to Marie Nesselrode (23 February 1841), *Lettres et papiers*, vol. 8: 129. For Nesselrode's views of France in 1815–1830, cf. Martens, "La Russie et la France pendant la restauration," *Revue d'histoire diplomatique* (1908), vol. 22: 161–248.
60. Gentz to Nesselrode, in G. Mann, *Secretary of Europe* (New Haven, 1946), 245.
61. Nesselrode to Alopius (23 December 1825), "État de St. Pétersbourg," *MAE* 333, SIM 560: Russie, vol. 33.

foreign policy they disliked, the conservation of European order, justified by the same rationale that had been employed against Kutuzov—that Russia's interests united her with the rest of Europe. As a defender of the new policy, Nesselrode was compelled to oppose both revolutionary change in Europe generally and the national movement in Russia.

The personal views of Alexander I and his extensive involvement in diplomacy made Russia's support for the European system fairly secure in the first decade after 1815. But Nesselrode, largely responsible for administering European policy, faced a challenge in the conduct of Near Eastern policy in a different spirit by a rival of subordinate rank in the ministry, Joannes Capodistria. Capodistria, who was Greek, Orthodox, and philhellene, was favorable to deeper Russian involvement in the Near East to support the Greek independence movement against Turkey. In this he was backed by Russians who for their own reasons were dissatisfied with the status quo. The rivalry continued through the period of the congresses of Aix-la-Chapelle in 1818, which both attended, and Troppau in 1820, by which time the founders of the concert realized that it was not as solidly established as they had hoped it would be. The Greek War of Independence in 1821 presented Russia with an opportunity to intervene, and Alexander's refusal to send the army against Turkey was a disappointment not only for Capodistria, who soon resigned, but for Russians who had long coveted Constantinople and the straits. Nesselrode afterward assumed greater responsibility for Near Eastern policy, and those who had backed Capodistria suffered. "Capodistria's patronage was enough to win me the enmity of his mortal foe, Nesselrode," Gorchakov recalled.[62]

The remaining years of Alexander's reign confirmed the trend that nationalists found unsavory, particularly the rise of Nesselrode's influence and collaboration with Metternich.[63] In

62. A. M. Gorchakov, "v ego razskazakh iz proshlago," *Russkaia starina* (1883), vol. 40: 169. Several Russians involved in Near Eastern affairs, including G. A. Strogonov, Envoy at Constantinople, were removed from their posts, apparently for having collaborated with Capodistria.

63. Nesselrode's ties with Metternich, while close, were exaggerated by his opponents and have been by subsequent historians, tsarist and Soviet. But Russian criticism focuses less on the character of Metternich's system than on the specific belief that Russia's real interests, economic and geopolitical, could be reconciled with Austria's. Such

1821 the two men worked closely to prepare the declaration of conservative principles at Laibach, and Nesselrode was appointed to the Supreme Council of State. His newfound prominence in policy regarding the Eastern Question was evident at the Congress of Verona in 1822 and especially in talks with Metternich at Vienna in 1823, after which Alexander made him Privy Counsellor. By this time, the era of congresses presided over by Metternich was coming to a close, but Russian support for the concert was to continue.

Alexander was painfully aware that the European system was unpopular with his own people. In 1825 he told a French emissary, la Ferronays, that while he had "kept the general welfare constantly and solely in view" in the effort "to maintain the peace of Europe," he had been pressured to do otherwise. There were those who wanted Russia to adopt an independent policy, particularly in the Eastern Question, and if his reign came to an end they might prevail. "I am a man, I am mortal, and perhaps it will please the Lord not to grant me a long life," he said. Hence it was imperative to move ahead toward agreements that would bind Russia to the concert. "Nesselrode has several new ideas to present to you," he told la Ferronays.[64]

The negotiations with the Western powers, prominently Britain, for a more secure arrangement in the Near East lapsed shortly before Alexander died in December 1825, and the possibility of a major revision of foreign policy was raised. The new ruler, Nicholas I, did not fully understand his brother's policy or share his ideals, and was more receptive to nationalistic influence. Nesselrode's opponents, led by General A. A. Arakcheev, urged Nicholas to get rid of him. They advanced Baron G. A. Strogonov, who favored an aggressive policy in the Near East, for the job. But Nesselrode, at forty-five, held advantages of experience and established position. As a tutor in foreign affairs, he had already impressed Nicholas with his views, not only on the Eastern Question, but on the subject of Britain prior to the Tsarevich's visit in 1816–1817. In addition he was backed by the Grand-Duke Con-

---

a condemnation of Nesselrode's policy appears, for example, in N. S. Bliukh, "Ekonomicheskoe sostoianie Rossii," *Vestnik Evropy* (1877), vol. 67: 304–358, 748–779; vol. 68: 202–237.

64. "Extrait d'une conversation entre S. M. l'empereur Alexandre et M. le comte de la Ferronays" (n.d. February 1825), *Lettres et papiers*, vol. 6: 218–219.

stantine, who had declined the throne on account of his mor-
ganatic marriage to a Roman Catholic.

In February Nesselrode submitted a memorandum stating
the policy he would advise, with the implication that another
policy would require a new minister. He proposed, according to
Polievktov, to treat the Eastern Question as a "general European
question, beyond the immediate interests of Russia."[65] When
Nicholas decided to retain him as minister, he elected a policy
that was highly controversial in Russia and destined to be the
pivotal issue in the contention between the "German" and "Russian" factions until the Crimean War.

Factional politics were not new in Russia, and antagonism
between Russians and Germans on matters of policy had been a
recurrent theme in eighteenth-century Russian history. But the
cleavage under Nicholas I took on unusual significance as a result
of the search for a viable approach in relations with the great
Western powers. The lines between the *nemetskaia partiia*, literally the "German" or "foreign party," and the *russkaia partiia*
were clearly drawn on many issues, with the former standing for
an "European" and the latter for a "Russian" orientation.[66] Leadership of the former in the 1830s and 1840s was suggested by
occasional references to it as the "Nesselrodian party."[67] "Nesselrode is the Chief of the German Party," wrote Golovin.[68] The
"Russian party," consisting mainly of official nationalists, was
called the Old Russian Party, True Russian Party, Great Russian
Party, National Party, and so forth, both in Russia and abroad.

65. M. A. Polievktov, "Nessel'rode, Karl Vasil'evich," *Russkii biograficheskii slovar*, vol. "N": 249. Cf. *Ocherki istorii Ministerstva
Inostrannykh del*, 100.
66. The factional contention was a well-recognized feature of Russian
politics. Schiemann finds "numerous occasions to speak of the opposition between the German and Russian parties in Petersburg,"
Geschichte Russlands unter Kaiser Nikolaus I (Berlin, 1904–1914),
vol. 3: 402. According to Grimm, Nesselrode's "many enemies" in
the government were partisans of "the national movement" and
the "old Russian party." *Alexandra Feodorowna*, vol. 2: 64. The
entry for "Nesselrode, Charles-Robert, Ct. de," *Grand dictionnaire
universel du XIX siècle* (Paris, 1874), states: "He always represented the German party in Russia, in opposition to Prince Menshikov, who represented the Russian party."
67. Cf. N. Barsukov, *Zhizin i trudy M. P. Pogodina* (St. Petersburg,
1899), vol. 13: 19.
68. Golovin, *Russia*, 315.

Of course there were no "party" politics in Russian autocracy, and no concept of loyal opposition. In a fictional interlude by Paul Grimm, Nesselrode announces, "I have written to Prince Gorchakov, one of the principal representatives of the Russian party," and is stopped cold by the Tsar's admonition, "In my empire there is no place for parties."[69] But factional politics did occur, and other governments watched the give and take for signs of change in policy. According to a British explanation, to understand Russian policy it was essential to recognize the "antagonistic principles" that pitted the "so-called Russian and German parties" against one another.[70] The French Ambassador, Barante, summed it up with the observation that "three things influence the course of policy . . . first, the opinions and momentary impressions of the Emperor" which, second, were "modified, corrected, and guided by the prudent and well-calculated actions of M. de Nesselrode," and third, were subject to nationalistic pressure "which never troubles itself about European affairs and would prefer that the Tsar did not."[71] Nesselrode referred to it as a contention between "common sense" and "ultra-Russian fanaticism" or the "patriotism of kvas."[72]

As the ultimate decision-maker, Nicholas I could incline toward one or the other position, but generally his perceptions of choices were heavily influenced by their representation. He wavered because, in Barante's words, while he wanted "to be Russian and to advance the development and progress of the national potential . . . one idea that neither he nor cultivated Russians would be able to accept is to be isolated from Europe."[73] In favor of Nesselrode's side was the Tsar's own German background; his fidelity to German connections in the conservative alignment; the glory of what he imagined to be Russia's leading position in Europe after his brother's victory over Napoleon; and to some extent his fear of revolution, possibly even a fear of the revolutionary tendencies of nationalists. On the other side was his desire

69. P. von Grimm, *Les Mystères du palais des czars (sous l'empereur Nicolas I)* (Warzbourg, 1870), 162–163.
70. "Russia's Actual Policy," *Foreign Quarterly Review* (London, 1839), vol. 23: 163–165.
71. In Guizot, *M. de Barante* (London, 1867), 144–145.
72. Nesselrode to Meyendorff (30 May 1846), *Lettres et papiers*, vol. 8: 320.
73. Barante to Thiers (20 April 1836), *Souvenirs*, vol. 5: 347.

to dispel the implications of his German background and fit the image of a true Russian Tsar. "Nicholas, annoyed at his German origin, does his best to pass for a Russian," wrote Golovin.[74] "No one is more Russian at heart than I am," said Nicholas.[75] Moreover, the Russian faction counted on his growing realization that cooperation with the German states and Britain did not serve Russian interests, and on the ascendant influence of official nationalism itself.

Nesselrode's first important moves under Nicholas I revealed his desire to resolve the Eastern Question, and to achieve this if possible through rapprochement with Britain.[76] He and Prince Lieven conducted the negotiations with Wellington that led to the St. Petersburg Protocol of April 4, 1826, the purpose of which was to prevent another clash between Greece and Turkey and to preserve the status quo in the principalities. This milestone in a promising détente was not a new departure; it had been planned before the end of Alexander's reign and Princess Lieven had been sent to London to promote it. Hence it was the fruit of Alexander's foreign policy and evidence of continuity. The old principles were reiterated. Nesselrode told Wellington that the "union" of their two countries was vital to European equilibrium.[77] The status quo was insured by the Akkerman Convention of October 7, by which Russia recognized Ottoman rights to govern the principalities. That these steps were leading toward renewal of the concert became evident when France joined Russia and Britain in the London Convention of July 6, 1827. Nesselrode expected that Metternich would soon fall into line, and that Prussia, without any real interest in the Near East, would join in any arrangement the others found agreeable. With several successes to his credit, he was nominated for the Vice-Chancellorship.

But the new system came to a premature end between 1827 and 1829, when Nesselrode had to meet the first serious challenge

74. Golovin, *Russia*, 268.
75. A. L. L. de Custine, *La Russie en 1839* (2nd. ed. revised, Paris, 1843), vol. 2: 46.
76. Cf. S. M. Solov'ev, "Vostochnyi vopros 50 let nazad," *Drevniaia i novaia Rossiia* (1876), vol. 2: 129–141, containing several extracts from documents by Nesselrode.
77. Wellington, *Despatches, Correspondence and Memoranda* (London, 1868), vol. 3: 212.

to his policy during the reign. The Russo-Persian War, precipitated in part by the bellicosity of a nationalist, Prince A. S. Menshikov, led to the annexation of Erivan and Nakhichivan by the Treaty of Turkmanchai in 1828, and it darkly overshadowed Nesselrode's efforts to create a favorable disposition toward Britain. The Russian army did well, and when the Russo-Turkish War began in 1828, nationalists expected to see a victory with conquests.

They were disappointed. The army was placed under Diebitsch's command, and after a series of methodical, successful moves he called a halt. For Russians to whom it seemed that Constantinople and the straits were virtually in their hands, the explanation was obvious. Diebitsch "was not purely Russian, not in his spirit, not in his upbringing, not in his religion"; furthermore their diplomacy "was conducted under the influence of another German, Nesselrode, who was incapable of understanding what needed to be done, because he wanted to keep the foreign powers happy and piddle around with a conservative policy."[78] Later it was said that "the ancient jealousy between the Russians and Germans was vigorously revived, and found expression in open hatred" in the wake of the war's disappointments.[79]

The war inspired Nesselrode to take a solid stand against Russian aggrandizement in the Near East. He had accompanied the Tsar into the field for part of the campaign and become concerned with war aims. Returning to Petersburg, he convened a special committee to discuss Russia's objectives. Kochubey was appointed chairman; the other members were A. N. Golitsyn, P. A. Tolstoy, D. V. Dashkov and A. I. Chernyshev,[80] the Minister of War. Kochubey had first made his mark as an opponent of an expansionist policy in 1802 when the possibility of partitioning the Ottoman Empire with France had been raised. He had argued that the traditional policy should be abandoned, and that

78. M. N. Pokhvisnev, "Dnevnik," *Russkii arkhiv* (1911), vol. 2: 202–203.
79. Grimm, *Alexandra Feodorowna*, vol. 2: 53–54.
80. Cf. R. J. Kerner, "Russia's New Policy in the Near East after the Peace of Adrianople. Including the Text of the Protocol of 16 September 1829," *Cambridge Historical Journal* (1937), vol. 5: 286–290; Martens, *Recueil*, vol. 4: 438–440; Martens, *Die russische Politik in der orientalischen Frage* (St. Petersburg, 1877), 27–31.

Russian interests could be secured by agreement to uphold the status quo.[81] Nesselrode had been a faithful student of his, in this as in other ways. Kochubey had been pleased by Nesselrode's handling of Near Eastern policy after Capodistria's resignation. "Our position is difficult," he told Nesselrode, "but it will become even more so if by some unforeseen act of fate the direction you have given affairs is changed—a direction for which, without intending any kind of flattery, I want you to have my most sincere compliments."[82] Since Golitsyn and Tolstoy had previously been aligned with Kochubey and Nesselrode on policy, the character of the committee's recommendation to the Tsar was probably a foregone conclusion, although Chernyshev represented the General Staff and Dashkov was a bright nationalist, a writer and a friend and admirer of V. A. Zhukovskii.[83] The recommendation, passed on September 16, 1829, closely conformed with the views Nesselrode presented. Whatever occurred in the Near East affected the interests of the Western powers, and they must be a part of it, he said.[84] In a formal Protocol, the members unanimously agreed that Russia must uphold the status quo. Although Capodistria, now in Greece, had submitted a proposal to the Tsar that Turkey should be partitioned, this was rejected. In the end, even Dashkov affirmed the opinion that the probable result of failure to support the concert would be a general European war.[85] The whole procedure was unusual, and apparently intended to justify a policy sure to be unpopular after military victory.

The Treaty of Adrianople, signed two days before the Kochubey committee issued its Protocol, did not alter existing conditions and great power relationships in the Near East, although Russia won territorial concessions, mainly in the Caucasus. Nesselrode pointed out that although Turkey had been "in our hands," the Tsar "decided to follow the noble dictates of his

81. On Kochubey's memorandum, "Etait-ce un avantage pour la Russie de s'en tenir au principe de la conservation de l'empire ottoman?" see Goriainov, *Le Bosphore et les Dardanelles* (Paris, 1910), 47–50.
82. Kochubey to Nesselrode (23 August 1823), *Lettres et papiers*, vol. 6: 152.
83. It may be noted that Nesselrode patronized Dashkov for several years, as he did other nationalistic Russians who openly disagreed with his policies.
84. Martens, *Recueil*, vol. 4: 438.
85. *Ibid.*, 439.

generosity" and "permit the continued existence of the Turkish government in Europe."[86] He thought this should be appreciated in the West. "The foreign newspapers are already beginning to print nonsense about our peace treaty," he wrote to Diebitsch in October, but "all reasonable, objective, calm, and unprejudiced men" would refrain from rash conclusions.[87]

European politics were already affected by Anglo-Russian polarity when the revolutions of 1830 suddenly focused attention on the ideological divergence of liberal and conservative states. Nesselrode happened to be in Karlsbad in July 1830, and soon after the outbreak in Paris he went to see Metternich, who asked for a promise that Russia would not intervene. When Nesselrode returned to Petersburg, Nicholas I was ready to send his army to Paris to depose Louis Philippe. Nesselrode advised him not to, arguing that the new French regime did not endanger the rights of other states. If, as Tatishchev asserts, he was responsible for changing the Tsar's mind, Grunwald is probably correct that "Nesselrode alone prevented an absurd war."[88]

Nesselrode could not, however, counteract the divisive effects of the Polish uprising and its suppression by the Russian army in 1830–1831. To many Westerners it seemed that Russia had unveiled the real character of her policy—Asiatic, despotic, and brutally aggressive when not subtly subversive. Many of the revolutionaries themselves had hoped desperately for Western intervention against Russia. Independent Poland would be aligned with Britain and France. But for precisely the same reason, Poland had gained greater importance as a factor in Russian security. Nesselrode, who afterward became firmly convinced that Russia should keep a close watch on Poland, held that the constitution Alexander I had granted would have remained in effect if the uprising had not occurred. This was the line he took in attempts to explain Russian actions to Britain, underlining the main point later with the argument that Ireland's relationship with Britain

86. Nesselrode to Potemkin (28 April 1830), in B. Jelavich, ed., *Russia and Greece During the Regency of King Othon 1832–1835* (Thessalonika, 1962), 138.
87. Nesselrode to Diebitsch (15 October 1829), in N. K. Schilder, ed., "Imperator Nikolai I i Vostochnyi vopros," *Russkaia starina* (1901), vol. 4: 18.
88. Tatishchev, "Vneshniia snosheniia Rossii v epokhu Krymskoi voiny," *Russkii vestnik* (1885), vol. 179: 38; Grunwald, "Nesselrode," 186.

was analogous to Poland's with Russia.[89] But the Polish tragedy had taken its place among the irreconcilable differences between Russia and Western liberals.

A united Europe now seemed further from reach than it had in 1815. Metternich wrote to Nesselrode that his "most secret thought" was "that the old Europe has come to the beginning of the end" while "the new Europe has not yet reached the beginning."[90] Nesselrode, with 1789 in mind, replied that the Europe Metternich was clinging to "hasn't existed for forty years," and that to try to restore the past was "to attempt the impossible." He admonished Metternich to concern himself with the present, "and if things don't get too bad, we will achieve something of immense value. . . . With this conviction one has the courage to face up to affairs, and not abandon hope for Europe."[91]

Emergent bipolarity kept concert diplomacy out of operation in the Near Eastern crisis that followed. The crisis began when Egypt overthrew Ottoman rule, and with French backing launched a military campaign against Turkey that turned out to be more successful than the one Diebitsch had waged. The Sultan's army was defeated, and Russia suddenly faced the possibility that Constantinople might fall under the influence of another great power. Metternich was among the first Western statesmen to realize that this would be intolerable for Russia and that the prospect was likely to provoke intervention, which it did. But the Western reaction was generally one of shock.

Anticipating trouble with the Western powers as a consequence, Nesselrode advised against intervention. But the Tsar listened to other advisers and sent a squadron to the Bosphorus. Nesselrode's opponents were pleased. "Thank God that Russian genius inspired the Emperor to take responsibility for the consequences of eastern affairs, keeping an eye on the West, when Vice-Chancellor pigmy was blinded by the political scrutiny of the rest of the world!" Severin wrote to Zhukovskii.[92] Britain and

89. Cf. Nesselrode to Palmerston (22 December 1831/3 January 1832), FO 181/93.
90. Metternich to Nesselrode (1 September 1830), Lettres et papiers, vol. 7: 149.
91. Nesselrode to Metternich (5 September 1830), Lettres et papiers, vol. 7: 151.
92. Severin to Zhukovskii (13 January 1833), in A. P. I. [Izvolsky], "Zametka," Russkii arkhiv (1899), vol. 2: 452.

France sent their fleets into Near Eastern waters, but the worst of Nesselrode's fears, a confrontation between Russia and the Entente Cordiale, did not materialize. Tension abated when Egypt and Turkey agreed to terms of peace.

Russia next secured the Porte's formal acknowledgment of her right to intervene, particularly if Turkey should fail in her obligation to close the straits. This was done by the Treaty of Unkiar Skelessi, July 8, 1833, which was composed by Nesselrode and negotiated by a nationalist, Count Alexei Orlov, whom Diebitsch had recommended on grounds that he was intelligent and truly Russian. Orlov, who had negotiated the Treaty of Adrianople, went to Constantinople at the head of a glittering regiment of guards with the title "Commander in Chief of the Russian Forces in the Ottoman Empire." But the whole procedure was laced with ambiguities—above all ambiguities in the treaty, which falsely gave the appearance that Russia had gained special influence. Russian intervention under the circumstances stipulated by the treaty was to be expected, a contingency which existed de facto if not de jure. But the treaty did serve as a reminder of Russian interests. Perhaps it also served as a fanfare, pleasing to Russians, to turn attention away from the obvious return to the status quo ante in great-power relationships in the Near East when Russia withdrew from the straits. Afterward, Nesselrode consistently held that it was intended to preserve the status quo.

After 1827 Russia had passed perilously close to isolation calling for an independent policy which the nationalists would have welcomed. Now it was time for reconstruction. In September 1833, after Nicholas, Orlov, and Nesselrode met with Metternich at Münchengrätz, an agreement to cooperate in Near Eastern and other affairs of general importance was signed. When joined by Prussia after negotiations at Berlin in October, it was announced as a revival of the Holy Alliance. It was an important step, indicative of Russian intentions, but it had drawbacks. The gulf between Russia and the Entente Cordiale was not bridged, and the problem of Russia's isolation was not really solved because, as Nicholas and Nesselrode realized fully after they met Metternich at Toeplitz in 1835, Austria and Prussia would be neutral in any Russian confrontation with the liberal entente over serious issues. Münchengrätz, Berlin, and Toeplitz merely gave the appearance of conservative solidarity. For Nesselrode, the defense of the European system had been reduced to a holding action to prevent Russia's isolation.

Nesselrode's position was complicated in the mid-1830s by the rise of Russian opposition. Barante noted that the men coming to the fore in government were "Russian and purely Russian, and know little about what is happening in the West."[93] The most coherent expression was the advent of Official Nationality as the state ideology in 1833. Belief in a secularized Orthodox Church, one Tsar, and one Fatherland carried the thrust of a reaction against diversity, and against the eighteenth century concepts of freedom and liberty which had made their fleeting appearance in Russian thought. It held modern, revolutionary implications: "the total subjection of numerous populations of different origin, races, and languages, together with their respective civilization, customs, and laws to the nationality of the Muscovites," as a British observer put it.[94] It was a weapon against foreigners and foreign influence, against the very kind of cosmopolitan pluralism which Nesselrode—who was not Orthodox, who it was said did not know the true Russian Tsar, and who was not himself Russian—symbolized at its worst. "To be sure, the Russian God is great," Prince Viazemskii quipped, mocking Nesselrode's catholicism, "But why should I say He is a Russian God? The same God is German and greater still, the sublime God playing whist with Nesselrode."[95] As a guiding ideology in foreign relations, it opposed "Europeanism" with pervasive xenophobia, and belief in unity with a deep, schismatic hostility to the West.

It was true that the nationalists saw the blessings of independence in isolation. But the one country they knew, and loved, and wished to court, was France. They believed that if Russia had allied herself with France and backed Egypt and Greece instead of Turkey, she might have gained a slice of territory extending to the Bosphorus, and an advantage over Austria in the Balkans and Britain in the Mediterranean. But the affinity for France ran deeper than geopolitics. Russian writers were stirred to a far greater extent by the war in 1812 than by the liberation of Europe and the Congress of Vienna, and there was a lingering feeling, a

---

93. Barante to Molé (24 March 1837), *Souvenirs*, vol. 1: 554.
94. *British and Foreign Review* (October 1840), vol. 11: 547–548.
95. Viazemskii to Zhukovskii (17 August 1840), *Russkii arkhiv* (1900), vol. 1: 385.

sense of regret, that Alexander I made a mistake when he did not follow Kutuzov's advice. It was less a matter of strategy than of honor: their opponent had been a worthy genius, a great hero. Next to Napoleon, Metternich was a villain. Among nationalistic officials the British were treated with suspicion, the Germans with contempt, and the French with warmth.

Meanwhile the foreign faction declined. Many of Nesselrode's friends, including Diebitsch, Kochubey, and Speransky, died in the 1830s, and their philosophy attracted no new blood. Leading German families, such as those of Benckendorff and Lieven, had their influence sharply undercut by rivals, and Balts in lofty positions were helpless to prevent forced Russification in their home provinces. A number of Catholic and Protestant families moved to Western Europe. This was expected to have an impact on policy. The French Ambassador reported: "The number of men who have come down from a bygone era, who have been schooled in the old policy, and who have been involved in European affairs and know Europe, diminishes day by day, and no one who possesses this special virtue—which each day becomes less appreciated and less useful—comes along to take their place. M. le comte de Nesselrode stands almost alone as a man of good knowledge of foreign countries and cabinets."[96]

There were signs that Russia stood at a crossroad in the mid-1830s, a point of fateful decision between cooperation with Europe and an independent course, not only in foreign policy but in many areas of life. To some extent, this was suggested by the great debate between the Slavophiles and the Westernizers. But there were other stirrings which held portent. It was the eve of a decade remarkable for its rich yield in thought and literature; a period, 1836–1843, which according to Professor Pintner "could easily be described as the beginning of a new and vigorous era of state-sponsored economic change"; the period, 1837–1842, which Professor Weidlé has called "the crack," when the new Russia diverged from the old, giving rise to the revolutionary movement and the rejection of Petersburg's "worn-out symbols of European grandeur."[97] In 1836 Glinka produced his ultra-

96. Barante to Molé (24 March 1837), *Souvenirs*, vol. 1: 554.
97. W. M. Pintner, *Russian Economic Policy Under Nicholas I* (Ithaca, 1967), 121–122; W. Weidlé, *Russia: Absent and Present* (New York, 1961), 64–80.

patriotic opera *A Life for the Tsar*, and work began on the first
Russian rail line; in 1837, the year of Queen Victoria's coronation, Pushkin died and his masterpiece "The Bronze Horseman"
was published. In it Peter the Great is portrayed as a true if terrible Russian Tsar whose dauntless will conspires with forces
arising in the hinterland to inundate Petersburg and purify Russia. In the same year Chaadayev composed his "Apology of a
Madman," in which he advanced the idea that Russia's salvation
lay in the West, in a Catholic community of Europe. When Kochubey died in 1836 and Orlov supported V. N. Tatishchev to replace him, the official attitude seemed to be in the process of
transformation. "More than others," it was said of Tatishchev,
"he believes in what is called a 'Russian policy,' that is, a policy
of being isolated as far as possible from Western Europe, of
avoiding its influence, and of retreating from contact with it."
"Perhaps it would be better to place more value on the civilization that arises from its own foundation," said Nicholas, com-
menting that Peter may have been wrong to have moved the
capital to Petersburg.[98] When the Winter Palace burned in 1837,
V. A. Perovskii, Governor-General of Orenburg, speculated hope-
fully that it might provide "a motive for the return to Moscow."[99]
Viazemskii recalled Pushkin's hatred for the Nesselrode family,
that symbol of Petersburg's "cosmopolitan Areopagus." "With
the end of one Count N.," he said, "a halt will come at last to so
many things that have weighed heavily upon us and have made it
barely possible to carry on."[1]

The stage was set for Nesselrode's most brilliant diplomacy
—in his exertions to advance the rapprochement with Britain
and insure the continuation of his policy for Russia. In 1836–
1839 he extricated Russia from a series of crises of confrontation
in Asia and the Near East, any one of which could easily have
touched off war with Britain. In each he had to counteract his
Russian opponents and outmaneuver British actions intended to
contain and isolate Russia; against countervailing pressure on

98. As reported in Barante to Molé (29 December 1836), *Souvenirs*, vol.
    5: 518–519. Barante to Broglie (30 January 1836), *Souvenirs*, vol.
    5: 259.
99. I. N. Zakharin, *Graf V. A. Perovskii i ego zimnii pokhod v Khivu* (St.
    Petersburg, 1901), part 2: 128.
1. Viazemskii to Bulgakov (8 April 1837), in "A. S. Pushkin (1816–
    1837)," *Russkii arkhiv* (1884), vol. 2: 440.

both sides, he argued that common interests outweighed differences and that the reasons for rivalry were shallow and best put aside. In 1839–1840, with the last of the severe crises passing, he turned his attention more fully to constructive possibilities he saw in the rapprochement. His logic was simple: the concert was inoperative as long as Europe was divided by the opposed alignments; bipartisan cooperation offered the most direct way of counteracting this division. He made overtures to Britain to settle the crucial Eastern Question, and the resulting agreement served as the basis for reopening the concert in 1840–1841. But the rapprochement stemmed from the principles of a coherent Weltpolitik, and Nesselrode's achievement in bringing about the treaties of 1840 and 1841 belongs to the history of an approach to a "new order." The character of this approach is suggested, in part, by his preoccupation with economic interests which, as he asserted repeatedly, united Russia and Britain (the rapprochement began with the lowering of restrictions on trade with Britain at the end of 1836, and concluded with the disappointing treaty on trade and navigation in 1843). There were coordinated moves toward other countries which, taken together, reveal the desire for a large community in which trade and commerce would unite Russia with Asia and Europe. It held a grand design, but it contained what Grunwald has termed "the most important grand error that Nesselrode made in all of his calculations"—his assumption that "it was possible to form a durable accord with the English."[2]

There can be no doubt that Nesselrode's Anglophilism led him to grossly miscalculate the realities of international politics. His mistake was that he perceived the rivalry with Britain as a collision of national prejudices and narrow, exclusive policies. Britain, he held, was "torn by two conflicting tendencies, by democracy and by catholicism."[3] The first, expressed in "public opinion," was all too responsive to national feeling to be allowed to influence foreign policy. The second, rooted in Tory philosophy, seemed to favor a clear separation of "high politics" from the domestic arena, allowing diversity. In the 1830s Russia had to contend increasingly with Russophobia in a "democratic" for-

2. Grunwald, "Nesselrode," 190.
3. Nesselrode to Meyendorff (8 November 1851), Lettres et papiers, vol. 10: 67.

eign policy for which he leveled much of the blame on Palmerston and the Liberal Party. "We can hardly ignore that the nature of public opinion on certain questions may impose conditions on the ministry of a representative state, sometimes against their most friendly intentions," he said. "We constantly have to take these things into consideration."[4] Unfortunately, Russia did not take part in parliamentary politics. "Consequently, when they reproach us or make an allegation against us within their chambers or Parliament, and it would be in our interest to answer them, we are at a relative disadvantage. . . . In our effort to counteract it publicly we can often do no better than make some tardy comment, which, like all of the communications from cabinet to cabinet, usually winds up being classified secret."[5] However, the fact that the Liberals were in power between 1836 and 1841 did not restrain him in his conciliatory efforts during those years, as we shall see. He certainly preferred a Tory ministry; "with the Tories there would always be very ready means to reach understanding on questions of general politics," he remarked later.[6] But, whichever was in power, he believed that there was "no real cause for rivalry, but to the contrary, every possible motive for union and cordiality."[7] "In the end, we will see that Russophobia is so much nonsense," he predicted.[8]

In 1843–1844 those who believed that the reasons for rivalry were real began once again to come to the fore, both in Russia, where Nicholas I suddenly adopted a more nationalistic policy, and in Britain, where the more popular Entente Cordiale quickly regained favor. The change in Russia was manifest in mounting friction between Nesselrode and the nationalists, and in major differences between Nesselrode and Nicholas over foreign policy. Before Russia had decided to support the constitutional government established in Greece in 1843, the foreign diplomatic corps in Petersburg became aware that Nesselrode

4. Nesselrode to Brunnow (18 July 1842), *BMAddMSS* 43144; and (20 August 1853), *Lettres et papiers*, vol. 10: 272.
5. Nesselrode to Brunnow (18 July 1842), *BMAddMSS* 43144.
6. Nesselrode to Khreptovich (27 March 1852), *Lettres et papiers*, vol. 10: 184.
7. Note congratulating Peel on a speech commemorating the founding of the British Russian Company, in Nesselrode to Brunnow (16 March 1844), *BMAddMSS* 40541.
8. Nesselrode to Meyendorff (21 February 1844), *Lettres et papiers*, vol. 8: 239.

was for it and Nicholas against. The British minister, Baron Bloomfield, reported that Nesselrode had taken a stand consistent with the British position, and that he "deplored" the Tsar's attitude.[9] But a more serious disparity was revealed in the same year, when Nicholas decided that the status quo could not be upheld in the Near East, and initiated overtures to Austria for a division of the spoils—a plan for a partition not unlike the one Nesselrode had defeated in the 1820s when Capodistria proposed it. Metternich was not receptive, although Orlov was sent to Vienna to try to persuade him. The crowning blow came in 1844, when Nicholas went to London and, instead of dispelling anti-Russian feeling, reawakened old suspicions. Nesselrode then went to England himself, and tried to repair bipartisanship with a promise of cooperation contained in the famous Nesselrode Memorandum. Within a few months, however, Britain had reaffirmed the Entente Cordiale. Russia was slipping precipitously into diplomatic isolation. The era of the rapprochement was over.

Along with the Russian reaction against cooperation with Britain, a sweeping rejection of the "Germanism" and "Europeanism" of the whole preceding era in foreign relations gathered momentum. For example, in *Russia in 1844*, addressed to Nicholas I by an official, V. S. Pelchinskii, "the system of Russian foreign policy maintained with such effort and such detrimental effect" was attributed to the "diplomatic doctrine" which had "permeated all governments with great subtlety" during the Congress of Vienna. The Holy Alliance had demonstrated "the complete nullity, the complete absurdity of the politics of diplomacy."[10] And the idea of cooperation with Britain had been insane. "There can be no doubt that the outstanding, vital interest of England is to see that the Russian fleet decays or is reduced and that her manufacturing and commercial industries are paralyzed."[11] While Pelchinskii thought that "Russia's involvement" in "all of the affairs of Europe" had been "completely detrimental" and had "served only to satisfy the vanity and opinions of her diplomatists," Golovin observed that the alien character of Russian diplomacy had "most contributed to injure its cause,

---

9. Cf. Bloomfield to Aberdeen (26 September 1843), *BMAddMSS* 43144.
10. V. S. Pelchinskii, *La Russie en 1844* (Paris and Leipzig, 1845), 117–118, 102.
11. *Ibid.*, 119.

for none any longer believe its necessity, and all dislike its proceedings."[12] In *Russia Invaded by the Germans*, published in
1844, Vigel wrote: "Above all, you must perceive the disagreement, the profound aversion existing between the Russians and
the Germans to see how very difficult it would be to revitalize the
alliance of the northern powers, the alliance of 1815."[13]

There was a note of impending change in the open expressions of nationalist discontent. Yet Nesselrode, promoted to
Chancellor in 1845, continued to involve Russia in affairs that
reached well beyond immediate national interests. A few months
after the trip to England, he went to Vienna to discuss Prussia's
possible annexation of Schleswig-Holstein and the Eastern Question with Metternich. He found himself in accord with Metternich
that Prussia's claims would have to be weighed in legal terms
against the Danish territorial status quo as a factor in European
equilibrium. His determination to uphold the concert as vital to
prevent "a general conflagration in the Orient" remained un-
shaken,[14] although his inability to press his policy forward and
alter Nicholas's views caused Metternich some uneasiness and
consternation. He continued to be "more favorable to newly constituted Greece than the Emperor," according to a French memorandum in 1846, and Russian policy conformed with his attitude.[15]
He obviously served as an ambassador of good will, and this may
have been due in part to an awareness in Petersburg, after the
Tsar's opinions had been aired along with those of Orlov in
Vienna and London, that Nesselrode's policy was more welcome
to the Western powers and more comfortably pursued.

His influence in this period is difficult to assess; there is
evidence of strong disagreement with Nicholas, even personal
antagonism, but he maintained a grip that allowed him to act effectively. In 1845, for example, he persuaded the Tsar to make
what was the last of the great imperial pilgrimages to the West,
a trip to Rome—remarkable enough for a Tsar in any time and
even more so in the era of Official Nationality. That the idea was
advanced by Nesselrode suggests that he remained a defender of

12. *Ibid.*, 99; Golovin, *Russia*, 208.
13. Vigel, *La Russie envahie*, 138.
14. Nesselrode to Persiany (20 July 1845), *BMAddMSS* 43144.
15. "Mémoire sur l'état des relations politiques extérieurs de la Russie,"
     (St. Petersburg, 20 February 1846), *MAE* 333, SIM 560, Russie,
     vol. 43.

the Holy Alliance in spirit as well as in diplomatic calculation. He also went to Rome, and his personal efforts led to the signing of the Concordat of 1847 with the Vatican—an agreement that the Tsar later chose to disregard, to Nesselrode's intense regret. On his way back to Russia in January 1846, Nicholas stopped in Vienna, and there indulged in thoughtless candor in interviews with Metternich. When Nesselrode learned about it, he confided to Meyendorff a fear that Nicholas would "poison our political relations and do great damage to our interests." [16]

In 1846 it became still more obvious that Russia's relationship with Britain had changed substantially and no longer served the purpose Nesselrode had intended in the rapprochement. As late as 1843 the two powers had cooperated, in the Belgian question for example, to sustain "the political system of Europe"; but two events in 1846 indicated that such cooperation was unlikely to continue. They were the return of a Liberal Government in Britain and the Austrian annexation of Cracow. Nesselrode, in the habit of keeping a close watch on British politics, had anticipated the Liberal victory. It was logical to expect a reversion to an anti-Russian policy, but he hoped the Liberals would see the wisdom of the Tory attitude toward Russia. He instructed Brunnow in London to prepare a paper giving an overview of relations between the two countries under the Tory ministry in 1841–1845, emphasizing their successful cooperation, and to submit it with a request that it be passed along to the next Government. But he suffered a seizure of despair when Lord John Russell as Prime Minister appointed Palmerston Foreign Secretary. Palmerston had lived to regret consorting with Russia in 1839–1841, and some believed that he was now motivated by a desire for revenge. Nesselrode did not think he would respect the concert, it was "a thorn in his foot." [17] But if there was still a chance of preventing Europe's division into "two camps," it disappeared with the annexation of Cracow. Cracow had been placed under joint administration by the conservative powers in 1838, and when they agreed that Austria should annex the city in 1846, Russia more than others bore the brunt of Western criticism, led in Britain by

16. Nesselrode to Meyendorff (17 January 1846), *Lettres et papiers*, vol. 8: 283.
17. Nesselrode to Meyendorff (25 July 1846), *Lettres et papiers*, vol. 8: 327.

Palmerston and the active Polish exile group. Nesselrode thought that Cracow was not important by itself in comparison with Palmerston's larger "strategy" to isolate Russia. "He wants to force us to back down, and will torment us plenty to achieve his aim," said Nesselrode.[18] But the danger was not great in an issue in which Austria and Prussia shared real interests with Russia. "I know that France and England will not go to war with us over Cracow," he said.[19]

Russia was falling back on the conservative alignment, the "German system," now buttressed less by common conservatism than by realities of geopolitics, a host of agreements and precedents, and, not least, ties that united the Romanovs with the German nobility. It was weak and destined to be a casualty in the Russian reaction against "Germanism."

The romantic movement in Germany itself involved a rejection of the Europeanism and cosmopolitanism of the *ancien régime*, and when this movement influenced the Russian intelligentsia it quite naturally turned Russians against the conservative system. Under the influence of Schelling, Schlegel, Baader, Herder, and others, although occasionally to the perturbation of German romantics themselves, the Slavophiles sought escape from German influence in government and the Pan-Slavs forged ideological weapons against Austria in the Balkans. The 1840s in Germany saw the beginning of the Pan-German movement with new concern for the far-flung minorities in Poland, Bohemia, the Ukraine, and the Balkans, and also of the new realism that educated Bismarck's generation of statesmen-strategists. The idea of the unity of the Volk was a justification for the extension of influence in both Pan-Germanism and Pan-Slavism in the 1840s.

Nesselrode's Germanism came under more intense fire in connection with Balkan policy as official nationalism developed a stronger Pan-Slav character. His position was intimated by his daughter when she accused "the ardent defenders of this system of persecution" (Official Nationality) of being critical of the regime only insofar as they were more anxious to "bring about

18. Nesselrode to Meyendorff (7 September 1846), *Lettres et papiers*, vol. 8: 342–343.
19. Nesselrode to Meyendorff (5 January 1847), *Lettres et papiers*, vol. 9: 5.

that glittering utopia ... Greco-Slav unity." "You must go along with Karamzin, Samarin, and Mukhanov in their gross absurdities or, if you happen to disagree, be accused of betraying your faith and your country."[20] Serbia provides an interesting example in which Nesselrode's "Germanism" antagonized Pan-Slavs. "Do we have hopes and plans for the independence of Serbia?" Nesselrode asked Barante in 1836, "What would we gain?"[21] In 1842 the independence movement gathered new strength, and the Pan-Slavs wished to support it; it was not until the spring of 1843 that Nesselrode managed to prevail. "You cannot imagine how much this affair has worried me," he wrote to Meyendorff. "We, the other Russians with German names, have our troubles now and then, and in this question the great current of national feeling aroused was more than those Serb bandits deserved."[22]

"If the peoples' passions were ever allowed to influence the calculations of high politics, it would be enough to turn all of Europe upside-down," he told Nicholas in 1848.[23] Fearing an upheaval that would upset European equilibrium and produce a great war, he saw no alternative to intervention in Poland and Hungary. He advised against abandoning Austria to the consequences of her weakness, although he realized that the "German system" collapsed with Metternich, and that the end result of the brutal actions of Paskevich's armies in Hungary, as well as in Poland, was to accentuate division and Russia's isolation. The European system ceased to exist. "The history of peoples and

20. Marie von Seebach to Dmitry Nesselrode (25 February 1846), *Lettres et papiers*, vol. 8: 294–295.
21. In Barante to Thiers (21 May 1836), *Souvenirs*, vol. 5: 388.
22. Nesselrode to Meyendorff (2 May 1843), *Lettres et papiers*, vol. 8: 213.
23. Nesselrode to Nicholas I (11 September 1848), in Martens, *Recueil*, vol. 12: 251. The Tsar's reply was written on the margin. On his attitude, see Riasanovsky, *Nicholas I*, 4–5. He issued a bombastic manifesto which resembled a declaration of war on the liberal West, and Nesselrode promptly published an explanation intended to counteract this impression, cf. *Journal de St. Pétersbourg* (19 March 1848), and instructed his staff abroad to read his own statement in addition to the Tsar's to know "la ligne politique que le gouvernement imperial comte suivre au milieu de cette crise." Nesselrode to Fonton (2 April 1848), *Lettres et papiers*, vol. 9: 78. While the West took the Tsar's manifesto as the index of Russian policy, Russians found Nesselrode's position "un-tsarist" and "un-Nikolaievan." K. N. Lebedev, "Iz zapisok," *Russkii arkhiv* (1910), vol. 3: 239.

certainly the history of our time offers few examples of a year so disastrous and rich in ruin," he said.[24]

He was disoriented after 1848. "Everything is so uncertain that it is impossible to form an opinion about what we should plan even for the nearest future," he complained.[25] But he tried to follow the old principles, for example in the role of arbiter at the Olmütz Conference in 1850. He had always regarded German unity as advantageous to Russian intercourse with the West. Now this was a ridiculous assumption, and with Metternich gone there was little chance of strengthening the concert by cooperation with Austria. When Britain took independent action in Greece in 1850, all he could do was cite precedent illustrating Russia's "common interests and actions with the British Cabinet," and warn solemnly against the destruction of "relations between powers which have signed the same agreements and have been linked for many years by a common solidarity."[26] But he knew that there was little reason for Britain to support the concert when she could assert her influence advantageously through the "Entente Cordiale of baneful memory, so dangerous and so great a peril to the peace of Europe."[27] He dreaded war. In England there was talk now of the coming of a great war, a struggle between Western democracy and Asiatic despotism. "A war with England would be the worst of all possible wars," he said. "She is beyond our reach and we are the ones who would pay the price. May it be God's will to protect us from it!"[28]

For official nationalists 1848 was a sobering year, but it was an invitation to return to things that mattered. "What do we see when we look at the past?" Zhukovskii asked in 1849 in a letter to Paskevich, in command of the forces in Hungary. He saw a protracted conflict with Britain in which Russia had been isolated. "Is there anyone who does not find friendship with England

24. Nesselrode's annual report for 1848, in Martens, *Recueil*, vol. 12: 245.
25. Nesselrode to Khreptovich (27 October 1851), *Lettres et papiers*, vol. 10: 58–59.
26. Nesselrode to Brunnow (7 February 1850), in N. I. Grech, *La Vérité sur le différend Turco-Russe* (Brussels, 1853), 37, 45.
27. Nesselrode to Meyendorff (16 January 1852), *Lettres et papiers*, vol. 10: 137.
28. Nesselrode to Meyendorff (12 December 1851), *Lettres et papiers*, vol. 10: 72.

when he causes a revolutionary upheaval? Is there any rebel who is not known to be supported by her government?" The "advocates of British freedom" aimed to found "a new Rome" ruled by capitalists with an empire built on trade.[29] He believed that Britain had rallied the West against Russia, and if his view was distorted by his conviction that liberalism was a weapon, it was perhaps not entirely his fault; in Britain it was widely believed that "constitutional government" was a means of "securing the nationality of Western Europe," because "a people who acquire freedom, must, on the day when their liberties are secured, become the natural enemies of Russia and the natural allies of England."[30] Zhukovskii concluded that there was no effective way for Russia to counteract the revolutionary movement in the West. The European system, ill-conceived from the Holy Alliance onward, should be abandoned. Russia should go her own way, "without haste, without racing, along the path assigned to her by her history" toward "a prosperous self-realization, independent of Europe." Russia, he predicted, "will not be part of Europe, and not of Asia—she will be Russia, a separate world isolated from all, internally harmonious, externally unapproachable."[31]

An independent course spelled the end of Nesselrode's influence. The poet Tyutchev, an official nationalist and a onetime employee in the foreign ministry, expressed his own preoccupation with historical determinism in a few lines dedicated to his former chief's eclipse: "No! my dwarf, coward without equal... / ... / You, with your soul of little faith / Will not lead Holy Russia astray... / ... / The universal destiny of Russia— / No! This you cannot change!"[32] Nesselrode was blamed, as Stremoukhov has said quoting Tyutchev, for carrying on "the false system, the inept and anti-national system" introduced under Alexander I as "the result of 'a profound deviation' in Russia's historical life, of

29. V. A. Zhukovskii, "Russkaia i Angliiskaia politika. Pis'mo V. A. Zhukovskago k kniaziu Varshavskomu, grafu I. F. Paskevichu-Erivanskomu," *Russkii arkhiv* (1878), vol. 2: 428–434.
30. T. McKnight, *Thirty Years of Foreign Policy: A History of the Secretaryships of the Earl of Aberdeen and Viscount Palmerston* (London, 1855), 186–187.
31. Zhukovskii, "Russkaia i Angliiskaia politika," 436.
32. F. I. Tyutchev, "Graf K. V. Nessel'rode," (1850), *Polnoe sobranie stikhotvorenii* (Leningrad, 1939), 93.

an alien civilization imposed upon intellectual society" while "the historical life, the national life, remained intact in the masses."[33]

Nesselrode saw Europe marching steadily toward the brink of war. In December 1852 he instructed Brunnow to warn Aberdeen, now Prime Minister, that France was reopening the Eastern Question,[34] entertaining "imperialist ideas" and pursuing an "ambitious and aggressive policy . . . to the woe of Europe."[35] In January 1853 he sent a remarkable dispatch to Brunnow, "an hypothesis pure and simple," in which he explained that Russia alone could not be expected to preserve peace if France forced a confrontation. "Even if we are conciliatory in our language and our actions, it is to be feared that sooner or later we will fail to avoid war." Speaking as if he were the French ruler, he said that he would confront Russia with a crisis in which she had two choices—to back down and withdraw her influence in the Near East with detrimental effect, or to fight, with equally detrimental effect. In a war, "carried on in the name of the independence and integrity of the Porte," Russia will "face the whole world alone and without allies, because Prussia will be of no account and indifferent to the question, and Austria will be more or less neutral if not favorable to the Porte." It would be a limited war, for the specific purpose of destroying Russian naval and maritime power on the Black Sea. "The theater being distant, other than soldiers to be employed as a landing force, it will require mainly ships to open the straits of Constantinople to us, and the united naval forces of Turkey, England, and France will make quick work of the Russian fleet" and "destroy Russian commerce, burn their bases." In the end, "the endeavor of 1815 will be annihilated." His hypothesis proved quite accurate, from first to last.[36]

A few months later, with war imminent, Nesselrode conjectured that there would be no move to reopen the concert. Would France, he asked, "demand to know whether her claims and conduct were in accord with the treaty of 1841, and would she consent to have the question decided by an areopagus of the five

---

33. D. Stremoukhov, *La Poésie et l'idéologie de Tiouttchev* (Paris, 1937), 139.
34. Brunnow to Aberdeen (24 December 1852), *BMAddMSS* 43144.
35. Nesselrode to Meyendorff (19 January 1852), *Lettres et papiers*, vol. 10: 138–139.
36. Nesselrode to Brunnow (2 January 1853), *BMAddMSS* 43144.

powers?"[37] His answer was negative, because peace was no longer the foremost consideration.

In the crisis, some Western statesmen still expected Nesselrode to step in as he had in the past, counsel moderation, and save the Tsar from another blunder. Sir G. H. Seymour confidently asserted in January 1853 that Nicholas "occasionally takes a precipitate step; but as reflection arrives, reason and Count Nesselrode make themselves heard."[38] But this did not happen. It was said that the Tsar ignored his minister's advice because the issues involved the Holy Places, and that Nesselrode was excluded from Orthodox affairs. Yet Nesselrode had often taken a leading role in the diplomacy of the Eastern Question, which was always interwoven with religious issues, and he had handled Orthodox affairs in the past. He had conducted the diplomacy that Alexander I had hoped would lead to a reconciliation with the Vatican on matters of policy in 1816. He had mediated relations with Polish Catholics and the Uniats, had helped plan and arrange Porfirii Uspenskii's mission to the Near East in 1840–1842, and, after sitting on a committee to study relations with the Vatican, had conducted the negotiations that led to the Concordat of 1847. What is surprising is that with his ideals of a Christian community of Europe, he exercised influence for as long as he did, despite the importance of Orthodoxy as a pillar of Official Nationality. "There is one fact which cannot be put aside, cannot be guarded against, and cannot in any way be entrusted to diplomacy," he remarked in June 1853. "This fact is the sympathy and community of interests binding our population of fifty million Orthodox with the twelve million comprising the majority under the Sultan (in European Turkey)."[39] Nicholas, who expressed regret that he had sacrificed "his religious beliefs" and "the traditions of Russian policy," according to Martens, may well have considered the Menshikov mission to be the expression of a patriotic policy.[40] In any event, he ignored the alternatives

37. Nesselrode to Meyendorff (23 June 1853), *Lettres et papiers*, vol. 10: 240–241.
38. Seymour to Russell (12 January 1853), in G. B. Henderson, "The Seymour Conversations, 1853," *History* (October 1933), vol. 18, no. 3: 245.
39. Nesselrode to Brunnow (1 June 1853), in M. I. Bogdanovich, "Venskiia soveshchaniia i Parizhskii traktat. 1854–1856," *Russkaia starina* (1876), vol. 17: 381.
40. Martens, *Recueil*, vol. 4: 443.

pointed to by the "Nesselrode Memorandum" of 1844 and, above all, by the straits convention of 1841. Menshikov's rash ultimatum to Turkey, delivered without regard for Western interests in the Near East, directly contradicted Nesselrode's policy.

After the war began, Nesselrode found one last opportunity to use his influence effectively against a course advocated by nationalists. The logical strategy for Russia was to send the fleet to the Bosphorus and an army through the Balkans to close the straits. When Nicholas was set to do this, Nesselrode counselled against it. "Of all my duties," he told the Tsar, "there is none more painful to discharge than to submit opinions to Your Majesty which may sometimes not be in agreement with his ideas and views." Austria would oppose Russia, he warned, and other states would follow suit. "Instead of having three adversaries, we would be in a struggle against the whole of Europe."[41] Given this vision of a titanic war between Russia and the West, Nicholas adopted the purely defensive strategy that confined the fighting mainly to the battle for Sevastopol.

To Nicholas, the Crimean War seemed pointless, a dreadful accident—"So many lives are sacrificed for nothing!" he said shortly before he died in 1855.[42]

"I have a profound feeling that everyone I see around me is participating in one of the most solemn moments in the history of the world," said Tyutchev.[43] His emotions took a strange twist, perhaps typical among nationalists; he welcomed the war and the patriotism it awakened, even in defeat. The rumbling guns were like a refreshing summer thunderstorm that would sweep away the stultifying atmosphere of the old regime. Now Russia was certain to follow a nationalistic policy; there was, as Kiselev said, "no alternative but to forge the power with which to turn power aside."[44]

When Nesselrode announced his wish to retire, the reasons he gave were personal, not the war and the failure of his policy.

---

41. "Mémoire présenté à l'Empereur Nicolas I par le comte Ch. de Nesselrode, contre un projet de déclaration de guerre a l'Autriche" (7 September 1854), *Lettres et papiers*, vol. 11: 74.
42. "Doktor Mandt o poslednikh nedeliakh Imperatora Nikolaia Pavlovicha," *Russkii arkhiv* (1905), vol. 2: 479.
43. Tyutchev, "Iz pis'em . . . vo vremia Krymskoi voiny. 1854 god," *Russkii arkhiv* (1899), vol. 2: 270.
44. In A. M. Fadeev, "Vospominaniia," *Russkii arkhiv* (1891), vol. 2: 26.

"An honest man must admit that he no longer has the energy or capacity to manage difficult affairs when, as is my case today, he has had an active and toilsome career of 59 years and has reached the age of 75." It would have been time to quit even "if Providence had preserved the sovereign I had the good fortune to serve through the most crucial periods of a glorious reign."[45] In accepting his resignation, Alexander II made a brief, reserved reply. "You have been the constant supporter of the Emperor Alexander I and of my venerated father, who in their policies desired no more than to uphold the established treaties and peace in Europe."[46] In 1856 the crucial periods of Nicholas's reign clearly overshadowed the glory, and Russians felt that something more should have been desired.

The great reforms initiated by Alexander II carried Russia over the threshold of a modern, revolutionary transformation, and held the most traditional of the aims of tsarist statecraft: they were intended to make Russia powerful, independent, autonomous, and invulnerable. A new foreign policy was called for to serve and complement domestic reform. Prince Gorchakov, hailed by official nationalists as a true patriot, was selected over Nesselrode's protégé, Brunnow, to administer it. Gorchakov had served under Nesselrode, but in contrast with Brunnow he disliked the European system, particularly the concert, and had been an outspoken antagonist of Nesselrode's for years. He had wanted to send the army to the straits, and Nesselrode blamed him for "the incontinent order to occupy the principalities" in the train of events that led to war.[47] Gorchakov for his part alleged: "Nesselrode forgot that it was in the era of Alexander Pavlovich's victories that Russia and Europe stood together in an entirely amicable frame of mind," whereas "in 1854 everyone and everything conspired against Russia."[48] He advocated a policy of *recueillement*—of spurning the kinds of European entanglements Nesselrode had promoted, while gathering strength. "They reproach

45. Nesselrode to Alexander II (n.d. November 1855), *Lettres et papiers*, vol. 11: 109.
46. Alexander II to Nesselrode (15 April 1856), *Lettres et papiers*, vol. 2: 15.
47. Nesselrode to Meyendorff (25 June 1853), *Lettres et papiers*, vol. 10: 242.
48. A. M. Gorchakov, "Kniaz Aleksandr Mikhailovich Gorchakov v ego razskazakh iz proshlago," *Russkaia starina* (1883), vol. 40: 169.

Russia, telling her to isolate herself and be silent," he said, "Russia must stand aside they say. Russia will not stand aside. Russia gathers her strength."[49]

Brunnow advocated a return to the concert. He had conducted the negotiations in London for the straits conventions of 1840 and 1841, and now proposed that Russia should strive "to secure, by common accord, the well-being and religious freedom of the Christian populace in the Near East, without discrimination respecting the rites they profess; to place religious and civil rights under a collective guarantee," and "to concert in this spirit for the renewal of the treaty of 1841." "You will understand the great care I have taken to explain, as well as possible, the purpose and importance of the treaty of 1841," he wrote to Nesselrode.[50] But such a policy was not to be enacted, and Brunnow, who had been groomed to be Nesselrode's successor since the 1830s, attended the Congress of Paris and then returned to his former post at London.

The treaty of 1841 did influence the statesmen who framed the Treaty of Paris, but the concert was not renewed in 1856, and a systematic approach based on classic principles was not reintroduced. Nesselrode, whose attitude since 1854 was virtually "peace at any price," favored relatively easy concessions on specific terms.[51] Far from interpreting the treaty as a vehicle for participation in the European system, Gorchakov and nationalists saw it as an onerous burden to cast off at the first opportunity.

Ultimately Gorchakov failed to live up to the expectations of the nationalists, especially the Pan-Slavs, although the military victories scored in Asia gave *recueillement* an appearance of effectiveness it did not have in the Near East. Unable to impose a "Russian solution," Gorchakov yielded to the Western powers at the Congress of Berlin, and attracted criticism for having failed to

49. Gorchakov, *Sbornik izdannyi v pamiat dvadsatipiatiletiia upravleniia Ministerstvom Inostrannykh del* . . . (St. Petersburg, 1881), "Depeshi i tsirkuliary," 5. It was believed that Gorchakov was initiating "a new era" in Russian foreign relations. Cf. Prince V. A. Cherkasskii, memoir (3 June 1856), "Protokoly Parizhskago kongressa," *Russkaia beseda* (1856), vol. 2: 26.
50. Brunnow to Nesselrode (n.d. 1855), *Lettres et papiers*, vol. 11: 111. Text of the proposal and enclosed note to Nesselrode.
51. For important dispatches by Nesselrode regarding the Peace of Paris, cf. "K istorii Parizhskogo mira 1856 g.," *Krasnyi arkhiv* (1936), vol. 75: 10–61.

make a clean break with the past in 1856. "Much has been said in our press about the long and injurious influence of Prince Metternich, assisted by Nesselrode, on the foreign and to a certain extent the domestic policy of Russia," said one critic, "but that damage hardly equals the extent of this, which has placed us under the influence of Prince Bismarck."[52] " 'Russia gathers her strength,' said Prince Gorchakov in his first message after succeeding his ill-starred predecessor Nesselrode. 'Be it declared that in questions of domestic and foreign policy alike, Russia has liquidated her accounts with the recent past' . . . Woe to you! How many horrible sins were continued!" wrote A. A. Kochubinskii, a Pan-Slav.[53] But if the rapprochement with France after Gorchakov left office relieved the government of criticism for "Germanism" to some extent, it also gave freer reign to the nationalistic, Pan-Slav ambitions that led to the calamity at Tsushima Straits and propelled Russia into the Great War. After half a century of gathering strength, Russia was still weak in comparison with the other great powers. But in 1856 the policy of *recueillement* expressed Russian expectations and was greeted, not as an entirely new course, but as a return to traditions of tsarist policy put aside in the idealistic rush to embrace Europe after 1801, a return to the laws of Russian history which Karamzin had been the first to invoke in protest against Alexander's innovations.

Nesselrode and Brunnow did not welcome it. They saw it as a return to isolation, to imperialistic policies at odds with the status quo, and to historic hatred of the West. But they saw no alternative. "It is entirely unimportant that you, Prince, are the one who will be minister," Nesselrode said to Gorchakov. "After the Peace of Paris, the Russian minister of foreign affairs will have absolutely nothing to do."[54] Russia would be cut off from the rest of the world. Two months before his retirement he had advised Alexander II that "Russia should adopt a system of foreign policy different from the one she has followed to the present time." He continued, "The extent and consequences of the sacrifices imposed upon the country by the war are not precisely known. But it is clear that from the present day Russia must ac-

52. D. I. Ilovaiskii, "M. N. Katkov," *Russkii arkhiv* (1897), vol. 1: 141.
53. A. A. Kochubinskii, "Nashi dve politiki v slavianskom voprose," *Istoricheskii vestnik* (1881), vol. 5: 463.
54. Gorchakov, "v ego razskazakh," 171.

cept the absolute necessity to concentrate on internal affairs and the development of her own material and moral strength. Because this domestic work is the country's first need, all foreign relations that would impede it must be carefully avoided."[55]

Russia had not withdrawn from Europe, she had been forcibly isolated. Britain bore much of the blame. "It is a tragedy for the whole of Europe," said Brunnow. "The peace, the prosperity, and the union of the nations that form the great European family would apparently be the ruin of England."[56] He expressed the forebodings of those who had believed that the European system offered not only a guarantee of peace but the benefits of access to Western culture:

"Before, the upper classes of society were making headway for the cause of the European family. . . . What is happening in Russia today? The country recoils in pain inflicted by the West, and with an irresistible resurgence of national feeling it is returning to an old eastern foundation, hostile to Europe. It is beginning to repudiate Western ways, to reject the pacific genius for modern society and civilization that was invading and conquering this mass of sixty and ten million people. 'So much the better,' they are saying. Russia has no choice but to withdraw for a century and a half. She will return to the ancient barbarity, to the times of the grand dukes of Muscovy, she will transport her capital from the Baltic to the Kremlin."[57]

The unanswered question was whether Sevastopol, the "Russian acropolis" where hard realities were revealed amid the debris of shattered illusions, was a consequence of Nesselrode's policy or a consequence of its failure. From some viewpoints, there was no distinction to be made, but from others, including Nesselrode's, the distinction was important because in the first case the motives and principles which lay behind a half-century of diplomacy would be condemned. His nationalistic opponents saw Sevastopol as a direct result of his policy. A policy foredoomed to failure was folly. His recommendation in 1856 that Alexander II adopt

---

55. Nesselrode to Alexander II (11 February 1856), *Lettres et papiers*, vol. 11: 112–113.
56. Brunnow, *La Guerre d'Orient, ses causes et ses conséquences* (Brussels, n.d.), 117. The date of publication is 1854. A reply was published the same year, cf. T. Anguetil, *Réponse d'un soldat à un diplomat, sur la question d'Orient* (Brussels, 1854).
57. Brunnow, *La Guerre*, 92–93.

a new foreign policy was taken as an admission that he had been wrong all along, and as a call for a "true Russian program, oriented to Russian society, placing Russia first and depending on native Russian understanding of her urgent needs and requirements."[58] But Nesselrode believed that the failure was an accident: the revolutions and war in 1848–1856 were connected events that allowed an inherent instability to surface.

This difference was evident in his defense of his policy against an attack by the Slavophile historian and official nationalist M. P. Pogodin, who accused him of having betrayed Russia's national interests.[59] Nesselrode replied that a policy should not be condemned simply because disaster had intervened, and that Pogodin had adopted a narrow, limited view in an attempt "to show that for fifty years Russian policy has been on the wrong track."[60] He wrote in defense:

"This policy had disadvantages, but is it humanly possible that any policy would not? One cannot always surmount all obstacles with equal ease by taking one course as opposed to another. The questions you must ask are these: Was it generally effective? Did it help to preserve Russia's domestic tranquility? Did it enhance Russia's importance and moral influence in foreign affairs? Surely no one would argue with the view that from 1815 to 1848 Russia's influence was acknowledged to be great, and that under the guidance of her rulers Russia held a leading position in Europe. But this position required sacrifices from Russia—moderation and relentless magnanimity. It required that she sacrifice her ambitions, even her private ambitions, so that the high interest of her policy would not be subordinated to lesser considerations. . . . No single event should be used to judge the highest achievements of the policy from past to present."[61]

After he retired, he retreated to a small circle of friends, mainly those who frequented the salon of the Empress Alexandra. Maria Kalergis looked after him and read Thiers' works to him,

58. V. S. N., "Neskol'ko slov po povodu zapiski gr. Nessel'roda," *Russkii arkhiv* (1872), vol. 1: 346.
59. Cf. N. Barsukov, *Zhizn i trudy M.P. Pogodina* (St. Petersburg, 1891), vol. 4: 253.
60. "Graf Karl Nessel'rode. Zashchita politiki Rossii i polozheniia, priniatago eiu v Evrope. 1854 g.," *Russkaia starina* (1873), vol. 8: 800.
61. *Ibid.*, 803–805.

which he found a fair and accurate record of events he had witnessed. He set out to write his memoirs, but dropped the project when he reach the year 1814—the eve of the Congress of Vienna and his ministry. His policy was in disrepute in Russia and not well known or appreciated in the West, and perhaps it seemed pointless to write about it.

Members of his circle, including Brunnow, acknowledged its failure and reluctantly accepted *recueillement*. For the most part, however, they did not join in the nationalistic denunciation, but held on to his reasoning that a policy should not be judged in terms of ultimate triumph or failure. This was the position taken, for example, by Alexander Jomini, a diplomat who had served under him since 1835 and was later a Senior Adviser in the ministry and a leading patron of the Imperial Historical Society. Speaking in particular of Nesselrode's effort to sustain the concert in relations with Britain, Jomini commented that his policy rested on "impossible ideals," then raised the question whether it would have been better to have followed these ideals than submit to "the realities that led to the Crimean War and everything since."[62] Jomini's major work, titled *Russia and Europe in the Epoch of the Crimean War* in the Russian translation, expressed his belief that "positive morality" stood above material reality.[63]

It may be noted that Jomini was not alone, and that the old principles retained a following despite the rise of nationalistic Realpolitik. Two of the leading protagonists were Friedrich Martens—diplomat, historian, Privy Counsellor, Professor of International Law at the University of St. Petersburg, and a moving spirit behind the Hague conferences on arbitration and arms limitation in 1899 and 1907[64]—and Sergei Goriainov, State Coun-

---

62. A. H. Jomini, "Rol i znachenie Rossii v Evrope pered Krymskoi voinoi," *Nabliudatel* (December 1885), vol. 12: 87.

63. Jomini, "Rossiia i Evropa v epokhu Krymskoi voiny," *Vestnik Evropy* (1886), vol. 117: 657–724; vol. 118: 176–242, 655–734; vol. 119: 253–311, 543–595; vol. 120: 204–260, 658–714; vol. 121: 179–235, 550–619. Since Jomini believed that the Crimean War contributed greatly to the unnatural separation of Russia from Europe, the Russian title is more significant than that of the first edition in French, *Étude diplomatique sur la guerre de Crimée* (St. Petersburg, 1874), 2 vols.

64. For Martens's treatment of Nesselrode's diplomacy and the rapprochement with Britain, cf. the *Recueil*, especially his commentaries

sellor, Director of the Imperial Archive and the Archive of St. Petersburg, noted historian and author of *The Bosphorus and the Dardanelles*, a study of Russian policy in the Near East.[65] As Jomini did, Martens and Goriainov praised Nesselrode's diplomacy for its ideals and principles and adroit management, yet with a clear recognition that it had failed and that conditions had changed. In contrast with the dominant interpretations—Russian and Western—they held that tsarist foreign policy was not necessarily aggressive or contentious. They maintained that a just legal order enforced by the community as a whole could control international conflict. With this emphasis, Martens emerges as the most outstanding protagonist. He was himself a statesman actively seeking means to secure peace, whose scholarly interest in the past went along with his own devotion to a classic approach. There were other similarities. As Nesselrode had, he believed that the political differences between Russia and the liberal Western powers were less important than their common interests; he also was German, and an object of vitriolic attacks for "cosmopolitan" tendencies.

The decline of the classic approach was indicated by the demise of the congress and concert systems by mid-century; but more than this, it involved a conscious rejection of a mode of perceiving alternatives and a whole guiding philosophy. Within Nesselrode's frame of reference, the "old conservatism" was nowhere in evidence after 1856. Not in Russia; not in Britain, where

---

in vols. 4 and 12; *Die russische Politik in der orientalischen Frage* (St. Petersburg, 1877); "Imperator Nikolai I i Koroleva Viktoriia. Istoricheskii ocherk," *Vestnik Evropy* (1896), vol. 182: 74–130; "Rossiia i Angliia v tsarstvovanie Imperatora Nikolaia I," *Vestnik Evropy* (1898), vol. 189, no. 1: 5–31, no. 2: 465–502. Also of interest are: *La Russie et l'Angleterre au debut de leurs relations réciproques* (Paris, 1891); *Russland und England in Zentral-Asien* (St. Petersburg, 1880); and reviews of the latter by V. P. Danevsky, *La Russie et l'Angleterre dans l'Asie centrale. Observations critiques* (London, 1881), and N. F. Petrovskii, "Rossiia i Angliia v Srednei Azii," *Drevniaia i novaia Rossiia* (1880), vol. 16, no. 1: 93–105.

65. Goriainov, *Le Bosphore et les Dardanelles*. Cf. Goriainov's sympathetic interpretation of the attempt in 1844 to keep the accord with Britain in effect, "O tainom soglashenii po delam Vostoka, sostoiavshemsia v 1844 g. mezhdu Nikolaem I i velikobritanskim pravitel'stvom," *Izvestiia Ministerstva Inostrannykh del* (1912), vol. 3: 201–203; English translation, "The Secret Agreement of 1844 between Russia and Great Britain," *Russian Review* (1912), vol. I, no. 3: 95–115, no. 4: 76–91.

the Peelite Tory approach with its free-trade philosophy had
been eclipsed by an imperialistic disregard for the commonweal
in both parties; not in France, the victim of vanity and aggressive
impulses under another Napoleon; not in Germany, which verged
on madness in his opinion. The modern school, in which war was
accepted as an instrument of diplomacy, not as the most palpable
evidence of its failure, was strange and repugnant to him. He met
Bismarck and found him no less pompous and narrow-minded
than Gorchakov. Bismarck sized up Nesselrode as "one of those
diplomats of the chancellery and salon we don't encounter any-
more, fortunately"; and Nesselrode, displaying his curious gift
for the incisive comment, remarked, "Certainly the good God
did not create him to solve the German question."[66]

But the future was no longer his worry. He had experienced
tumultuous times; he hoped his children and grandchildren would
see better; but he doubted that they would live in a world as
peaceful as that of 1815–1848.

"Count Nesselrode is dying," V. A. Mukhanov wrote in his
diary on March 21, 1862. "Opinions of him differ widely. . . .
Perhaps it is true that he did not meet things squarely and was too
faint-hearted to be the chief spokesman for Russia's interests in
Europe."[67] On the twenty-third he called his friends and relatives
to his bedside and made his exit as gracefully as he had conducted
his diplomacy—with a benediction: "May you all be as happy in
this life as I have been. Adieu."[68]

66. Grunwald, "Nesselrode," 192n.
67. V. A. Mukhanov, "Iz dnevnik zapisok," *Russkii arkhiv* (1897), vol.
    1: 63.
68. As told by A. D. Nesselrode, *Lettres et papiers*, vol. 11: 241.

II. The Danger of War:

The Bipolar Configuration of Power

In the mid-1830s the danger of war with Britain became one of Russia's major preoccupations. It may be accounted for by three related developments: first, the emergence of a bipolar configuration of power in which international politics were dominated by the contention between Russia and Britain; second, the projection of this into imperial rivalry as the expanding spheres of influence in Asia and the Near East intersected; and third, the associated competition in the extension of many aspects of national life, from the romantic search for identity to the realistic drive for economic independence. As a result, the possibility of a great European war was very much in mind. "Europe is divided into two camps, and however general and sincere the desire for peace may be, each side fears war and is wary of all the dangers," Barante wrote at the end of 1835.[1]

Nicholas I did not want war. "Russia needs peace," he said in January, 1836, "There is talk of war, but it is not necessary.

1. Barante to Broglie (20 December 1835), *Souvenirs*, vol. 5: 227.

. . . By choice not I nor any other real power desires war."[2] But in the West, and in Britain especially, there was a great deal of uneasiness over Russian ambitions, and serious thought was given to means of containing Russia and preventing further incursions into the Balkans, the Near East, and Asia. In February the House of Commons heard a discussion of the need to "impress Russia with the conviction" that Britain was "ready to go to war with her if necessary."[3] It was believed that all of the European powers would side with Britain in such a conflict. Nicholas, who affirmed that he would be "senseless if he attempted anything against the will of the whole of Europe," was aware of the possibility that Russia could be isolated.[4] This was reason for prudence, but not necessarily for fear. He tended to assume an arrogant, independent attitude, confident in the power demonstrated by the unbroken chain of victories that stretched back to 1812. Russia seemed to be unassailable. "It is impossible not to sense the grace of God and national pride when we see mother Russia standing like a pillar in the midst of all the chaotic conditions that agitate Europe, disdainful of the yelping envy and maliciousness, giving good for evil," he wrote to Field-Marshal Paskevich in February.[5] As Lobonov-Rostovsky has observed regarding the year 1837, the power of tsarist Russia was at its zenith, and conducive to aggressive adventures.[6]

In 1836 the British minister at Petersburg, the Earl of Durham, reported to Palmerston that the Tsar had confidence in only two men as advisers on foreign policy—Nesselrode and Orlov.[7] The two held different views of Britain. Nesselrode was well known for his Anglophilism and his professed hope "that His Majesty's policy will not be altered insofar as he is convinced that the union of both countries has proven advantageous for their commercial interests and indispensable to the larger interests of Europe."[8] He was instrumental in the first significant

2. In Barante to Broglie (12 January 1836), *Souvenirs*, vol. 5: 240.
3. Record of speech by Lord Dudley (19 February 1836), and discussion, *Hansard's Parliamentary Debates*, 3rd series, vol. 26: 636.
4. Barante to Broglie (20 December 1835), *Souvenirs*, vol. 5: 227.
5. Nicholas I to Paskevich (15 February 1836), "Imperator Nikolai Pavlovich v ego pis'makh," 18.
6. A. Lobanov-Rostovsky, *Russia and Asia* (New York, 1933), 115.
7. Durham to Palmerston (12 January 1836), *FO* 65/224.
8. Martens, "Rossiia i Angliia," no. 2: 447.

move toward rapprochement—an *ukaz* of December 18, 1836, providing for reduced tariffs and removing ninety-eight items, most of them manufactures, from the list of goods long excluded under Kankrin's policy, officially justified on grounds that "the admission of foreign products of superior quality . . . would encourage the producing classes to redouble their activity, by awakening them to a useful talent of emulation."[9] He announced it to Durham as heralding a fundamental change in economic policy. Russia was abandoning the old "system of prohibitions" and adopting a "system of protection."[10] This was not a complete surprise to Durham, who since 1835 had discussed trade and tariffs with Nesselrode on a number of occasions, and was familiar with his wish to see superior British manufactures made widely available in Russia and his general desire for freer trade and closer economic relations with Britain.[11] Nesselrode himself had encouraged Durham to tell Nicholas that relations between the two powers would be improved by lowering the barriers to trade, and Durham told the Tsar that "if any liberal change could be made in the Russian commercial policy it would have a very good effect." By his own account of the interview in May 1836, Durham said that "one of the main existing grounds in which those who were opposed to a Russian alliance made their stand was the system of prohibition which marked the policy of Russia, and which deeply affected the commercial relations of England."[12] He had discussed the subject with Kankrin and found him unhelpful. But he had been encouraged by Nesselrode's open disapproval of Kankrin's policy, and by Nesselrode's success, a few months before the passing of the *ukaz* of December 18, in eliminating some of the red tape which confronted British merchants entering Archangel and Kronstadt.[13] The *ukaz* was interpreted as promising economic rapprochement. Durham's biographer, Reid, writes that it was welcomed as a change "of great and far-reaching economic

---

9. *Tableau des marchandises étrangères admises à l'importation, et d'autres dont les droits de douane sont réduits ou modifiés*, printed by the Department of Foreign Commerce (St. Petersburg, 1836). Phrase quoted from Nicholas's formal announcement first published in the *Gazette du Senat* (6 December 1836).

10. Durham to Palmerston (1 January 1837), *FO* 65/233.

11. Cf. Durham to Palmerston (7 December 1835), *FO* 65/218.

12. Durham to Palmerston (16 May 1836), *FO* 65/225.

13. Cf. *ibid.* and Durham to Palmerston (21 September 1836), *FO* 65/226.

significance" and that "the British mercantile community regarded it as the turn of a tide."[14] Soon afterward, Durham reported that the Russian government was more open in discussing confidential economic matters than ever before.[15] He believed that if the new policy were greeted in a friendly spirit in Britain, commerce might flourish.

There were timely indications of a general responsiveness to potential Russian economic initiatives. In 1836, for example, Richard Cobden argued in *Russia, By a Manchester Manufacturer* that anti-Russian policies were leading toward war, and that it would be better and more economical to accept Russia as a partner and competitor than to isolate or crush her.[16] (Nesselrode came to regard Cobden as an ally, and later welcomed him to Petersburg "with a profusion of smiles," in Cobden's words, and "spoke of my Free Trade Labours, which he said would be beneficial to Russia.")[17] François Loeve-Veimars, a Frenchman, visited Petersburg in 1836 and in the following year published an article in which he made the remarkable assertion that Russian policy was changing; Russia, he said, wished to challenge the West "by the development of her merchant marine, and not through the conquests of her military navy, by the extension of foreign trade and not of frontiers."[18] There was even a realization that the desire for free enterprise was foreign to Russia and conflicted with national traditions. In 1837, for example, an English writer observed that if the Tsar wished "to render his nobles purely Russian in spirit and organization, his efforts to create and facilitate commerce and industry tend to foster a middle class necessarily European in their feelings and habits."[19] This was precisely what Nesselrode wanted.

Orlov, on the other hand, supported Kankrin's "prohibitive" system of trade in the spirit of economic nationalism, took a

14. S. J. Reid, *Life and Letters of the First Earl of Durham 1792–1840* (London, New York, and Bombay, 1906), vol. 2: 165–166.
15. Durham to Palmerston (13 February 1837), *FO* 65/233.
16. Cobden, *Russia, By a Manchester Manufacturer* (London, 1836). On Cobden's ideas about Russia, cf. J. A. Hobson, *Richard Cobden: The Industrial Man* (London, 1919), 29–36.
17. From Cobden's diary, in Morley, *Richard Cobden*, vol. 1: 451–452.
18. F. A. Loève-Veimars, "Des rapports de la France avec les grands et les petits états de l'Europe. I. De la Russie," *Revue des deux mondes* (1837), vol. 11: 227.
19. *Morning Chronicle* (11 October 1837).

jaundiced view of British capitalism, and was not anxious to promote free competition between the two powers, especially in domestic Russian markets. He portrayed Britain as a dedicated rival, if not an enemy (which Nicholas was not prepared to accept). He believed that Palmerston was mad, "capable of anything"—even a surprise attack, such as that on Copenhagen, "to burn Kronstadt." In 1836 he predicted war, and warned Barante that France should be ready to ally herself with Russia. "Your alliance with England is certainly not intended merely to plunge you into a senseless war at her side," he told Barante. "This would be a general war, a conflagration of Europe."[20]

Orlov's views were backed by convincing arguments based on military strategy, and enjoyed wide popularity among officers. The most influential strategist was Baron-General Antoine Jomini, who advised Nicholas during the campaign of 1828–1829 and in 1837 was chosen to instruct Alexander Nikolaevich in military science, at which time he also began work on his best-known strategical studies, including a secret report on all of the wars Russia might conceivably have to fight.[21] His approach contradicted Nesselrode's: he treated strategy and foreign policy as closely related, and regarded Britain as a threat to the continental balance of power because her naval and maritime supremacy gave her a disproportionate advantage. Jomini, who was French, advocated a policy of isolating Britain from all European alignments, chiefly by means of an alliance with France, which he believed should be the backbone of Russian policy.[22] Those who followed Orlov and Jomini could be expected to welcome events that drove a wedge between Russia and Britain, particularly a crisis in which France would be reluctant to go to war to defend British interests. Hence the first step in a nationalist policy would be the same as in a rapprochement with Britain, namely to break the Entente Cordiale. [23]

20. In Barante to Broglie (9 February 1836), *Souvenirs*, vol. 5: 284.
21. Jomini's most important published work is his *Précis de l'art de la guerre* (Paris, 1837–1856), n. vols.
22. "Une entente entre la France et la Russie a été jusqu'a la fin le plus caressé de ses voeux et de ses rêves." Sainte-Beuve, *La Général Jomini* (Paris, 1869), 224. This was referred to as a "continental strategy," and not surprisingly its Russian adherents had in many instances been Bonapartists before 1812.
23. For a nationalist's blueprint for this procedure, cf. "Mémoire sur les moyens . . . pour rompre l'alliance entre la France et l'Angle-

The possibility of an armed confrontation was heightened by the conflict in the Caucasus, where Russia had been drawn into an expensive, controversial war with the Murid tribes in an attempt to secure control of territory granted by the Treaty of Adrianople. It was an open invitation to trouble with Britain. Britain regarded the Caucasus as a barrier to Russian expansion, and aided the mountaineers with a clandestine flow of arms and supplies, some of which were carried to the Circassian coast by way of the Black Sea. The mountaineers put up a sturdy resistance to the Russian advance. Led by daring, brilliant tacticians, such as their chieftain Shamil, they scored victories, took a heavy toll in Russian prestige, and became popular heroes in the West and in the ranks of the Russian army itself. The illicit commerce and Russian exertions to halt it "escalated." The Russian navy had set up a blockade in 1831, but this proved largely ineffective, and in 1835 more energetic endeavors began. A fleet of six warships was assigned to the blockade and stationed at Gelendjik, about 250 miles to the east of Sevastopol by sea. At the same time the army started to build a military road for patrols and supply trains to Gelendjik. The government issued a warning that the blockade would be rigidly enforced. But when a British ship, the *Lord Charles Spencer*, was captured in international waters on the Black Sea, not in the act of supplying arms, Nesselrode denounced the actions of the Russian captain and secured the release of the vessel.[24]

In the spring 1836, British agents in the Caucasus told the mountaineers that Britain would soon be at war with Russia and that they could expect more extensive aid. The Russian government learned of this, and in August Nicholas remonstrated to Durham about it. Durham denied any knowledge of the agents. The Tsar replied that he was sure the British government was not directly involved because the intrigue came from the same source as an anti-Russian publication called *The Portfolio*. He may have intended this as a warning, because *The Portfolio* was edited and published by the First Secretary of the British Embassy at Con-

---

terre," (n.d. April 1834), G. F. Martens, *Nouveaux suppléments au Recueil des traités* . . . (Göttingen, 1839–1842), vol. 27 (3): 743–750.

24. Durham reported that Nesselrode severely faulted the officers of the Black Sea Fleet for seizing the *Lord Charles Spencer*. Cf. Durham to Palmerston (19 March 1836), FO 65/223.

stantinople, David Urquhart.[25] (Among other things it contained the testimony of Admiral Sir Edward Codrington, who had commanded the combined British, French, and Russian fleet at Navarino, that, "Were it generally acknowledged that Russia was at war with us, the only point to be considered would then be how to oppose her with the greatest ease and safety."[26]) The Tsar found in Durham a sympathetic listener, one who regarded *The Portfolio* as the work of an "industrious clique of Russophobists" which might "produce the very dangers it denounces."[27] But in September, Adjutant-General M. S. Vorontsov informed Nicholas that the agents were still spreading stories—"about the intentions of certain European powers to ally themselves with Turkey, declare war on us, and send auxiliary forces to Circassia with the aim of annihilating the Russians"—and Orlov, returning from a trip to Britain, said that he had never seen such preparations for war.[28] Durham reported that the Tsar was deeply disturbed.[29] This was the atmosphere in November when a Russian warship captured a British vessel near the Circassian coast.

The "Vixen" Affair

On the evening of November 24, 1836, the British schooner *Vixen* sailed into view of the *Anna*, flagship of the blockading fleet under the command of Rear-Admiral S. A. Esmant, and then put out to sea. The *Vixen* had not made a great effort to evade the blockade—the *Anna* was anchored at fleet headquarters at Gelendjik.

Esmant ordered Lt.-Captain N. P. Vulf of the brig *Ajax* to pursue the *Vixen* and bring her back. If Vulf met "the slightest resistance" he was "to use force of arms."[30] Nightfall and un-

---

25. Durham to Palmerston (14 August 1836), FO 65/225. The publication in question was D. Urquhart, ed., *The Portfolio. State Papers Illustrative of the History of Our Times* (London, 1836), 2 vols.
26. *Ibid.*, *The Portfolio*, vol. 2: 322.
27. Durham to Palmerston (11 August 1836), FO 65/225.
28. M. S. Vorontsov, "Vsepoddanneishii rasport Novorossiiskago general-gubernatora" (26 August 1836), *Russkii arkhiv* (1894), vol. 2: 219. N. N. Murav'ev, *Russkie na Bosfore v 1833 god* (Moscow, 1869), 459.
29. Durham to Palmerston (21 September 1836), FO 65/226.
30. P. Vulf, "Angliiskaia shkuna *Wixen*—voennyi priz, vziatyi brigom 'Aiaks' u beregov Kavkaza v 1836 godu," *Morskoi sbornik* (April 1886), 93.

favorable winds slowed his progress to Sudjuk Kalé, a small harbor which Esmant thought might be the *Vixen*'s destination. On the 26th, Vulf sighted the *Vixen* at Sudjuk Kalé, hailed her with a warning shot and asked where she was headed. The captain, Thomas Childs, answered that he had arrived at his destination. He had come at the direction of his supercargo, James Bell, to sell salt to the natives. Vulf ordered the *Vixen* to accompany him to Gelendjik, but Childs requested that they wait for Bell, who was ashore. When Bell arrived, in Vulf's opinion dressed like an "official of the English Kingdom,"[31] he apparently protested that Britain did not recognize the blockade.[32] But Vulf siezed the *Vixen* for a suspected violation of customs regulations. They sailed back to Gelendjik, where Esmant placed the *Vixen* and her cargo under guard. Vulf had not made a search, and in his report stated that Bell claimed her cargo consisted only of salt, but added that on the 24th and 25th she had "engaged in commerce with the mountaineers and, since the brig was unable to reach her, succeeded in unloading part of her cargo."[33]

Esmant ordered the *Vixen* held for a violation of customs regulations, on grounds of the admission of Bell and Childs that they had sold salt without passing through customs at a bonding port as required.[34] He called a commission of inquest composed of his own officers, and found that the vessel was privately owned by an English firm, and that although there was reason to suspect that she had carried contraband, the only solid evidence regarding the cargo was Childs' declaration that it consisted of one hundred casks of salt. The commission did note that two cannon listed in the ship's papers as part of her armament were missing. But it recommended that the *Vixen* be confiscated for a violation of customs laws and sent to Sevastopol.[35]

31. *Ibid.*, 95. From a report by N. P. Vulf.
32. Bell maintained afterward that he did protest the blockade. Cf. J. S. Bell, *Journal of a Residence in Circassia, during the years 1837, 1838 and 1839* (London, 1840), vol. 2: 168.
33. Vulf, "Angliiskaia shkuna," 94–95.
34. This was the second time the *Vixen* had been caught violating Russian customs regulations. In November 1835 she and another vessel were seized for an infraction of laws concerning the navigation of the Danube. Cf. Palmerston to Durham (11 December 1835), and enclosure by George Bell, *FO* 181/199.
35. The report is summarized in the *Journal de St. Pétersbourg* (31 December 1837).

Bell, Childs, and the crew were taken to Odessa where they were placed in confinement. Bell appealed to his government to intervene, by a letter dated December 12, 1836, and not forwarded to London by Durham until January 3, 1837.[36] He based his appeal on a contention that the *Vixen* was seized for running the blockade.

The first news of the incident to reach Europe through diplomatic channels made a surprising conjecture that "the seizure of the ship near the Circassian shore was deliberately planned by Lord Ponsonby," the British Ambassador at Constantinople, "and therefore by the British government, in order to categorically and pointedly raise the question of the blockade and try it."[37] The report went to the French Ambassador at Vienna, who revealed its contents to Metternich. It corroborated information the Austrian Chancellor had received from Constantinople, and he passed it along to the Russian minister.

Nesselrode's initial reactions are unknown, but it was apparent that he believed that the *Vixen*'s voyage had been planned by members of the British government. On January 2, Barante reported to Molé that Nesselrode "said that this affair was instigated by an intrigue in London and Constantinople; that he had received forewarning in the dispatches of the Russian Ambassador in England; that an article in the *Morning Chronicle* had given clear evidence of it, and that M. Urquhart . . . who wanted to embroil the two powers, was the principal instigator of the plan."[38]

Nesselrode had not yet spoken to Durham, who was indisposed, and the first British reactions came to him through the press, well before Bell's letter had left Russia.[39] He offered his first explanation of the seizure in the *Journal de St. Pétersbourg* on January 12 in response to an article which had appeared in the *Morning Chronicle*. The *Chronicle* had stated that the *Vixen*'s cargo included gunpowder and cannon. Nesselrode's article said

36. Durham to Palmerston (3 January 1837), *FO* 65/233. Enclosure by J. Bell (12 December 1836).
37. Shalle to Molé (11/23 December 1836), *Krasnyi arkhiv* (1940), vol. 102: 195.
38. Barante to Molé (2 January 1837), *Souvenirs*, vol. 5: 528.
39. On the public reaction in Britain, cf. J. H. Gleason, *The Genesis of Russophobia in Great Britain* (Cambridge, Mass., 1950), ch. 7, "David Urquhart—The *Vixen*."

that the *Vixen* had been seized because her owners sold salt to the Circassians without complying with Russian customs regulations. "The straightforward exposé of the deeds we have recounted here is enough to shed light on the conduct of the English merchants who . . . did not hesitate to trespass in order to engage in shameful commerce, or to carry out perfidious designs which the impartial judgment of all men of good will shall not fail to condemn and discredit." Consistent with the verdict of Esmant's commission, the potentially explosive view that the *Vixen* had been seized for running the blockade would be ignored and thus defused.[40]

The explosive interpretation would have been more acceptable to Russian nationalists. In fact there was a possibility that they might override Nesselrode. Admiral Lazarev, commander of the Black Sea Fleet, was not satisfied with the verdict of Esmant's commission. At Sevastopol he compiled new evidence, including a "secret report" by the commandant at a coastal post which stated that eight cannon, 200 casks of powder and a quantity of rifles and sabres had been landed. He convened a "prize commission" to reexamine the case, and it delivered a verdict that the *Vixen* was a "rightful prize of war," and recommended that Vulf be awarded the Order of St. Anne, Second Class, and 5000 rubles "prize money."[41] In terms of the chain of command it clearly nullified the decision made at Gelendjik. But Nesselrode simply ignored Lazarev's commission. If the *Vixen* were a prize, then a sharp protest to Britain would have been in order, and Bell and Childs would have been subject to severe punishment, even death, under international law. Instead, there was no protest, and Bell and Childs were released and sent to Constantinople where Ponsonby gave Bell a warm welcome.[42]

In the second week of January, Nesselrode discussed the matter with Durham for the first time. Durham came prepared

40. *Journal de St. Pétersbourg* (31 December 1836).
41. Vulf, "Angliiskaia shkuna," 95, 98. According to a "secret report" allegedly filed by the commandant at Anapa, Lt.-Col. Maklakov (15 January 1837), the *Vixen* put ashore four 3-pounders, four-6-pounders, 200 casks of gunpowder, and an unspecified quantity of rifles and sabres.
42. S. K. Bushuev, *Iz istorii vneshnepoliticheskikh otnoshenii v period pri soedineniia Kavkaza k Rossii (20–70e gody XIX veka)* (Moscow, 1955), 35.

with a protest that Palmerston had outlined. It rested on an assumption that the *Vixen* had been eight miles from shore when captured, and demanded restitution and questioned Russia's right to claim sovereignty over the Caucasus. Nesselrode refused to accept it or give any answer. Durham left with the impression that Britain should not press the matter; he apparently favored Nesselrode's interpretation. In a later report to Palmerston, Durham complained that he did not think it right that Bell and his associates should be allowed to raise important political issues and leave the government to bear the responsibility.[43]

Thus far, Nesselrode had presided over an impasse, with the stipulation that Britain was welcome to approach Russia on the basis of the interpretation he had published in the *Journal de St. Pétersbourg*. He now waited uneasily for this to occur, worried that someone would "raise a clamor in Parliament against Russia and move the English ministry further along the wrong course . . . and ultimately sow discord between the two countries and drive them into direct conflict." His instructions to his minister at London were to counteract this while quietly inviting the British government to make the correct decision: "We will strive to enlighten the public mind of England, and to provide the British Cabinet with an exit from the difficult position into which it willfully rushed." The procedure was to permit Palmerston to escape embarrassment without having to challenge Russia: "we will consciously refrain from uttering the name of Lord Ponsonby even though he has implicated himself," said Nesselrode; "we have decided to pay no heed to the circumstances which have cast a shadow over the conduct of Lord Palmerston." Russian actions would have a single aim: "to show that the confiscation of the vessel was itself an act of high justice."[44] If Palmerston took the "exit" provided, a crisis would be avoided, and Britain would acknowledge the legality of the Russian position.

Meanwhile, there was an attempt in Russia to gain acceptance for an approach conforming with the decision of Lazarev's commission. Nesselrode's Ambassador at Constantinople A. P. Butenev became alarmed when he received "circular notes"

43. Cf. Durham to Palmerston (12 January 1837), *FO* 65/233; Barante to Molé (14 January 1837), *Souvenirs*, vol. 5: 529.
44. Nesselrode to Pozzo di Borgo (4/16 January 1837), *Krasnyi arkhiv* (1940), vol. 102: 199–200.

from Lazarev and Vorontsov indicating that the *Vixen* was a prize of war. By coincidence, on the same day that Nesselrode wrote to reassure him that they intended "to lay the responsibility for this plot on the motives of its perpetrators alone, thus clearing the English government of suspicion of complicity,"[45] Butenev composed a dispatch saying that Lazarev and Vorontsov were leveling accusations at the British ministry. "It is not my place to hasten to submit a detailed statement," he said, uncertain which side prevailed at Petersburg, but Lazarev and Vorontsov "did not take any notice—not the slightest—of the unanimous reception we were counting on for the law." Their reaction was geared to the assumption that, as stated by Lazarev, the "voyage of the *Vixen* on the Black Sea originated under the direct influence of the English Ambassador at Constantinople." Butenev himself, no less than the others, was sure that the British government was responsible; but he realized that to contest its involvement as Lazarev and Vorontsov wished to do would carry Russia to the brink of war.[46]

In February the affair grew more menacing. As yet there had been no exchange of a formal character between the two powers. The British newspapers were calling for a hard line, and in some cases war to recover the *Vixen*. At the end of January Palmerston had "summoned" Ponsonby to London for a discussion of their policy, and Ponsonby had been knighted. Nesselrode finally instructed his minister at London, Pozzo di Borgo, to broach the subject with Palmerston, but the response, in the first week in February, was that Britain was studying the matter. Pozzo di Borgo believed that the government might split over the issue of whether to follow "the design of agitators and provocateurs of war." "Lord Palmerston is directly involved in this design," he told Nesselrode.[47] "Discussion continues without any cleavage," wrote Nesselrode, "and Count Pozzo di Borgo has tried to make Lord Palmerston understand that it is in the highest degree desirable to put an end to enterprises like the attempt by the

45. Nesselrode to Butenev (5/17 January 1837), *Krasnyi arkhiv* (1940), vol. 102: 202.
46. Butenev to Nesselrode (5/17 January 1837), *Krasnyi arkhiv* (1940), vol. 102: 203.
47. Pozzo di Borgo to Nesselrode (26 January/7 February 1837), *Krasnyi arkhiv* (1940), vol. 102: 206.

Vixen, which had a single aim—to break relations between the two governments."[48]

Durham, who had come to admire Nesselrode and now "made little secret of his personal opinion" that "to him the seizure appeared to be just,"[49] apparently received no important new instructions on the affair until mid-April. Before then, Nesselrode was informed of the beginning of the change he had been watching for. "Such dissension and scandal there is in the English Embassy in Constantinople!" Pozzo di Borgo wrote when the newspapers carried some of Urquhart's correspondence with Palmerston. Urquhart had submitted the documents in an attempt to show that Palmerston and the government had failed to defend British interests. Pozzo did not find their publication worrisome because they were so obviously a ploy. "They inevitably make a very foolish impression," he said, "since their argument is aimed entirely at destroying peace."[50] Urquhart, furious, had launched a sensational campaign in which he accused Palmerston of treason and called for discussion of the affair in Parliament.[51] It was put on the agenda three weeks after his first accusations appeared, but the heat of the moment had already died down, and what might have been a crusade against Russia deteriorated into a petty squabble. Palmerston was called upon to defend his inaction, and the cleavage became evident to all in an explanation finally presented to Parliament on March 17. He said that Britain did not recognize the Russian blockade, but that the paramount question was that of war and peace.

Toward the end of April, Palmerston made the incredible move of instructing Durham to ask Nesselrode for an explanation based on the verdict of Lazarev's commission. In essence, his argument was that Lazarev had justified the seizure on grounds

48. Nesselrode to Butenev (2/14 February 1837), *Krasnyi arkhiv* (1940), vol. 102: 207–208.
49. Barante to Molé (28 February 1837), *Souvenirs*, vol. 5: 543.
50. Pozzo di Borgo to Nesselrode (12/24 February 1837), *Krasnyi arkhiv* (1940), vol. 102: 209.
51. For Urquhart's views, cf. his *Diplomatic Transactions in Central Asia from 1834 to 1839* (London, 1841). Palmerston is accused of treason in the preface. Reeve writes that after having patronized the Urquhart faction, "Lord Palmerston suddenly became violently opposed to them, and disclaimed all knowledge of those whom he had employed." *The Greville Memoirs*, vol. 1: 118n.

that the *Vixen* ran a blockade; a blockade had to be effective to
be legal; since the *Vixen* had no difficulty in reaching Sudjuk Kalé
and spent several hours there before she was captured, it was not
effective. "Your Excellency is aware that there is no matter with
respect to which the public mind in this country is more watchfully
jealous," Palmerston admonished, "than the forcible interference
of a Foreign Power with the peaceful voyages of British Subjects
engaged in the occupations of commerce."[52] In a dispatch written three days later, he argued that the *Vixen* had been outside
of the three-mile zone of territorial waters when she was captured—ignoring Russia's well-established twelve-mile limit on
territorial seas.[53] Then, in a meeting with Pozzo at the end of the
month, he claimed that the Treaty of Adrianople was invalid
because it was signed under duress—an empty argument in international law. Pozzo replied that Russian policy in the Near
East was moderate, not aggressive, and Palmerston retorted, as
the Russian minister related it, "Yes, Europe has slept too long.
She rouses at last to put an end to this system of aggrandizement."[54] Pozzo wrote to Nesselrode to say that Palmerston's
attitude and British "prejudices" were likely to carry the country
into war, but in his next dispatch apologized for a false alarm.
His warning had been "written under very distressing impressions gained from the hypocrisy and malice that Lord Palmerston
displayed."[55]

Palmerston finally came around. Durham was instructed to
ask for an official Russian explanation, for the first time since the
Vixen had been captured, and did so on May 6. Nesselrode
quickly provided one: "The vessel was confiscated because it
carried illegal cargo into Russian territory granted by the Treaty
of Adrianople . . . without observing the laws . . . which prohibit
a foreign vessel from visiting a port having neither customs nor
quarantine."[56] It was forwarded to Palmerston with Durham's
recommendation that it be accepted, and it was submitted to

52. Palmerston to Durham (19 April 1837), *FO* 181/132.
53. Palmerston to Durham (22 April 1837), *FO* 181/132.
54. In Martens, *Recueil*, vol. 12: 63.
55. Pozzo di Borgo to Nesselrode (20 April/30 May 1837), *Krasnyi
    arkhiv* (1940), vol. 102: 224.
56. Nesselrode to Durham (27 April/9 May 1837), *Krasnyi arkhiv*
    (1940), vol. 102: 225.

Parliament with all documents relating to the case on May 18.[57] On the 23rd the British government announced that the confiscation was just for the reasons given in Nesselrode's explanation.[58] The affair was closed.

Nesselrode had utilized the danger of war to preserve the status quo, in effect to win British adherence to the principles of Russian policy. He assumed that Britain was motivated by a desire to force Russia to make a choice between war and the Treaty of Adrianople, virtually between war and her influence in the Near East. There is evidence that his paradigm was well-founded. Palmerston had shown an inclination to use brinkmanship against Russia, as in 1835 when Wellington had to countermand his secret orders to force the straits and send the British fleet into the Black Sea. This procedure might well have been carried out in a crisis over the *Vixen*'s capture, assuming as Nesselrode did that Palmerston had backed the voyage. Certainly he knew about it. Ponsonby had reported a visit by Bell before the incident, during which Bell had "said he expected to have his vessel seized —that he had no intention of acting under any disguise." Ponsonby said he had advised Bell to be careful to show the *Vixen*'s exact position in the log when she was captured, and not to give any appearance of trying to evade the blockade.[59] This was an incredible way of announcing an event of such importance if Palmerston did not know about it beforehand. If the *Vixen* had been taken as a "prize of war," as the more aggressive parties on both sides wished, Britain would have demanded restitution, and a major crisis would certainly have ensued. Perhaps it would have served as a pretext for sending the British fleet through the straits.

"This affair has been strange to observe," wrote Barante. "I could see all of the prudence of Russian policy in addition to its good management, especially regarding England."[60] Nesselrode was pleased with his success: "What concerns us is that we should

57. Durham to Palmerston (10 May 1837), *FO* 65/234. Cf. documents relating to the formal exchange in *Parliamentary Papers* (1839), vol. 40.
58. Palmerston to Durham (23 May 1837), *FO* 65/232.
59. Palmerston to Durham (15 December 1836), enclosure Ponsonby to Palmerston (28 October 1836), *FO* 181/129.
60. Barante to Molé (28 February 1837), *Souvenirs*, vol. 5: 544.

rejoice because this tricky affair led to results that were so wel-come—because in securing our full rights we did not in any way damage peaceful relations between Russia and England."[61] His main concern was not merely to avoid a crisis, but to preserve an atmosphere in which close relations between the two countries could develop. In his formal explanation to Britain he had expressed the hope that "the longstanding credit and thriving English commerce in Russia will not be interrupted by simi-lar attempts."[62] In acknowledging the British acceptance of his explanation, he remarked: "The notes we have exchanged in resolving this controversy, in our view, create a new pledge of the reciprocal intentions of the powers to uphold full har-mony in relations, since Russia and Britain are equally united by large commercial interests and foremost leadership of the community."[63]

Confrontation in Asia

The *Vixen* affair opened a series of volatile crises that in-volved both Asian and Near Eastern affairs. As will be seen, war probably would have been the result if Nesselrode had not acted decisively, or if his Russian opponents had prevailed. This is amply illustrated by the "great game" in Asia, as the imperial rivalry has been called. There was a real prospect, dear to Rus-sians while it sent cold chills down the spines of the British, that Russia would forge an alliance with Persia, the Afghan khanates of Kabul and Gandahar, and perhaps Bokhara, securing access to the Persian Gulf and a base for the conquest of Khiva and the khanate of Herat and a thrust into the Punjab and British India, and also for the pacification of the Caucasus and a campaign through Anatolian Turkey. It was the kind of plan that Peter the Great would have taken up with alacrity had he possessed the means (he had envisaged such a project). Added to the strategic attractions, official nationalists revered Asia as the true cradle of their past, and their future civilization. They held tenaciously to

61. Nesselrode to Butenev (30 March/11 April 1837), *Krasnyi arkhiv* (1940), vol. 102: 223.
62. Nesselrode to Durham (27 April/9 May 1837), *Krasnyi arkhiv* (1940), vol. 102: 225.
63. Nesselrode to Pozzo di Borgo (22 May/3 June 1837), *Krasnyi arkhiv* (1940), vol. 102: 227.

the habit, which Alexander I had neglected to counteract, of treating Central Asian affairs as entirely separate from other areas of foreign policy—as an aspect of domestic policy, in fact. Hence Nesselrode faced a complicated problem: he had to effect a coherent Weltpolitik in a region traditionally regarded as having a special relation to Russia, and he had to hold his opponents in check when they were on the verge of a crusade against Britain that they regarded both as a realistic defense of national interests and a fulfillment of manifest destiny.

"It must be emphasized that it will be a completely satisfactory course for us to enter into a long-lasting period of commerce with Persia," Nesselrode had written in 1828 to his minister at Teheran, the writer A. S. Griboedov, in an effort, according to the British Envoy, "to cultivate the best understanding with the British Mission."[64] His instructions contrasted with the assertive policy in Persia and other parts of Asia advocated, for example, by the Viceroy of the Caucasus, General A. P. Ermolov.[65] But seven months later Griboedov was dead; he had been dragged from the Russian Embassy by an angry mob and murdered. The post remained empty for a time, and was filled again in January 1832 by Colonel I. O. Simonich, a "military agent" who also functioned as minister.[66] "Thanks to whose influence he was appointed as Russian representative in Persia after Griboedov, I do not know," wrote A. O. Diuhamel (who was later selected by Nesselrode to replace Simonich), "but it definitely may be stated that it would have been impossible to make a more un-

---

64. Nesselrode to Griboedov (1/13 May 1828), in A. P. Berzhe, "Aleksandr Sergeevich Griboedov. Deiatel'nost ego kak diplomata 1827–1829," *Russkaia starina* (1874), vol. 11: 518. D. M. Lang, "Griboedov's Last Years in Persia," *Slavic Review* (1948), vol. 7: 323.

65. J. S. Curtiss writes that the government "disregarded the repeated warnings of Gen. A. P. Ermolov . . . that many of the Persians regarded Nesselrode's conciliatory policy as weakness." *The Russian Army Under Nicholas I, 1825–1855* (Durham, 1965), 21.

66. Terent'ev, *Rossiia i Angliia v bor'be za rynki*, 247. A Russian translation of Simonich's memoirs edited by N. A. Khalfin is *Vospominaniia polnomochnogo ministra 1832–1838 gg.* (Moscow, 1967). Simonich was born near the Adriatic, entered Russia with Napoleon in 1812, was captured, joined the Russian army in 1815, held a number of assignments in Central Asia, and was wounded in 1826 while serving under Paskevich, then Ermolov's deputy, at Elizabethpol. It is probable that Paskevich and Ermolov were responsible for his appointment to the post at Teheran.

fortunate selection."[67] From the outset, his appointment meant
that the commercial and diplomatic enterprises Nesselrode wished
to advance were subordinated to a "hard Persian policy" of the
type Ermolov called for.[68] Within a few years of his appointment,
Simonich provoked a crisis with Britain.

A large part of the difficulty arose because the appointment
allowed the military to interfere in diplomacy. In Teheran Simonich received orders from four sources: the General Staff, the
Governor-General of the Orenburg Military District, the Asiatic
Department, and the Ministry of Foreign Affairs. His first responsibility as an army officer was to the General Staff. The General Staff was very active in deciding and directing Asian policy,
and its procedures in Persia had been laid down largely in 1826–
1827 by Paskevich, who believe that Nesselrode had played into
the hands of the British and lost Russian advantages there in the
period of Griboedov's murder.[69] The Governor-General at Orenburg, General V. A. Perovskii, wished to coordinate Simonich's
activities with his own moves in Khiva, Turkestan, and Bokhara.
The Asiatic Department, under K. K. Rodofinikin from 1819 to
1837, often operated without any but the most tenuous link with
its parent institution, the foreign ministry; Rodofinikin antagonized Nesselrode by serving the views of men like Vorontsov,
Ermolov, and Paskevich in the General Staff. This bizarre command arrangement led to trouble; orders from the General Staff
and from the ministry reflected differences between Ermolov and
Nesselrode, and Simonich did not fail to remain loyal to his
superior officers. Simonich's estrangement from the ministry was
made worse because his strongest personal ties were with officers,
numerous in Asian administration, who were Francophile to the
point of being Bonapartists, who not only saw Britain as Russia's natural enemy but even wanted revenge for the defeat of
France.[70]

There were signs of impending difficulty between Russia and

67. A. O. Diuhamel, "Avtobiografiia. . . ," *Russkii arkhiv* (1885), vol.
    2, no. 8: 90.
68. Curtiss, *The Russian Army*, 21.
69. Cf. V. K. P., "Fel'dmarshal Paskevich i diplomatiia v 1827–1829
    godakh," *Istoricheskii vestnik* (1892), vol. 4: 507–510, "Original-
    'nost Nessel'rodovskoi diplomatii."
70. "Simonich was a zealous Bonapartist," wrote Diuhamel, recounting

Britain over Persia and Afghanistan early in 1836, when Mohammed Shah of Persia began active preparations for a long-projected
campaign to depose the ruling dynasty at Herat, the capital of
one of the three independent Afghan khanates. The time seemed
opportune because the two other khanates, under Dost Mohammed in Kabul and Kohundil Khan in Gandahar, were interested
in putting down the dynastic heirs of their old enemy, Shah Sudju-
el-Mulk, who passed most of his time in retirement on a British
pension in India. Simonich enthusiastically supported the idea of
a campaign against Herat.

The British Ambassador at Teheran did his best to discourage Mohammed Shah, and when his failure was beyond doubt
he turned to Simonich with a warning. By his own account he said
that Afghanistan "must be considered as frontier to our Indian
Empire; that no European nation had relations, either commercial
or political, with that country; that accordingly I could not con-
ceive that the British government would view, otherwise than with
jealousy, any interference, direct or indirect, in the affairs of
Afghanistan."[71]

Such considerations no doubt influenced the choice of the
new British ambassador to Persia in 1836. Before taking his post,
Sir John McNeill published *Progress and Present Position of Russia in the East*, in which he advanced a view that Russian foreign
policy was based on a preconceived design that in Asia as elsewhere called for subversion and conquest.[72] All of Russia's efforts to extend her influence, whether by diplomacy and trade
or by military conquest, were to be vigorously opposed because
they stemmed from the same design.

"It would be difficult to find two men less able to live in
harmony," wrote Diuhamel about Simonich and McNeill, "and
I can assert absolutely that if Simonich had remained an additional year at his post in Persia, he certainly would have precipi-

---

that he had a picture on the wall of his office in Teheran depicting
Napoleon's ghost, bearing the inscription, "I bequeath the dis-
honor of my death to the ruling house of England." "Avtobiografiia. . . ," vol. 2: no. 8: 90.
71. Ellis to Palmerston (16 April 1836), *Parliamentary Papers* (1839),
vol. 40: 10.
72. J. McNeill, *Progress and Present Position of Russia in the East* (London, 1836).

tated war between England and Russia."[73] In a sense, Simonich and McNeill were well-suited to fulfill each other's expectations. Simonich, a swaggering, boastful expansionist and militarist, was the Russian menace personified. And McNeill, a pompous, clever, mercantilist and imperialist, embodied traits that Simonich associated with the march of the British Empire. The two clashed immediately, and a crisis began to unfold.

Before the end of 1836 McNeill complained to Palmerston about Simonich's efforts to encourage the Persian attack on Herat, and Palmerston soon instructed Durham to ask Nesselrode to explain why Simonich's behavior contradicted "all the professed principles" of Russian policy.[74] In a statement earlier publicized in England, Nesselrode had stated that the Russian government expected "to see the representatives of Russia and England in Persia authorized to act in concert in a spirit of peace and union."[75] Durham was to protest if Nesselrode defended Simonich; if he renounced Simonich, the British government would expect "that the Russian Cabinet will put a stop to a course of conduct so much at variance with its own declared policy."[76]

Nesselrode assured Durham that he had instructed Simonich "to dissuade the Shah from prosecuting the war at any time and in any circumstances." He told Durham that the "folly and impolicy of the course pursued by the Persian monarch" was seriously magnified by its detrimental effect on relations between Britain and Russia.[77] Although he expressed doubt about the reliability of McNeill's reports, his response satisfied Palmerston: "The answer of Count Nesselrode to this inquiry was plain, direct, and unequivocal . . . he declared that if Count Simonich had acted in the manner represented, he had done so in direct opposition to his instructions."[78] Nesselrode offered to show Durham his own instructions to Simonich as proof of his words,

73. Diuhamel, "Avtobiografiia. . . ," vol. 2: no. 8: 91.
74. Palmerston to Durham (16 January 1837), enclosure McNeill to Palmerston (3 November 1836), FO 181/130.
75. This phrase from Nesselrode's statement was published by Urquhart, *Diplomatic Transactions*, 21, as an illustration that the professed policy was not the real one. Urquhart accompanied McNeill for part of the latter's journey to Teheran in 1836.
76. Palmerston to Durham (16 January 1837), FO 181/130.
77. Durham to Palmerston (24 Febraury 1837), FO 65/233.
78. Palmerston, "Draft of Note to be presented by Lord Clanricarde to Count Nesselrode" (26 October 1838), BMAddMSS 36469.

and invited him to discuss the matter with Rodofinikin. After these conversations, Durham believed that Simonich would soon be recalled.[79]

But the quarrel between Simonich and McNeill had only begun. McNeill continued to report progress in the projected campaign against Herat.[80] Simonich, who remained at Teheran, refused to be received by Mohammed Shah at official functions if McNeill was present. The tension increased. McNeill was upset because Simonich went confidently ahead with his preparations, as if he were under orders to do so. What was occurring within the Russian government may never be known, but Simonich received no reprimand sufficient to change his approach. Durham reported to Palmerston in May 1837 that Nesselrode had repeated his intimations that Simonich would be recalled.[81] Two weeks later Nesselrode instructed Simonich to offer his good offices to mediate peace between Persia and Herat.[82] In June McNeill reported having received Russian assurances that Simonich would not support Mohammed Shah in a war against Herat.[83] But Simonich, in step with a different drummer, ignored Nesselrode's instructions and worked even harder to bring about the attack on Herat.

Nesselrode reacted in August by appointing a replacement, Diuhamel, and trying to hasten Simonich's recall.[84] He thought that Diuhamel was "sufficiently well-known for the moderation of his character that this nomination alone would serve as the most certain index of" Russia's "line of conduct."[85] However, for reasons which are unknown but probably involved the countervailing influence of the General Staff, nine trying months were to elapse before Simonich returned to Petersburg.

In the interval Mohammed Shah was at last persuaded to attack Herat.[86] Simonich joined the Shah at the walls of the city

79. Durham to Palmerston (28 February 1837), *FO* 65/233.
80. Palmerston to Durham (14 April 1837), enclosures by McNeill, *FO* 181/132.
81. Durham to Palmerston (2 May 1837), *FO* 65/234.
82. Nesselrode to Pozzo di Borgo (20 October/1 November 1838) *BMAddMSS* 36469.
83. McNeill to Palmerston (30 June 1837), *FO* 60/49.
84. Diuhamel, "Avtobiografiia. . . ," vol. 2, no. 8: 91.
85. Nesselrode to Pozzo di Borgo (20 October/1 November 1838) *BMAddMSS* 36469.
86. Cf. Simonich, *Vospominaniia*, chs. 9 and 10.

and helped direct the siege. At the same time he succeeded in negotiating an important step toward an alliance between Russia, Persia and the Afghan khanates, which he had been promoting with the assistance of an agent, J. V. Witkiewicz, in the khanates. He brought Mohammed Shah and the Kohundil Khan together in a treaty which Dost Mohammed was expected to join. He pledged Russian adherence.

These events were more than McNeill could tolerate; he broke diplomatic relations with Persia and left the country, taking his entire staff with him. Lord Auckland, the Governor-General of India, dispatched a British army toward the khanates, and Mc-Neill recommended to Palmerston that five thousand troops also be sent to occupy Teheran.[87] A British naval force appeared in the Persian Gulf and landed troops for an assault on the Persian fortress of Karrack. Karrack soon fell. Britain was at the brink of war with Persia and Kabul, and with Gandahar and Russia if they sided with Persia.

The turning point came in May 1838 when the Tsar, no doubt impressed with the danger of war, ordered Simonich to renounce Russian support of the treaty he had mediated and recalled him.[88] The siege of Herat was given up when Mohammed Shah realized that he could not count on Russian backing against Britain. A few days later the Marquess of Clanricarde, who had replaced Durham, read a "stentorian" note to Nesselrode demanding that Simonich be relieved of his post, and Nesselrode was able to quiet him with the information that it had been done.[89]

Nesselrode later told Pozzo di Borgo that "the gist of the instructions with which General Diuhamel was equipped when he went to Teheran" was to influence Mohammed Shah "to reestablish his friendly relations with England."[90] This is substanti-

87. For a discussion of McNeill's proposal, cf. Hobhouse to Palmerston (20 October 1838), *BMAddMSS* 36469.
88. Nesselrode to Pozzo di Borgo (21 February 1839), G. F. Martens, *Nouveau Recueil*, vol. 24 (16): 306.
89. Terent'ev, *Rossiia i Angliia v bor'be za rynki*, 248. Terent'ev considered Simonich's recall to be a setback for Russia, signifying a larger failure to contend with Britain.
90. Nesselrode to Pozzo di Borgo (21 February 1839), G. F. Martens, *Nouveau Recueil*, vol. 24 (16): 304.

ated by Diuhamel's account of the audience in which the Tsar charged him with his new mission: "You must adhere strictly and candidly to this assignment, using the influence granted to us by law to prevent us from being placed in a hostile relationship with the English," said Nicholas. "We and the English have one and the same interest in Persia, and with them we wish to conserve the present order of things." If peace were to be maintained, Britain must be convinced that Russia did not aim to subvert the status quo. "They think that our influence accounts for everything that happens in the East," he said. "You must, by your candid manner and actions, reveal the groundlessness of these nonsensical calumnies."[91]

When Diuhamel went to Teheran, one of his first actions was to order another officer to return to Petersburg. He was Jan Witkiewicz, a romantic Polish intellectual with vague Pan-Slav sentiments and a burning desire to fight British imperialism He. had been serving as a Russian agent in Bokhara and Afghanistan under orders from Simonich and Perovskii to strengthen relations between the khanates, Persia, and Russia.

Witkiewicz was the most unlikely of Russian expansionists —a Polish patriot who had written some revolutionary poetry that enabled the authorities to trace his membership in a secret society, "the Black Brothers," for which he was arrested and banished to Orenburg in 1824. There he found the officers in charge, themselves more or less exiles sent to the outpost because their views were not welcome in Petersburg and elsewhere, more patronizing than repressive. Writers and scholars interested in Slavic and Asian history, languages, and culture visited Orenburg frequently in the 1820s and 1830s, and Witkiewicz was encouraged to pursue his own studies of languages and literature. He soon became fluent in Persian and several Kirghiz dialects, and his talent received special recognition in 1829 when he was a translator for the German scientist Baron Alexander von Humboldt, who passed through Orenburg on his Central Asian expedition. At the end of the expedition, Humboldt praised Witkiewicz highly, and requested that he be rewarded, preferably by being freed to return to Poland. His reward was to be made an

91. Diuhamel, "Avtobiografiia. . . ," vol. 2, no. 8: 83–84.

officer and adjutant to the Governor-General. In the 1830s
Perovskii sent him on missions into the Kirghiz steppe, Khiva,
Bokhara, and the Afghan khanates, usually in native dress under
the name "Omar Beg," alone or in the company of a few cos-
sacks. Beyond his talent for languages he held a romantic vision
of Asia's future, a vision that Perovskii thought was true in spirit
and Nesselrode found obnoxious. It was not an original vision,
but one shared with other romantic intellectuals including Slavophiles. Witkiewicz believed that a new civilization would arise
in Asia, drive out the Western commercial empires, unite with
Russia, embracing the Oriental facets of her culture and over-
throwing her superficial Europeanism, and advance on Europe.
Poland would once again absorb the shock of a collision between
East and West, and when peace came she would be the intermediary between convalescent Occident and strident Orient, con-
veying Western enlightenment to the East while she helped to
liberate Europe from her oppressive materialism. It was, in fact,
similar to the notions of a number of the proponents of Official
Nationality, and clearly a prototype for an ideological world-
view justifying a crusade against Western imperialism in Asia.

In the summer of 1837 Perovskii assigned Witkiewicz to
serve under Simonich, and in October "Omar Beg" went to
Kabul.[92] Simonich told McNeill that Witkiewicz was on a strictly
commercial mission. McNeill reported to Palmerston, "I cannot
doubt that the effect of the establishment of a Russian agent at
Cabool must be seriously detrimental to British interests in India
and in the Punjant." He said it was "one of those advances
which I regard as the more dangerous because it is not avowedly
hostile."[93] In Kabul Witkiewicz came face to face with the British
agent Alexander Burnes, who was trying to negotiate an alliance.
He immediately exerted his influence to wreck the British plan
and promote an alliance with Russia instead. Dost Mohammed
insisted that he wanted Peshawar in exchange for an alliance with
Britain, and there was a strong possibility that he would seek the
same objective in an alliance with Russia. Witkiewicz encouraged

92. Witkiewicz probably continued to file his main reports uith Perovskii.
    Cf. G. L. Ivanin and D. Golosov, "Pokhod v Khivu v 1939 godu.
    Otriada russkikh voisk, pod nachal'stvom general-adiutanta Perov-
    skago," *Voennyi sbornik* (1863), vol. 1: 68n.
93. McNeill to Palmerston (30 October 1837), *FO* 60/57.

Dost Mohammed to hold out in this demand, and Britain interpreted it as a threat to India.[94]

The British negotiations for alliance with Kabul impressed
Simonich with the need to act quickly. It was at this point that
the confrontation entered the crucial phase.[95] When Russia and
Britain were locked in conflict, the wisdom of attacking Herat
would be proved. His decision to instruct Witkiewicz to offer
Dost Mohammed an alliance would be vindicated.

Witkiewicz was more than a match for Burnes. As soon as
Dost Mohammed realized that Burnes would not concede Peshawar, "Omar Beg" offered his services as the representative of
Russia and Mohammed Shah of Persia as well. Burnes, who
himself held a romantic view of the duel with Russia in Central
Asia and could not have taken the defeat lightly, gave up and departed in April 1838.[96] By his failure, Burnes left the Governor-
General of India the alternative of forming an alliance with the
enemies of Kabul and Gandahar. (Later in 1838 an alliance between Britain, the Punjab, and Herat served to justify the first
Afghan expedition against Kabul. As it turned out, however, even
the fact that Dost Mohammed had been deprived of the alliance
negotiated by Witkiewicz and Simonich did not prove decisive,
since the Afghans defeated the British armies without Russian
assistance.)[97]

94. For reactions to Witkiewicz's activities, cf. Palmerston to Millbanke
    (27 March 1838), enclosures 88, 89, and 105, *FO* 65/241.
95. Cf. Schiemann, *Geschichte Russlands*, vol. 3: 296.
96. Cf. A. Burnes, *Travels into Bokhara* (London, 1834), 3 vols., and
    Cabool (London, 1842).
97. The question is whether the activities of Simonich and Witkiewicz
    were enough to give cause for a British reaction to Russian aggres-
    sion, even after the two men had been recalled. The predominant
    Western view—cf. J. A. Norris, *The First Afghan War, 1838–1842*
    (New York, 1967) for a recent exposition—is that the British re-
    sponse advocated by Lord Auckland was well justified. This inter-
    pretation may be contrasted with the Soviet view that Simonich
    and Witkiewicz were doing what was needed to counter the British
    menace. Cf. N. A. Khalfin, ed., Simonich, *Vospominaniia*; and
    "Britanskaia ekspansiia v Srednei Azii v 30–40–kh godakh XIX v.
    i missiia Richmonda Shekspira," *Istoriia SSSR* (1958), vol. 2: 103–
    112. On another side, there is evidence that "hysterical Russopho-
    bia" was a factor in British policy in the years 1838–1842, as A. P.
    Thornton contends; cf. "Afghanistan in Anglo-Russian Diplomacy,
    1869–1873," *The Cambridge Historical Journal* (1954), vol. 11, no.
    2: 205.

Witkiewicz was sent back to Petersburg soon after Diuhamel's arrival in Teheran. In the capital he met with Nesselrode.
We do not know what occurred at this meeting. Clanricarde informed Palmerston that it had taken place, but declined to guess
what Nesselrode said to Witkiewicz.[98] (Nesselrode had previously
defended Witkiewicz on the basis of information from Simonich,
who had lied that the mission to Kabul was for the negotiation of
a commercial treaty alone.) A few days after the meeting Witkiewicz destroyed his papers and shot himself.[99] The incident was
cloaked in mystery. "The Government took much pains to con-
ceal the event, and the remains of Witkiewicz were disposed of
like those of a private," wrote Golovin.[1] It was rumored that
Nesselrode had accused him of disloyalty, and nationalists felt
that the act was a defense of his honor and a protest against Nesselrode's policy. Rodofinikin tended toward this view, but Seniavin, who had replaced him at the head of the Asiatic Department,
took steps to dispel it. Witkiewicz "was discontented with the
whole world," he said in a letter to Perovskii, adding that Nesselrode had received Witkiewicz graciously and that the meeting
had had nothing to do with the tragedy. Witkiewicz had plunged
into despair "out of misanthropy, out of Polonism, the latter having most to do with the decision." With implicit contradiction,
Seniavin then asserted that "it was Simonich who should have
shot himself and not Witkiewicz, who was merely a tool in his
hands."[2]

With Diuhamel in Teheran and Seniavin at the head of the
Asiatic Department, Nesselrode was a more effective administrator of Asian policy than ever before. The General Staff and the
nationalists had experienced a major setback. Diuhamel's first
task was to mediate a renewal of diplomatic relations between
Persia and Britain. "Instantly, with the first glance, it was easy
to be convinced that my role in Persia would be exceedingly dif-

98. Clanricarde to Palmerston (25 May 1839), FO 65/252.
99. Cf. report from Seniavin to Perovskii, reproduced in part in Ivanin
    and Golosov, "Pokhod v Khivu," vol. 1: 69n. Also Ia. Ia. Polferov,
    " 'Predatel' iz vremen grafa Perovskago," Istoricheskii vestnik
    (1905), vol. 100: 502.
1. Golovin, Russia, 204.
2. Seniavin to Diuhamel (1 August 1839), in Diuhamel, "Avtobiogra-
    fiia . . . ," vol. 2, no. 8: 109; and Diuhamel, ibid.

ficult."[3] He noted, for example, the difficulty of having to exert pressure while discouraging the projects Simonich had promoted. Simonich had told the Persian government that his recall was temporary and that he would return in a short time to take up where he had left off, thus undermining Diuhamel's effectiveness.[4] Three months passed before the Russian government viewed the situation as being less than critical.

Until the siege of Herat, Palmerston had remained moderately satisfied with Nesselrode's earlier statements of Russian policy. The siege compelled him to recognize the danger of escalation to war. Countering McNeill's proposal for direct intervention in Persia, Hobhouse had argued in a memorandum to Palmerston that "it is not probable that Russia would refuse to support her ally"; therefore "a conflict between the British force and that of Russia would naturally ensue, and from that moment the struggle would assume a new and totally different character, and be transferred from the (uncivilized) tribes of Central Asia to the (two) great powers (of the civilized world)."[5] Hobhouse thought that this would be a momentous war for mastery of Asia and the Near East. "Without professing or feeling any alarm at the probable result of such a contest," he continued, "we would still refrain from commencing it under disadvantageous circumstances, and we do not consider the proposed invasion of Southern Persia by a British force of the number suggested by M. McNeill as the suitable mode in which the armies of Her Majesty and the East India Company should make their first appearance in the field." In the end, Palmerston sided with Hobhouse and denied McNeill's request.[6]

There was another exchange in October. Palmerston wanted a firm answer as to "whether the intentions and policy of Russia towards Persia and towards Britain are to be deduced from the declarations of Count Nesselrode and M. Rodofinikin to the Earl

3. *Ibid.*, 94.
4. *Ibid.* Simonich "went so far as to induce Hadji-Mirza-Agassi to write a peculiar letter to Nesselrode urgently demanding that Count Simonich again be appointed to Persia, since this man alone could meet the extremely difficult circumstances of the time." *Ibid.*
5. Hobhouse to Palmerston (20 October 1838), *BMAddMSS* 36469. The words "uncivilized" and "two" were scratched out and "of the civilized world" inserted in the margin.
6. *Ibid.*

of Durham, or from the acts of Count Simonich." He responded to Nesselrode's words that the interests of the two countries were the same in Asia. "Persia is an immediate neighbor" of Russia, he said, and "Great Britain has regarded Persia as a Barrier for the securing of British India against attack." Given the strategic consideration, "The interests, therefore, of Great Britain and Russia with regard to Persia, are not merely compatible, but almost the same." Hence Russia and Britain should "Endeavour to pursue . . . a common course," should "concert" together, as "has frequently been urged by the Russian Govt. and acknowledged by that of Great Britain."[7]

If military strategy were the main consideration, the fact was that Simonich had maneuvered Russia into an advantageous position, and if Nesselrode's approach had been thrown out and a "hard policy" taken up in the alliance with Persia, Kabul, and Gandahar, Britain would have faced real trouble. The question of Palmerston's intent revolves around what he meant when he conceded that Russian and British interests were "almost the same." Since he later bragged, "we drove Russia to the wall about Count Simonich," suggesting that he thought he had gained some advantage, it seems very unlikely that he was warming to the conservative concept of identity of interests.[8]

Nesselrode's response focused on the heart of the issues Palmerston had skirted, the deeper reasons why the interests of the two powers should be regarded as identical. It turned out to be the most forceful overture for bipartisan cooperation in Asia that Nesselrode, or the Russian government, had ever made. He wrote to Pozzo di Borgo:

"Great Britain and Russia must have one and the same interest at heart: that is to maintain peace in the center of Asia and to see that a general conflagration does not begin in this vast part of the globe.

"Now, in order to prevent such a great tragedy, it is necessary to conserve carefully the repose of the intermediate countries which separate the possessions of Russia from those of Great Britain. To consolidate the tranquility of these countries; to refrain from exciting one against the other by feeding mutual animosities; to confine rivalry to trade, and not to engage in a contest for political influence; finally, above all else, to respect the independence of the intermediate countries which separate us: this in our judgment is the system which it is in the interest of the two Cabinets to follow invariably. In order to avoid the possibility of a conflict between the two great Powers, in order to remain friends, they must not touch and must not collide in Central Asia."[9]

The moving idea behind the initiative contained in the full message became known as his "theory of buffers."[10] The essence of Nesselrode's theory was rooted in the conditions he thought necessary for the independence of the countries lying in converging Russian and British spheres of influence. The buffer states had to be neutral—free to pursue their own policies without being "Russified" or subjected to the British "civilizing mission." In one way, however, these countries were not to be free: they were not to be free to align themselves with either power, not even to extend preferential treatment, especially economic concessions.

The principles of free trade must prevail. Nesselrode, critical of Britain's "exclusive and jealous" imperial monopolies, said that in her attitude to Asia, Britain behaved as if it were necessary "to totally deprive" Russia "of the benefits which she pretends would vanish entirely if shared—if the products of our factories were allowed in all of the markets" of Asia. "We demand nothing," said Nesselrode, "other than to be permitted to participate in an open competition for the advantages of commerce in Asia." Guarantees of nonpreferential treatment were necessary to secure "a state of prosperity and of calm that would render this region accessible for the commerce and business of all interested nations." If Britain would agree to such an arrangement peace would have a more solid foundation, and the buffer countries would enjoy a greater measure of independence than they would under imperial rule by one power or the other. The status quo was the modus vivendi. "The policy the Emperor follows" in Asia, said

9. Nesselrode to Pozzo di Borgo (20 October/1 November 1838), *BMAddMSS* 36469. Full text also in *FO* 65/247; G. F. Martens, *Nouveau Recueil*, vol. 24 (16): 291–299; *Russkii arkhiv* (1885), vol. 2: 94–104.

10. Cf. Martens, "Rossiia i Angliia v tsarstvovanie Imperatora Nikolaia I," 498; *Recueil*, vol. 12: 75.

Nesselrode, "is guided by the same principles which direct it in Europe."[11]

In his response to Palmerston, he said that "public opinion in England ascribes a decisive role to Russia's influence in events that occur today in Persia, and attributes dangerous motives to our Cabinet." Hence Britain felt compelled to take up the defense of the independence of the countries she regarded as the outer perimeter of her imperial domain. "This consideration is so grave," he said, and "it produces an influence so unfortunate on all our relations with Great Britain, that we do not hesitate for a moment to go before the English Cabinet with a frank and candid explanation to reassure it completely about the intentions and the views of our Govt. with respect to the affairs of Asia." It "could never be compatible with a sane and rational Policy" for Russia to reach for India. He hoped that "every enlightened and objective man" might discover "that no hostile design towards England could direct the development of the policy of our Cabinet regarding Asia."[12]

It was obvious that a great deal of importance was attached to Nesselrode's message. Nicholas I gave Clanricarde a preview of its contents in a special audience at Tsarskoe Selo on October 28. "The Emperor has frequently said to others, what he did the honor to repeat to me," reported Clanricarde, "that he should be mad to meditate an invasion of the Queen's Indian Territories."[13] Pozzo di Borgo handed the document over to Palmerston on November 11, 1838. Palmerston returned a formal acknowledgment on December 20. The British government fully accepted Nesselrode's assurances. But the novel content of the message was ignored, although not entirely; Palmerston made the reservation that his government "desire that their Silence may not be understood as implying acquiescence in the Reasonings, the

---

11. Nesselrode to Pozo di Borgo (20 October/1 November 1838). Divov wrote in his diary that Nesselrode said, "the policy of Russia is guided by the same principles in Asia as in Europe," and that a contentious approach in relations with Britain "would be completely incompatible with the requirements of sound policy." P. G. Divov, "1838 god v Peterburge," *Russkaia starina* (1902), vol. III: 644.

12. *Ibid.*, and attached note by Nesselrode.

13. Clanricarde to Palmerston (6 November 1838), *FO* 244/5.

Views, or the Statements of any Passages in that Despatch, to which I have not specifically adverted in this letter."[14]

Nesselrode accepted it gracefully. "These explanations have given the two Cabinets occasion to receive and to offer on both sides assurances which bear the quality of just reciprocity, and which are inseparable, the one from the other," he said.[15]

Pozzo di Borgo had informed Nesselrode that the correspondence on Asia might be submitted to Parliament. Nesselrode found this highly encouraging. It was not easy for Russia to reach the British public. The letters he had exchanged with Palmerston, "in setting forth the facts exactly as they are, will enlighten the opinion of all men of good will, and dispel the misgivings that malice seeks to cast over the intentions of Russia."[16] He enclosed another lengthy, detailed essay on Russian relations with Asia, and reiterated his "theory of buffers" in briefer form, without the treatment of the economic aspects that Palmerston had refused to acknowledge. He thought that Russian actions not only in recalling Simonich but in patching up relations between Britain and Persia after they had been broken, were consistent with his statements. "Certainly an exclusive, jealous, and narrow policy would have guided us to profit from the present circumstance and perpetuate the quarrel between the two Governments in order to exploit the rupture in their relations to our advantage," he said. Then, after stating the need for agreement to preserve peace, he appealed for bipartisan leadership: "We leave it to the enlightened judgment of the English Cabinet to reflect on these things in its wisdom . . . [for] the peace of Asia can only be secured by mutual accord of views and peaceful initiatives. It is important that in this respect there be complete reciprocity between the two Powers that together influence the destiny of this vast part of the globe."[17]

Having received the Russian guarantee of non-intervention and having decided that "the establishment of a permanent British influence in Afghanistan" was vital, the British government went

14. Palmerston to Pozzo di Borgo (20 December 1838), *BMAddMSS* 36469.
15. Nesselrode to Pozzo di Borgo (29 January/10 February 1839), G. F. Martens, *Nouveau Recueil*, vol. 24 (16): 302.
16. *Ibid.*, 303–304.
17. *Ibid.*, 307–308.

ahead with its decision to send an army into Afghanistan.[18] The Afghans would not have Russia's support, and it seemed certain that there would be no real Russian opposition to the move. As the expeditionary force advanced, British newspapers blossomed with articles about the need to contain Russian aggression.

Diuhamel, who later complained that one had to present things "in a rosy light" to keep Nesselrode happy, began to suspect that the move to propitiate Britain had been "a mistake." "This question may be more weighty than it is thought to be in St. Petersburg," he wrote to Seniavin in March 1839. "When the English consolidate their influence in Khiva and Bokhara and are strong enough to send out a Mullah to stir up our Moslem tribes, then we will realize perhaps too late that it was a mistake to allow the English to advance beyond India, and that it was a mistake not to support the brothers Barakzeev"—the khans of Kabul and Gandahar.[19]

Such doubts became widespread, especially among Russian military officers, but Nesselrode held fast. He learned of Diuhamel's opinion, and composed instructions to counter it. Simonich had provoked the British expedition, he argued, and the Russian pledge of non-intervention had nothing to do with the British decision. As he wrote to Diuhamel, "We very clearly saw that we would have to endure hard times. We never deceived ourselves about the issue of the English-Indian expedition; we did not hold out a small hope for the Afghans' capacity to resist. All of the considerations you put forward in your last dispatches have already occurred to us. . . . But if they give rise to a proposal that we must contain the English by helping the Sirdars of Gandahar and Kabul, then I shall inform you that we remain at an impasse and a thousand times condemn Simonich for his thoughtlessness and improvidence."[20]

But the British expedition hardly seemed to mark "an impasse." It aroused strong feelings in Russia. "England has been allowed an aggression in Afghanistan," wrote General F.-W.-R. Berg, expressing a thought not uncommon among his fellow officers.[21] Watching events close at hand and perhaps sensing the

18. McNeill to Palmerston (27 October 1838), *BMAddMSS* 36469.
19. Diuhamel to Seniavin (25 February 1839), in Diuhamel, "Avtobiografiia . . . ," vol. 2, no. 8: 109.
20. Diuhamel, *ibid.*, 103.
21. Berg to Diuhamel (8 November 1839), *ibid.*, 114.

possibility of change at the insistence of the General Staff, Diu-hamel had decided that "the imagined schemes of Russia were none other than cavils, fabricated to justify their own ambitions for conquest." Some Russian response seemed to be in order. "If my advice were asked," he said, "I would say above all take pos-session of Khiva."[22]

The desire to conquer Khiva was nowhere more strongly felt than in Orenburg, where for years Perovskii had been compiling maps and plans, some put together on the basis of information Witkiewicz had collected. He had proposed a campaign against Khiva in 1834, but had been turned down, largely because of Nesselrode's interference. Now it seemed that the project might be passed over Nesselrode's objections.

Perovskii, later remembered in Russia as having "laid the foundation of our power in Central Asia," was an outstanding officer, in whom experience, courage, and a keen, realistic intel-lect were combined with sensitive, romantic patriotism.[23] He fought the French in 1812, when he was barely old enough to hold a commission, and was captured and held prisoner for two years. Later he enjoyed Menshikov's patronage, and served as his Chief of Staff in the Turkish campaign in 1828, when he was gravely wounded. In 1833 he was appointed Governor-General of Orenburg—a high rank, in "a place of banishment for criminal and political offenders," as a result, it was said, of pressure by the "German party . . . to get rid of men incompatible with its interests."[24] It was true that Perovskii's zealous nationalism and advocacy of an aggressive, expansionist policy drew him into a clash with Nesselrode, whom he came to despise.[25] But it also should be noted that he belonged to a family which, although it included a Minister of the Interior, his brother, L. A. Perovskii, chafed restlessly under both Alexander and Nicholas, worried them, and formed part of the crust of old nobility that protected some of the outspoken critics of foreign influence. Among his close friends were Viazemskii, Murav'ev, Karamzin, Pushkin, Zhukovskii, Khitov, and Dal—most of whom visited him in Oren-

22. Diuhamel, ibid., 115, 109.
23. P. B., "Graf V. A. Perovskii," Russkii arkhiv (1881), vol. 3: 475.
24. I. N. Zakharin ("Iakunin"), Graf V. A. Perovskii i ego zimnii pokhod v Khivu (St. Petersburg, 1901), part 1: 9.
25. Cf. I. N. Bozherianov, ed., "Pamiati V. I. Dalia," Russkaia starina (1907), vol. 132: 279.

burg. Dal, who lived there for eight years and has been referred
to as Perovskii's "shadow,"[26] believed that Russian culture had
been shaped largely under Asian influences, and that unification
with Central Asia would be mutually beneficial. "The entire region
and peoples form a brotherhood with us, giving them direction
and organization," he said, while prospects for trade and development of resources meant that "here, almost within sight of our
borders, one of the vital regions of Russia may be raised from
nothingness." In contrast, British culture had little in common
with Asian, and British imperialism was destructive to it."[27]

While Perovskii was anxious to take Khiva, the projected
campaign needed other justification. The reason given was to
secure routes of commerce for the caravan trade and free the
large numbers of Russian prisoners held by the Khivan Khan for
sale in the thriving Asian slave market. As presented to the Tsar,
Perovskii's plan was to march to Khiva, secure the release of the
prisoners, reach an agreement beneficial to Russia, and march
out again. (When this plan had been presented before, Nesselrode
had succeeded in squashing it with the argument that diplomacy
and outright bribery would be less expensive and more successful
in the long run than a direct assault. "Therefore I most humbly
ask you Dear Sir, to change your view on this and offer money
to expedite the negotiations for the prisoners," Nesselrode had
written to Perovskii.[28] The project had been shelved, and Perovskii ordered to build a wall between Orenburg and Khiva, which
he reluctantly set about doing, completing about eighteen of the
projected hundred versts before the British expedition gave him
a new argument.)[29] But there was intense disagreement over the
campaign before it was approved. At the end of February 1839,
Perovskii was called to Petersburg to explain his plan and aims.
He met with Nesselrode and Chernyshev, and in the course of

26. N. Modestov, ed., "K istorii osvobozhdeniia russkikh plennykh."
    Russkii arkhiv (1915), vol. 1: 42. Perovskii was also close to
    Zhukovskii. Cf. Zakharin, "Druzhba Zhukovskago s Perovskim,
    1820–1852 gg.," *Vestnik Evropy* (1901), vol. 208, no. 2: 524–552.
27. Dal, "Statia," in Modestov, ed., "K istorii," 42.
28. Nesselrode to Perovskii (1834), *Russkii arkhiv* (1914), vol. 3: 105–
    107. The "Philanthropic Society" is mentioned in Ivanin and
    Golosov, "Pokohd v Khivu," vol. 1: 45.
29. Cf. Ivanin and Golosov, *ibid.*, 67.

these meetings drew up an extraordinary document—virtually a treaty with Nesselrode in which he agreed to hold himself to certain stipulated lines of conduct. Signed on March 24, it contained six points: (1) Nesselrode's concession that the expedition should go forward and with the cooperation of his ministry; (2) that Perovskii should keep the preparations secret as long as possible, and say that he was outfitting a scientific expedition to the Aral Sea, allowing Nesselrode extra time to prepare Britain; (3) that his departure should not occur until the end of the British Afghan expedition, but if the British had not stabilized the situation by the spring, 1840, it could be undertaken then; (4) that if he reached Khiva, Perovskii was to find a reliable potentate for the throne, a ruler who would promise "to establish order and security so far as possible, to release all of the prisoners, and to give full freedom to Russian commerce;" (5) and (6) provide for funding and logistics. Perovskii did not have permission to plant the Russian flag in Khiva. The administration after a victorious campaign was to be Khivan, not Russian.[30]

In the period of preparation, there were additional diplomatic negotiations, although we do not know the extent of Nesselrode's role in them. The Khivan Khan did release some prisoners and send an envoy to Orenburg. Perovskii wrote to Nesselrode that the message brought by the envoy "may be summed up as no more than bombastic prattle" and that he would continue to "follow your previous instructions, Dear Sir, if you approve."[31]

On November 24, Perovskii, Dal, and an army of about five thousand set out into the wintry steppe. Perovskii addressed his soldiers: "Comrades! Awaiting us are cold and blizzards and all of the formidable difficulties of a long campaign in the steppe. . . . For the first time the troops of the Orenburg corps are marching against the enemy in great force. . . . In two months, God willing,

30. Cf. M. Ivanin, *Opisanie zimniago pokhoda v Khivu v 1839–1840 g.* (St. Petersburg, 1874), 3; Perovskii, "Pis'ma k A. Ia. Bulgakov," *Russkii arkhiv* (1878), vil. 5: 36n.; Perovskii, "Voennoe predpriatie protivu Khivu," *Chteniia v imperatorskom obshchestve. Istorii i drevnostei rossiiskikh pri Moskovskom Universitete* (January–March 1860), vol. 1: 47 (authorship indicated by Perovskii, "Pis'ma," above, 34).

31. Perovskii to Nesselrode (21 August 1839), in Modestov, ed., "K istorii," 34–35. According to Modestov, the draft of the letter was prepared by Dal.

we shall be in Khiva, and there for the first time in the capital of the khanate Russians will offer fervent and thundering prayers for Tsar and Fatherland."[32] Perhaps Perovskii did not expect that the first time would be the last. But in a "Declaration" sent to Petersburg he gave the rationale that Russia held historic interest in commerce with Central Asia, and that freedom of trade was blocked by Khiva.[33]

Nesselrode's main motive in the agreement of March 24 was to control the effect of the expedition on relations with Britain. A week before Perovskii left Orenburg, Nesselrode explained the objects of the campaign to Clanricarde, saying that the foremost was to obtain the release of Russian prisoners. Later in the same month, Perovskii's speech was published, and Clanricarde began to speculate that a Russian garrison might be stationed at the city of Khiva.[34] The Russian government offered further explanations in order to protect talks on the Eastern Question that Brunnow had just initiated in London. Nicholas personally assured the British ambassador that Russian aims did not even indirectly involve British India or Afghanistan; the object was to "establish tranquility for the future."[35]

In London, Brunnow also explained to Palmerston that the campaign was intended solely to secure the release of the prisoners and halt raids on Russian commerce. He tried to show Palmerston that the expedition was not a response to the British Afghan campaign, but Palmerston answered that Russia seemed merely to be taking a different road to India. Brunnow rejoined that this idea ought to be dispelled by Russian efforts to reestablish good relations between Persia and Britain and by the fact that he was in London on a special mission of friendship.[36] Palmerston admitted that Brunnow's thoughts had some force, but cautioned that there could be no foregone conclusions while he had "to deal with public opinion, which is deeply imbued with distrust and

32. Perovskii, "Prikaz otdannyi . . . pred vystupleniem v Khivinskii pokhod 1839 goda," *Russkii arkhiv* (1879), vol. 3: 342.
33. Perovskii, "Deklaratsiia" (14 November 1839), M. Ivanin, *Opisanie zimniago pokhoda*, 225–227.
34. Clanricarde to Palmerston (18 November and 30 November 1939), FO 65/253.
35. Clanricarde to Palmerston (14 January 1840), FO 65/260; the phrase quoted was underlined in pencil.
36. As related in Palmerston to Clanricarde (24 January 1840), FO 65/258.

jealousy of Russia."[37] He said that the government of British India felt menaced, and referred to a passage in Perovskii's "Declaration" which indicated that Russia had historic and rightful interests in Central Asia. Brunnow then brought up the subject of Afghanistan, indicating that similar criticism might be made of British policy. Palmerston disagreed. The cases were not parallel; Afghanistan was vital to British defense. Since Russia had "determined that Afghanistan should no longer be left alone, and remain independent, we had resolved that it should be British and not Russian and Persian." Palmerston spoke with candor. Brunnow, frustrated by his narrow distrust, closed the conversation saying he would consult Petersburg.[38] Explanations were forthcoming; they were in the same vein, and they were the subject of lengthy discussions between Palmerston, Hobhouse, and Brunnow. On March 24 Palmerston raised a vision of a clash between the Russian and British armies.[39] The possibility of war between Russia and Britain in Afghanistan and the Hindu Kush was a subject of speculation, and it was generally agreed that it would be an interesting match, with both armies overextended and barely strong enough to protect themselves from the tribes whose independence they were supposedly trying to secure. As it was, the British met disaster at the hands of the Afghans and nature intervened to stop Perovskii.

An unusually severe winter descended on the Khivan desert, with heavy snow and intense cold. It was said that Perovskii's flask of Irish whiskey froze solid at his side. With his camels dying and his effective fighting force down to one-fifth, he called a council of his officers, decided that victory was beyond hope even if they reached Khiva, and announced a retreat. "Comrades!" he announced, "However painful it is to forego the victory which awaited us, we must now retrace our steps to our own frontier. There we will await new orders from the Gosudar Emperor. Success will yet be ours."[40] Dal, who was with Perovskii, said that they felt it was a "major misfortune for contemporary political relations," because "a strike on Khiva coinciding with the English occupation of Kabul would have been timely and well-

37. Palmerston to Clanricarde (14 January 1840), *FO* 65/260.
38. *Ibid.*
39. Palmerston to Clanricarde (24 March 1840), *FO* 65/258.
40. M. Ivanin, *Opisanie zimniago pokhoda*, 176–177.

placed;" it "would have given us much weight in Asia and Europe."[41]

Perovskii was not given "new orders" for another campaign, although for several months Nesselrode and Brunnow had to counter rumors that he had received such orders. Nesselrode's opponents felt that a second expedition should have been mounted as soon as possible. Perovskii himself returned to Petersburg in June 1840 to urge a new campaign. But he met a cool reception, and apparently found that those who opposed his views wished to emphasize his lack of success and have him "completely disgraced."[42] Whatever transpired, by the end of June, Clanricarde thought that the Khivan question had been stabilized. Although the British effort to control Afghanistan continued for nearly two years afterward, there was no Russian response to it, and the series of confrontations in Asia came to an end in June 1840.

Beginning as a small setback for Nesselrode in his contention against an expansionist policy, the Khivan campaign turned out in his favor by harmlessly demonstrating that Russian operations in Asia provoked the war party in Britain and endangered the cooperative spirit, which at the time had become very important in connection with the Eastern Question. This was suggested by a change in Diuhamel's opinion, which shifted with the suddenness of a weathervane: "Thank God that the expedition to Khiva is finished," he wrote to General Berg, "I tell you that it would have precipitated tragedy in Asia."[43]

It was true that Nesselrode had not made great gains. Russia was more or less holding the old expansionist policy in abeyance in observance of the territorial status quo. If real advances toward a new order were to come, they would have to follow British acceptance of the overtures for the creation of a neutral free-trade area, the buffer theory, as a basis for negotiation and agreement. But by this time the rapprochement was an ongoing affair, and there would be opportunities to raise the subject again.[44] The Tsar was in favor of the procedure, although he was reluctant to

41. Dal (14 February 1840), *Polnoe sobranie sochinenii* (St. Petersburg and Moscow, 1897), vol. 10: 497.
42. Perovskii to Bulgakov (27 June 1840), in Zakharin, *Graf V. A. Perovskii*, part 2: 143.
43. Diuhamel, *Avtobiografiia* . . . (Moscow, 1885), 115.
44. Brunnow brought it up at least twice during the negotiations of 1839–1840, but Palmerston's mind remained closed.

hold the General Staff as firmly in check as Nesselrode would have liked, and he had some reservations. But if he had followed the advice of his generals and decided to take decisive action, not merely sending the small army of five thousand through the snow toward Khiva, the status quo would have gone by the board, and in all probability there would have been war instead of rapprochement. Perhaps, as Perovskii and others later argued, it would have been more advantageous to meet Britain on a broad front in a prolonged conflict in Asia than at the ramparts of Sevastopol.

Confrontation in the Near East

In 1836 and 1837 relations between Russia and Britain began to pivot around the Eastern Question: each believed that the power that dominated the Near East would hold a weighty advantage in Asia and in Europe. Both governments acted as if vital interests everywhere could be decisively affected by changes in the deployment of their naval forces, especially if one fleet could pass freely through the straits. The strategic equation involved three factors of tremendous importance: (1) the Black Sea Fleet had entered a period of rapid growth, but was not yet a match for the British Mediterranean fleet; (2) the strength of the Russian fleet would have been greatly augmented if it could have used the Black Sea as a sanctuary from which to cruise the Mediterranean; and (3), as Crawley has said, "the Black Sea was in fact the only point at which England could touch Russia at all in case of conflict."[45] Dominant influence at Constantinople would have given either side the edge by opening the way to exclusive control of the straits.

Nesselrode wanted to avoid a contest for dominance. He believed that the closure of the straits to warships of all nations was vital to Turkish neutrality and the status quo. His nationalistic opponents, including the Minister of the Navy, A. S. Menshikov, were convinced that the strategic advantages should belong to Russia and wanted to open the straits to Russian warships.

Menshikov had long been interested in foreign affairs, particularly the Eastern Question, and considered himself to be something of a diplomatist. His experience in the Near East

---

45. C. W. Crawley, "Anglo-Russian Relations, 1815–1840," *The Cambridge Historical Journal* (1929), vol. 3: 71.

began during the Napoleonic period, when he saw action with the army in the war against Turkey, and afterwards served at Shumly, Nikopol, and elsewhere in the south. In 1823 he accepted a post in the foreign ministry, but the following year returned to the military. In 1826 he was named Ambassador to Persia, where he immediately frightened the Shah into thinking that a Russian invasion was imminent, alarmed the British, and helped to start the Russo-Persian War. This was not the last time that his brusque, insulting manner and penchant for hasty action led to diplomatic disaster. In 1828 he was appointed to the General Staff and took part in the Russo-Turkish War. He was also given the rank of Admiral, and three years later took charge of the Ministry of the Navy. He set out to renovate the fleet and was highly successful between 1833 and 1836, until funds were reduced and diverted to the army for Minister of War Chernyshev's development plans, which to Menshikov's chagrin simply demanded more soldiers, heavier artillery, and increased outlays for the unsuccessful war in the Caucasus.

It is interesting to compare Menshikov with Chernyshev. Menshikov was the grand strategist; he saw no beauty in a military organization which was a parade-ground symbol of order. For him it was natural to think in terms of a large plan for Russian aggrandizement in the Near East and Asia. Chernyshev, on the other hand, was thoroughly wrapped up in the formalities and details of managing the army and entertained few grand designs. But he was closer to the Emperor; neither Chernyshev nor Nicholas really saw the point of making an all-out effort to seize the straits and contest British naval power in the eastern Mediterranean. But the Tsar made adroit use of Menshikov when he appointed him Minister of the Navy: a contentious attitude toward Britain was desirable in the man who was to direct the first full-scale renovation of the navy since the reign of Catherine II.

The mid-1830s witnessed the beginning of what was regarded as a naval armaments race between Russia and Britain. Menshikov's program of development brought the Russian navy into the age of steam, replaced rotting hulks with new ships, and indolent routines with innovative training programs—such as the creation of communal sailors' societies to prepare peasants for maritime service. Menshikov could claim little nautical experience, but he was a strong advocate of modern sea power, and was highly esteemed by nationalists such as Lazarev and Vorontsov. Like most Russian strategists he was convinced that the Black Sea Fleet was more important than the Baltic Fleet. The Black Sea Fleet was less likely to be bottled up by Britain, and it was better situated to protect a world-ranging merchant marine. Because the Baltic Fleet was the show-case of naval progress, it received excessive attention. This increased the need to find ways of combining the fleets, which required, first, that the straits be opened. By 1836 it was clear that Menshikov had created a new navy. British observers maintained that Russian training was inferior, and that the Russian ships were slower than the British in maneuvers and firing. But they were watching with keen interest. When the naval armaments debate was re-opened in Britain in the spring of 1836, the Russian navy was pointed to as a justification for increased expenditures.

Rumors of impending naval war in the Baltic caused an economic panic among Petersburg merchants in March 1836. Foreign commerce declined sharply. Nesselrode, always preoccupied with trade, expressed his concern to Durham and conveyed a proposal that the Russian and British fleets join each other for a Baltic cruise to dispel the rumors. Britain did not respond favorably to this plan, but the Russian government eased fears by sponsoring a petition, signed by leading foreign and Russian merchants in Petersburg, which stated that there was no basis for the panic, that it was bad for business, and that Russia and Britain would continue to enjoy friendly relations; meanwhile, a group of British merchants petitioned their own government for public "assurances which may tend to allay apprehension, and strengthen that confidence which is indispensable to the successful prosecution of commercial enterprise."[46]

But Britain grew steadily more uneasy over the new Russian navy. Durham repeatedly asked for explanations of the purposes of Menshikov's program. Finally, Nicholas I held a personal interview with Durham and told him that the strength of the navy would remain inferior to that of the British navy and

46. Barante to Thiers (14 May 1836), *Souvenirs*, vol. 5: 377. Durham to Palmerston (20 March 1836), *FO* 65/223, and (9 May 1836), *FO* 65/224. Petition filed with the British Consul by British merchants in Petersburg, bearing 24 signatures, (24 April/6 May 1836), enclosure Durham to Palmerston (7 May 1836), *FO* 65/224.

that it should not be viewed as a hostile development. After he learned of the interview, Palmerston replied that the Russian program would necessarily affect parliamentary discussion of naval expenditures, and that while the Russian navy was not as strong as the British in quantitative terms, it did hold a certain advantage. It could bring a greater concentration of force to bear more quickly because the British navy had to be dispersed over the oceans of the world to protect imperial interests. In May 1836 he said, "If then the Russian Government is desirous of investigating the many causes which have tended to create in this country unfriendly feelings towards Russia, they ought not to overlook these apparently threatening Naval armaments which are so naturally calculated to give umbrage to the people of this country."[47] In July 1836 the largest Baltic Fleet Russia had ever assembled passed in review at Kronstadt. Durham and British naval officers were invited to witness the spectacle. It was as if Russia were announcing that she intended to be Britain's next rival at sea.

Menshikov understood that if Britain decided to destroy Russian naval power her main objective would be the Black Sea Fleet. The *Vixen* affair awakened the feeling in the General Staff that it was urgent to lay plans against a swift British attack.[48] If Britain made the first move without warning, Turkey probably would side with her and open the straits. It was thought that if given a small warning Russia might be able to close the Bosphorus, and in February 1837 Chernyshev issued secret orders to be ready for this move.[49] Menshikov did what he could to improve the efficiency of his command, but the conditions imposed by the closure of the straits confined him to a defensive strategy. Even when he anticipated trouble, closure prevented him from sending ships from the Baltic to reinforce the fleet in the Black Sea. This prompted him to advance a plan that would have opened the

47. Palmerston to Durham (31 May 1836), *FO* 181/123.
48. The possibility of a surprise attack that might place an enemy in an advantageous position was a relatively new development in Russian military thinking. It arose with a grasp of the implications of naval power in the 1830s, and was heightened by fear of a British attack at the time of the *Vixen* affair. Cf. Schiemann, "Russische-englische Beziehungen unter Kaiser Nikolaus I," *Zeitschrift für osteuropäische Geschichte* (1913), vol. 3; 488.
49. Chernyshev, (12 February 1837 and 16 February 1837), in Murav'ev, *Russkie na Bosfore*, Appendix K. K.: 085–087.

straits. He proposed to send two ships from the Baltic to the Black Sea, and won the Emperor's approval without Nesselrode's knowledge. On January 16, 1837, he composed a note to Nesselrode: "The Emperor has charged me to inform you, Monsieur le Comte, that His Majesty intends to send two ships of the line with one or two dispatch boats out from the Baltic this spring. They will leave under the pretext of going on maneuvers, and then proceed to the Dardanelles and pass into the Black Sea."[50] He wanted Nesselrode to arrange for the Russian ships to take on provisions at a Sardinian port.

But Nesselrode, confronted with what appeared to be the Tsar's final decision, did not react as Menshikov expected. Instead, he emphatically opposed the plan in a memorandum to Nicholas on January 28. He began by recounting what he had learned from Menshikov, and asked for Nicholas's "orders on this subject, as long as it requires the concurrence of the Ministry of Foreign Affairs." Then he stated that he did not expect any difficulty in complying with Menshikov's request regarding the Kingdom of Sardinia. His words were terse but polite.[51] The body of the message constituted an admonition; he proceeded to explain Nicholas's foreign policy to Nicholas:

"Regarding the passage of our fleet through the Bosphorus, the spirit of my duty and the profound devotion which I feel to Your service, Sire, compels me to reveal to You several considerations on this subject which involve the general system of Your policy. These considerations are so grave that my proper responsibility as a loyal servant to Your Majesty obligates me to submit them first for His deliberation with a respectful and complete frankness.

"In the midst of the difficult and often dangerous circumstances which surround the affairs of the Orient, Your Majesty has invariably followed the principle that Russia be rigorously vigilant to see that the Dardanelles stay closed to the foreign banner of war.

"This principle, in accord with interests which are well understood and with the ancient political traditions of the Porte,

50. Menshikov to Nesselrode (4/16 January 1838), P. E. Mosely, *Russian Diplomacy and the Opening of the Eastern Question in 1838 and 1839* (Cambridge, Mass., 1934), Appendix A: 141.
51. Nesselrode to Nicholas I (16/28 January 1838), in *ibid.*, 142.

was formally consecrated by the treaty concluded between Turkey and England in 1809.

"By this transaction the principle of the closure of the Dardanelles was clearly recognized "as an ancient law of the Ottoman Empire which should be respected in time of peace by every power, without exception. . . ."[52]

Nesselrode believed that parity should be maintained. Russia must not demand rights which she expected Turkey to deny to the other powers. The error of doing so was illustrated by the probable consequences, when the fleet, "after having made a tour of Europe and attracted the attention of all the maritime Powers, came to the Dardanelles and demanded to pass." This, he reasoned, "would then necessarily raise two alternatives: the Porte would refuse us passage; or it might well decide to accord it."

"In the first case, as I have already observed, we would not have a real, positive right *to insist* on passage. The Porte, in declining our demand, would invoke the strict observance of the treaties. It would be within its rights legally. We would have no grounds for contention against its refusal. But whatever the attendant circumspection with which such a refusal might be met, it is no less true that in the eyes of Europe it would comprise a wound to Russia's dignity. It would produce a dual disadvantage for us—for one part having sustained a blow against our credit, for the other having given birth to a wrong and provoked a cause for misunderstanding which would not fail to have an unfortunate effect on our relations with Turkey.

"In the second case, imagine that the Sultan granted us passage. England and France would in their turn speedily seize this pretext to demand permission from the Porte to allow some warships to enter the Black Sea."[53]

This would lead to other difficulties: it would invite a permanent British and French naval presence on the Black Sea and sharpen contention for influence over the Porte. Nesselrode argued that by demanding passage Russia "would accept the possibility of a war in which we would have nothing to gain and great commercial interests to lose."[54]

52. *Ibid.*, 142–143.
53. *Ibid.*, 144–145.
54. *Ibid.*, 145.

The Tsar thanked him, and promptly reversed the decision. Menshikov had been checkmated. It had been Nesselrode, not Nicholas, who understood that the plan contradicted the principle of closure. The nationalists would have gained ground if Nicholas had followed through with his mistake. For Menshikov, Lazarev, Vorontsov, and others concerned with military strategy, closure was a tremendous liability. Russia could not reach for a great naval and maritime future while the straits were closed. The disadvantages Nesselrode pointed out were real only if one assumed that Russia would not be able to meet the British and French challenge. But nationalists assumed that Russia would hold dominant influence at Constantinople and be able to close the straits in an emergency. This was what Nesselrode wished to avoid. It would have demolished the concert. Closure, he pointed out, was an established principle of general European law.

In his exertions to avoid a contest, he was trying to restrict Russian as well as Western involvement, although he knew that Russia's special interests required a "strong influence" in Turkey. "The geographical position of a State defines its needs and determines its interests," he had written; "it suffices to glance at the map to be convinced that on the day when Russian possessions approached the tributaries of the Black Sea, free commerce between this sea and the Mediterranean, along with a strong influence at Constantinople, became one of Russia's foremost needs."[55] From a defensive viewpoint, the straits were, as Chernyshev put it, the "vital key to the Russian hinterland." In his view, "No one would argue that we would be able to tolerate the establishment of a foreign power there, however eventual that might be. It follows that Russia must not only focus lively and constant attention on this area, but even be ready for action to take the initiative from any other power at the first signal."[56] Russian intervention would be provoked by any development which threatened to place the straits in foreign hands. But the straits were no less important as an offensive factor in Russian thinking. It made no sense to aspire, as Nesselrode did, to build a merchant marine capable of ranging over the world's oceans and assuming a larger

55. Grunwald, "Nesselrode," 181.
56. Chernyshev, "Vsepoddanneishii doklad grafa Chernysheva—Imperatora Nikolaia I," *SIRIO*, vol. 122: 305.

part of the commerce which reached Russia in foreign ships, if the main part of the naval force remained confined in the Black Sea.

That the straits were the most important single factor in the strategic balance between Russia and the Western powers was recognized in the West as well. The implications were discussed, for example, in an influential work by Marshal Marmont, one of the great strategists of the day, whose advice Ponsonby sought during the Near Eastern crisis. The work was first published in France in 1837–1838, and a translation by Lt.-Colonel Sir Frederick Smith of the Royal Engineers appeared in London in 1839.[57] Marmont observed that Russia suffered a disadvantage as a land-based power confronted by the Western naval powers, and that she must acquire naval power before she could meet them as an equal. She could become a naval power if she held the straits. The Treaty of Unkiar Skelessi had given her no real advantage, but there was nothing to stop her from gaining the objective if she made use of initiative and surprise. "I have already shown that with the greatest ease the Russians could take possession of Constantinople," he remarked, in which case "the most intimate alliance between France, England, and Austria, the most energetic effort of these three powers, would be ineffective to force the Russians to evacuate." There was only one way in which this could be prevented: the Western fleet would have to pass through the Dardanelles and secure Constantinople before Russia could, and pass through the Bosphorus into the Black Sea. "Then the Russians would have immense difficulties to overcome," and "the Russian fleet, having retreated to Sevastopol, would be bottled up there."[58] In the West, no less than in Russia, there was a feeling that if a severe crisis arose, decisive moves would place the enemy in a very difficult position without actual fighting.

A new Near Eastern crisis began to take shape a few weeks after Nesselrode had defeated Menshikov's move. For nearly a year Mohammed Ali, the Pasha of Egypt and ostensibly a vassal of the Turkish Sultan, Mahmud II, had been preparing to attack

57. Marmont, Duc de Raguse, *Voyage du Maréchal Duc de Raguse* . . . (Paris, 1837–1838), 2 vols. English translation, *The Present State of the Turkish Empire* . . . (London, 1839), with notes by Lt.-Col. Sir F. Smith.

58. *Ibid.*, *Voyage*, vol. 2: 127.

Turkey. He was widely expected to win an easy victory. The Egyptian army led by Ibrahim was recognized to be superior, and the threat to the tottering Turkish regime heightened Western fears that Russia would intervene. Early in the spring of 1838 Ponsonby held talks at Vienna with Austrian and French representatives on "means of defending the Turkish Empire against an attack from Russia."[59] Such a defense would have involved the risk of war between a Western coalition and Russia, a risk unacceptable to Austria and France, whatever Ponsonby had in mind. Soon afterward, a more peaceful plan for meeting the emergency was introduced—for a conference to sanction collective measures, including military intervention, and perhaps to adjudicate issues at stake between Turkey and Egypt. Among the first advocates of this plan were Mohammed Ali, who wished to isolate Russia and weaken Turkey, and Palmerston, who wished to isolate Russia and align Turkey with Britain. Meanwhile both sides put their military forces in readiness.

This led to a round of talks in London in June between Palmerston, Pozzo di Borgo, the French Ambassador Horace Sebastiani, and the Austrian Ambassador Prince Paul Esterhazy. Again, the powers were divided over whether or not the status quo should be the guiding principle. Sebastiani offered the following formula: the four would agree to constrain Mohammed Ali and preserve the existing order while they worked to settle grievances; however, if they failed, and war broke out anyway, no final settlement would be decided until the lines of the issues had been drawn on the battlefield. This generally conformed with Mohammed Ali's own proposal, and it appeared that if he did not gain his wishes through an agreement, he would simply go to war to get what he wanted, knowing that Russia would be constrained. Palmerston favored a collective resolution, and was receptive to Sebastiani's proposal. Esterhazy was noncommittal on specific issues, but favored a conference in any case. But Pozzo di Borgo could not agree: he maintained that the only collective action acceptable to Russia would be for the powers to cooperate in offering assistance to Turkey with the aim of upholding the status quo.[60] There was no point in sacrificing the Treaty of Unkiar Skelessi for collective action to unleash Mohammed Ali

59. Ponsonby to Palmerston (8 February 1838) FO 78/328.
60. Palmerston to Granville (3 July 1838), FO 27/557.

and redraw Turkey's borders. Nesselrode, who had repeatedly warned Mohammed Ali against attacking Turkey, could not entertain the proposals or join a conference which would only have magnified the differences between Russia and the others. A conference almost certainly would have aligned France and Britain against Russia.

Nesselrode found no prospect as ghastly as that of an entente between Britain, France, and Austria against Russia. In June and July of 1838 this seemed frighteningly close. Discussions between the Western powers had suddenly picked up in tempo and earnestness after having occurred sporadically for three years. At the end of June, Nicholas and Nesselrode went to Toeplitz to meet Metternich and try to head off such an accord by reaffirming the Münchengrätz agreement. While Nesselrode was at Toeplitz, Pozzo di Borgo and Palmerston ended their talks on a conference. Having followed Nesselrode's instruction to absolutely refuse a conference, the Russian Ambassador reported the interviews closed on July 3, with the observation that Palmerston had not given up the idea. Indeed, as soon as Palmerston had ascertained the Russian position, he sent off formal proposals for a conference. The first of these went out on July 6. Nesselrode felt compelled to respond immediately from Toeplitz. He did not swerve from the position he had taken in his warnings to Mohammed Ali, the same position Pozzo di Borgo had maintained. He explained Russian policy and the reasons for turning down Palmerston's conference proposal in a modest, straightforward message which came to be known as his "Toeplitz Declaration."[61]

Nesselrode pointed out that the powers should not be led into precipitate negotiations that might drive them apart. He said that the justification Palmerston gave in calling for a conference was a point of complete agreement between Russia and Britain. Both wished to prevent war in the Near East; both recognized the need to discourage Mohammed Ali from trying to win concessions on the battlefield. However, he thought that Mohammed Ali had counted heavily on "the jealousy of the European Cabinets in order to forward his designs." He expected that

61. Nesselrode to Pozzo di Borgo (11/23 July 1838), *FO* 65/247. The same text was communicated to the governments of France and Austria.

"once he had proclaimed the independence of Egypt, the accord between the Great Powers that exists to this day would cease to be, and that then the divergence of their opinions would contribute to the support of his own interests." This was the danger. The best way to avoid it would be for each of the great powers to make a similar declaration that Egypt must continue its peaceful relations with Turkey as before. If made "with energy by the representatives of Russia, Austria, England, and France" such a declaration "would not fail to have a salutary effect on Mohammed Ali by showing him that all the Cabinets are unanimously content to maintain the bonds that attach Egypt to the Ottoman Empire."

Nesselrode remarked that he had already instructed the Russian Minister Plenipotentiary at Alexandria, Count A. I. Medem, to sternly warn Mohammed Ali against attacking Turkey. He thought it would be highly "desirable for the representatives of the Courts of Europe to present this message simultaneously in order that by this coincidence the accord that subsists between them would be clearly impressed upon the Pasha." Such action, short of intervention on which consensus was not likely, did not prescribe a conference; it could easily be taken by the powers without a conference, employing the usual channels of diplomacy. Nesselrode supplied a sample text for use so that the wording of messages sent to Egypt by the other powers would be similar enough to impress Mohammed Ali with their "unanimity." This would serve, above all, "to convince Mohammed Ali that his hope to give birth to a divergence of opinion between Russia and England is illusory."[62]

Nesselrode's proposal was proof of Russia's good faith. Russia was prepared to sanction a British naval demonstration along the coast to Egypt or any other move short of intervention to conserve peace, but it Mohammed Ali endangered Turkey, Russia could be expected to intervene. The recommended course of action could stave off the need for intervention. It would "demonstrate to the Pasha of Egypt that an accord, which it is not to his advantage to disturb, exists between the European Powers regarding the affairs of the Levant." A conference would have the opposite effect. In order "to forestall the chance of a conflict" it was "important that the same unanimity which would direct the

62. *Ibid.*

action" of the European powers "presides also over the language that they employ at Constantinople." That is, the Sultan should be inspired with confidence that Mohammed Ali would not win his claims through collective measures imposed by a combination of the powers. A conference was rejected as being contrary to the interests of Europe and destructive to the political neutrality of Turkey. It would be better to proclaim agreement where it was known to exist, without entering a course that would divide the powers on hypothetical issues and greatly encourage Mohammed Ali to make a move. "The conservation *of the status quo* is therefore the true aim toward which our efforts must be directed, *above all else*," he said.[63]

The ideas Nesselrode expressed at Toeplitz were perfectly consistent with the policy he had advocated for many years. It was a policy calculated to insure Turkish independence and neutrality, insofar as this was possible given the converging interests of the great powers. He opposed Palmerston's conference because it would have produced divisions which would have encouraged Mohammed Ali to attack Turkey, and he thought that whatever followed, it could only bring Russia closer to the "regrettable but compelling necessity to intervene" at the straits.[64] Nesselrode did not wish to invoke the Treaty of Unkiar Skelessi; he did not wish to give his nationalistic opponents a second chance to entrench themselves at the straits.

Russia was now in grave danger of being isolated if Austria allied herself with Britain and France, and in August Nesselrode and Brunnow went to Vienna to persuade Metternich that Palmerston's proposal threatened the concert. They did not greatly strengthen relations with Austria, but Metternich at least adhered to a policy of impartiality.

The British diplomatic offensive was by no means ended, however. During the spring of 1838, McNeill at Teheran had kept Ponsonby informed about the growing possibility that war would erupt in Asia. Russia's alignment with Persia under Simonich's influence made it advantageous for Britain to use the danger of war to seek an alliance with Turkey. The Sultan valued his neutrality, but, since he leaned toward Britain as the more distant and less menacing of the two rivals, he might have been moved

63. *Ibid.*
64. *Ibid.*

further in this direction by a conflict with Persia. Dynastic and territorial disputes were already a cause of sporadic fighting along the border. Ponsonby, continuing the drive for an alliance against Russia, held out a promise of economic and military assistance to Mahmud. Such assistance, ostensibly to be used against Egypt, could as easily be used against Russia and Persia. A preliminary agreement had been drawn up in June, and early in July the Turkish Reis-Effendi, Reshid Pasha, had gone to London for the negotiations. A treaty was concluded between Britain and Turkey on August 16, 1838.

On the 15th, Palmerston brought the ambassadors of the four great powers together in one room for a chat about the Eastern Question—supposedly an attempt to open a conference.[65] However, Pozzo di Borgo was no doubt correct in his view that Palmerston could not have intended it as a move which would pave the way to a conference. Russia's position was well known. If Palmerston intended to emphasize the fact that Russia had been isolated on the question, he succeeded, because Pozzo sat in stolid silence while the others discussed the need to agree on collective measures.

The cause for concern was compounded when Britain signed the apparently innocent commercial treaty of August 16, an agreement negotiated by Ponsonby and surrounded by rumors that the Porte implicitly or secretly gave its word to open the straits to British warships in the event of conflict. Nesselrode examined the treaty closely and made a careful distinction between its "commercial" and its "political" effects. In a dispatch to Butenev he said that as for the commercial arrangements "the Emperor would not view other than with satisfaction the advantages which this transaction would bestow upon the Ottoman Government." He

---

65. Webster writes that Palmerston wished "either to confine Russia more and more in the bonds of a 'concert préalable' or else force her to reveal clearly by her refusal the true secret of her oriental policy," C. K. Webster, *The Foreign Policy of Palmerston, 1830–1841. Britain, the Liberal Movement and the Eastern Question* (London, 1951), vol. 2: 593. But Pozzo di Borgo's refusal was virtually certain under the circumstances Palmerston arranged. According to Mosely, Palmerston was making a "strange" but real "attempt to open a conference by surprise," *Russian Diplomacy*, 81–82. This too is a weak analysis, because it ignores the consideration that Palmerston could not have expected Pozzo to act against Nesselrode's instructions.

thought that Ponsonby's motives, however, were political, namely to encourage Mahmud to resist Russian influence under Unkiar Skelessi and perhaps to take stronger action against Mohammed Ali. He told Butenev to find out if the "insinuations" which surrounded the treaty were "destroying the political system adopted to this point by the Sultan," and if it was "subjoined by any secret engagements."[66] In the end he concluded that the treaty was essentially commercial, whatever the character of Ponsonby's innuendos.

Palmerston replied to Nesselrode's "Toeplitz Declaration" on September 3, saying that he was delighted to acknowledge the "unanimity" but thought that a conference would still be desirable.[67] Proposals for a conference were again addressed by the British government to France, Austria, and Russia. The treaty of August 16 had cut deeply into tenuous British bonds with France, and France turned down the proposal. Metternich did an about-face and also turned it down. Last of all, on September 21, Nesselrode instructed Pozzo di Borgo to once more turn down the conference proposal.

The European states were in as close agreement as Nesselrode expected could be achieved for the time being. "The crisis is past," he said, "and the accord between the great Powers is intact." Thus he expressed his main concern. "Why then bring on a deliberation about eventualities?"[68]

After acknowledging that a conference would probably divide Europe, aligning Britain and France against Russia, Palmerston told Clanricarde that even without the results a conference might bring, Britain would never again allow Russia to occupy the straits.[69] This was a cause of Russian concern in November, when Nicholas wrote, "Palmerston verbally proclaimed to Pozzo that England would never tolerate our intervention in Turkish affairs, as though war would issue from it." He added, "Whatever happens, we are ready."[70] Nesselrode still worried that Turkey

---

66. Nesselrode to Butenev (27 October 1838), in Mosely, *Russian Diplomacy*, Appendix C: 162.
67. Palmerston to Pozzo di Borgo (3 September 1838), FO 65/247.
68. Nesselrode to Pozzo di Borgo (21 September 1838), FO 65/247. Cf. Martens, *Recueil*, vol. 12: 73.
69. Palmerston to Clanricarde (10 October 1838), FO 65/243.
70. Nicholas I to Paskevich (21 October 1838), "Imperator Nikolai Pavlovich v ego pis'makh . . . ," vol. 1: 23.

might ally herself with Britain, and Butenev in Constantinople was instructed to learn if the British fleet was on the verge of passing the straits. During the first week in November Clanricarde emerged from solemn talks with Nesselrode and Nicholas to report, "I am convinced that Russia has every reason to dread war, and I do not think the Russian government would willingly incur even the risk of such a calamity."[71]

Palmerston instructed Clanricarde to tell Nesselrode that if Russia was interested in conserving peace, it ought to be recognized that "the menacing naval demonstrations of Russia" were having a negative effect on relations between the two countries. Nesselrode should be assured that "Her Majesty's Govt. are far from sharing the opinion, which is very prevalent in this Country, that the Russian Fleet is maintained in its present condition with views hostile to Great Britain." But the British government had to be responsive to public opinion. In this note, which was read verbatim to Nesselrode, Palmerston argued that since Russia was in no danger of attack, the fleet must be intended for aggression, "and Great Britain and Turkey are the Countries which publick opinion points out as likely, according to circumstances, to be threatened by the Russian armament."[72]

Nesselrode was openly annoyed when Clanricarde read the dispatch to him. He told Clanricarde that the British government was wrong in viewing Russian sea power as a threat. The straits were closed, and Russian warships could not pass into the Mediterranean; Russia was not engaged in aggression. The Russian government was building a maritime future, and since there was little prospect that a merchant marine would grow spontaneously, it was necessary to train sailors by means of a directed program. He said that the Russian government had given "proofs of its moderation and of its peaceable and unambiguous policy in its conduct towards Turkey."[73]

Clanricarde replied that the "English Government entertained neither apprehension nor suspicion of the designs of Russia," however, "it was with a view of quieting publick opinion in England, and throughout Europe generally" that the British government advised Russia to reduce its naval activity. The "suspi-

71. Clanricarde to Palmerston (6 November 1838), FO 65/244.
72. Palmerston to Clanricarde (29 December 1838), FO 65/243.
73. Clanricarde to Palmerston (21 January 1839), FO 65/251.

cions and accusations" about Russian policy "were not confined
to England," said Clanricarde. But Nesselrode disagreed. First, it
was not "throughout Europe generally" that anti-Russian feelings
were sustained in politics, but in the two maritime countries; he
said that "it was only in England and in France that any suspicion
or hostility to Russia was entertained." Second, public opinion
was not the source of the problem, because "the bad feeling, that
existed, would soon end if not encouraged by the Government."
Nesselrode treated the British protest against Russian naval power
as a political gambit.[74]

When the Near Eastern crisis reopened in April, Turkey
and Egypt did go to war, and Russia faced the necessity to intervene if the concert failed. It brought a moment of truth for Nesselrode, a crucial test. The war apparently came as a surprise.
On April 1, 1839, Clanricarde reported to Palmerston that Nesselrode predicted there would be no war in the Near East. The
British Ambassador also said that his colleagues believed the
Russian government honestly desired tranquility for Turkey.[75]
Twenty days later Turkey attacked Egypt, and Clanricarde reported that Nesselrode was disturbed. "I am convinced," he
wrote, "that this event has caused surprise and great annoyance
to the Imperial Government; that the Emperor will not seek, but
will avoid, as far as he can, recognizing any *casus foderis*, that
the Sultan may allege to have arisen under the Treaty of Unkiar
Skelessi." Russian expeditionary forces at Sevastopol were
placed in a state of readiness, it was true, but he later told
Palmerston that Russian intervention was so improbable that he
would not expect it unless the Turkish forces were rolled back
to "the walls of Petersburgh."[76]

In May the British government sent Admiral Stopford fresh
authorization to force the straits on either of two conditions: first,
if the Turkish government submitted a request for naval assistance
through the British ambassador; second, if Russia, even in response to a Turkish request, intervened. In the second case the

74. *Ibid.*
75. Palmerston to Clanricarde (1 April 1839), *FO* 65/251. It is possible
that Palmerston was simultaneously seeking an alliance with Turkey
against Russia. Cf. Schiemann, *Geschichte Russlands*, vol. 3: 378–
379.
76. Clanricarde to Palmerston (8 June 1839) and (8 July 1839), *FO*
65/252.

British fleet was ordered to force the straits even if it meant war with Turkey, and presumably Russia.[77] At the same time, the French government considered forcing the straits and decided that three conditions would be required for success: favorable winds, coordination with a land assault force, and British support or acquiescence.[78] A test of the Marmont doctrine was in the offing. But Britain and France were not coordinated on strategy in the eastern Mediterranean. France was still Egypt's benefactor.

In May and June Nesselrode continued to resist any arrangement in which Russia would have to sit down opposite a Western coalition led by Britain. In July he worked to secure Austrian neutrality and open direct negotiations between Turkey and Egypt, without much success, before he turned to the solution of a concert approached through bilateral agreement with Britain.

In June the Turkish army was defeated, on June 30 Mahmud died, and two weeks later the whole Turkish fleet surrendered to Egypt. People who had been expecting Turkey to crumble to pieces thought that they were witnessing the event. Now, as never before, there seemed to be a grave danger that the Russian and Western forces would suddenly converge on the straits and start "a terrible European war."[79] Clanricarde reported that Russia was convinced of the danger.[80] Metternich proposed a conference at Vienna, and Palmerston was favorable, but Russia rejected the proposal. Nesselrode would have nothing to do with a conference mediated by Metternich. He thought that the powers were moving toward accord on general principles, and that a conference might bring back the old problems. "Metternich," he complained to Meyendorff, "out of sheer wantonness would complicate a very simple matter" which was better left alone "because all of the cabinets are falling into accord."[81] It was best to wait, keeping the issue in abeyance, "since by desiring to put it on the agenda, we would risk being forced into embroilment, by desiring to remain united, being forced into disunity, in the end shaking the Ottoman Empire by the force of our desire to

77. Crawley, "Anglo-Russian Relations," 61.
78. Bourqueney to Soult (17 June 1839), in Guizot, *Mémoires pour servir à l'histoire de mon temps* (Paris, 1872), vol. 4: 338–339.
79. Martens, *Die russische Politik*, 36.
80. Clanricarde to Palmerston (8 June 1839), *FO* 65/252.
81. Nesselrode to Meyendorff (24 July 1839), *Lettres et papiers*, vol. 7: 287.

conserve it."[82] He did, however, think that the feeling of amica-
bility Metternich conveyed with the proposal offered hope for
strengthening whatever remained of the Münchengrätz ties. The
high point in a series of moves in that direction was a general
statement of Russian policy which came in the first week in July.
Nesselrode warned that the Russian government could not alter
its position on the central issue, that of closure. He said that "the
question of the closure of the Dardanelles is for us a question of
honor, that we are obliged to defend at all cost and without ever
recoiling from real sacrifice."[83]

To achieve peace in the Near East, the powers should arrange a direct settlement between Egypt and Turkey. "We ought
not, and cannot set ourselves up as arbiters of what affects the
interests of the Porte to such a degree," wrote Nesselrode in instructions to Butenev. "The Emperor allows you full latitude to
open the way, in concert with your colleagues, for a pacific arrangement between the Porte and Egypt."[84] Without recounting
the course of these efforts, it is enough to say that direct negotiation fell through because no compromise could be reached on
important issues, such as whether Turkey or Egypt should acquire Syria. The collective note signed by the five powers on July
27, 1839, was not a move toward a conference, but an adaptation
from the principle of direct negotiation.[85] According to Nesselrode, the five powers were to offer their "good offices" to mediate
a direct settlement, not to resolve the issues. It was the kind of

82. Nesselrode to Struve (18 July 1839), in Goriainov, *Le Bosphore et les
    Dardanelles*, 55–56. Cf. Martens, *Die russische Politik*, 37.
83. Nesselrode to Struve (4 July 1839), in Martens, *Recueil*, vol. 4: 479–
    482.
84. Nesselrode to Butenev (n.d. 1839), in L. Blanc, *Révolution français.
    Historie de dix ans. 1830–1840* (Brussels, 1843), vol. 5: 477.
85. Another interpretation, namely that the note was an attempt to impose
    a settlement on Turkey and Egypt by a concert of the European
    powers, is found in most studies of the subject in the English language.
    Cf. H. W. V. Temperley, *England and the Near East. The Crimea*
    (London, 1936), 107–109; Webster, *The Foreign Policy of Palmer-
    ston*, vol. 2: 635–636. Nesselrode was not in favor of any such
    attempt because he believed it would be divisive; the collective note
    was acceptable to him only insofar as it was not a prelude for action
    by the great powers. Similar considerations rendered it acceptable
    to Admiral Roussin, who signed it for France, a fact that Temperley
    (*England and the Near East*, 108) finds "remarkable." And in the
    end, the positive effect of the note evaporated when Palmerston
    pressed to use it as if it were more than a statement of "unanimity."

expression of "unanimity" he had called for during the first phase of the crisis. The "five powers are perfectly agreed upon the Eastern Question," the note said, and their participation in the settlement was limited by "the interest they conjointly feel and exert."[86]

But "unanimity" did not survive. France withdrew because it appeared that Turkey's claims to Syria would be supported by the other powers. And Nesselrode, alarmed that Palmerston was intending the note as the beginning of a conference, disclaimed it. Baron Bourqueney, the French minister at London, reported that Palmerston was "strongly impressed with a fear that the Russian cabinet may urge the authorities at Constantinople to a direct settlement between the Porte and Mohammed Ali."[87] But despite its early demise, the collective note left Russia and Britain in closer cooperation than ever before, and it opened the way to the diplomatic paradigm Nesselrode favored as holding the best advantages for resolving the European side of the crisis—specific bilateral agreement with Britain. "Metternich himself wished to convene a conference at Vienna," writes Grunwald, "but in order to avoid a division of Europe into two camps the Vice-Chancellor preferred an accord direct with the cabinet of St.-James."[88] The Russian move toward Britain came as a surprise to Metternich, who, after receiving Palmerston's overtures for a year and a half, was convinced that direct agreement between Russia and Britain on the Eastern Question was close to impossible.

As the new accord began to take shape Palmerston was reluctant to yield in his belief that Russian policy was aggressive. In a dispatch to Lord Granville at the end of June, he claimed that the Western powers probably had prevented Russian aggression because Russia might possibly have made a secret agreement with Egypt and then played off one side against the other to weaken Turkey and thereby arrange circumstances for intervention. If there were such a plan it had been foiled, he thought. In July he still believed that Britain and France should be ready to move against Russia.[89] But the evidence of Russia's conciliatory

86. *Correspondence Relative to the Affairs of the Levant*, vol. 1: 157.
87. Bourqueney to Soult (27 July 1839), in Guizot, *Mémoires*, vol. 4: 347. Nesselrode's desire to promote direct negotiation is mentioned *ibid.*, 345.
88. Grunwald, "Nesselrode," 188.
89. Palmerston to Granville (29 June 1839), *FO* 575/265.

attitude was mounting. The Treaty of Unkiar Skelessi had not been invoked, and even when Britain had decided that it would be prudent to send Stopford to the straits, Russia had acquiesced without hesitation, proving the genuineness of Nesselrode's assurances.

The Russian decision to make a bid for a concert built on an arrangement between the two powers came in August. Nesselrode argued his case in a memorandum to Nicholas on August 15, saying that there was no alternative. The effort to promote direct negotiations had shown that "the crisis in which the Ottoman Empire is involved does not admit of any but a single means of resolution . . . a prompt and definite transaction designed on one side to return repose to Turkey, and on the other to consolidate the gains which the Viceroy presently holds and which he certainly will not lightly abandon." A settlement between Turkey and Egypt was in the offing, whereas it had not been before, and Britain, France, and Austria would probably reach agreement to sanction it. Russia must take the lead or stand alone. "Contracted without our concurrence," he said, "such an engagement would at once have the dual disadvantage of isolating us completely from the other courts and bringing them together in a combination which, under the pretext of being organized in favor of the Porte, would in reality be directed against us." The Treaty of Unkiar Skelessi could be offered in exchange for a concerted agreement to uphold the status quo. If Russia secured "the closure of the Dardanelles as a general principle of public European law," then "the Treaty of Unkiar Skelessi will cease to have practical value for us."[90] Nicholas decided in favor of the proposal within a week, and Nesselrode selected Brunnow to deliver the overture to London. He called Clanricarde for an interview and informed him that since the two governments held similar views, Russia wished to offer Britain a blueprint for a general agreement as a basis of discussion.[91] A few weeks later, the arrangements for Brunnow's mission were underway.

Shortly after Nesselrode had acted on the Tsar's decision,

90. Nesselrode to Nicholas I (3 August 1839), in Goriainov, *Le Bosphore et les Dardanelles*, 58–60.
91. Clanricarde to Palmerston (22 August 1839), *Parliamentary Papers* (1841), vol. 29, no. 290: 407.

it was learned that the agreement between Britain, France, and Austria on a Near Eastern settlement was not as feasible as he had represented it in his proposal. France let it be known that she would not join Britain in negotiating terms between Turkey and Egypt. Conditions were substantially different than he had portrayed them. But this was encouraging: Britain would not negotiate as the spokesman for a Western coalition.

Retreat from the Brink

The decision to send Brunnow to London coincided with spectacular army maneuvers commemorating the Battle of Borodino in 1812 and ending with the roar of seven hundred and ninety-two cannon—a reminder of the last great European war. War had been much in mind since the *Vixen* affair. It gave Nesselrode his most effective rejoinders in favor of the policy he had advocated throughout his career. "Any good Russian," he had earlier written, "can have but a single, reasonable aim in the politics of our time—the preservation of peace."[92] This aim united Europe. "All governments which are friends of order have an equal interest in preventing the occurrence of a catastrophe a few fanatical men seem to want to bring down on Russia and the whole of Europe, all of the horrible consequences of which their imaginations refuse to envision."[93]

In Britain the crises of the late 1830s capped a longstanding trend. Opinion was divided because it seemed, and perhaps correctly so, that to retreat from the brink of war Britain would have to be content with something less than world primacy. There were those who, realizing the implications of their position, came to believe that it would be a courageous act of fearless responsibility to cross it. "If we choose to seek the evil—if we choose to meet Russia on the Black Sea; if we resolve that she is no longer to interfere in the affairs of Turkey or Europe," the problem would be solved, wrote Urquhart in *England and Russia* a year before the *Vixen* affair.[94] A strike at Sevastopol

---

92. Nesselrode to Marie Nesselrode (28 December 1820), *Lettres et papiers*, vol. 6: 116.
93. Nesselrode to Pozzo di Borgo (10 May 1833), in Schiemann, *Geschichte Russlands*, vol. 3, Anlage 7: 461.
94. Urquhart, *England and Russia* (London, 1835), xii.

might eliminate the naval threat that gave the Eastern Question its real importance, and drive Russia out of European affairs. "The fact is," Palmerston once boasted, "that if England were fairly to go to work with her, we should throw her back half a century in one campaign."[95] The retreat turned out to be as deliberate and painful in British as it was in Russian statecraft. The change of attitude required was described by Durham, from his experience at the British Embassy in Petersburg: "The great difficulty I had, at first, to encounter was the being beset by persons who had been in the habit of working up every event into a plausible article of anti-Russian manufacture . . . I felt however that if I had, at their bidding, and, in compliance with current prejudices, counselled the proceeding which they insisted on, England, nay all Europe, must have, as a natural consequence, been involved in a war, the extent and termination of which, no man, however wise and experienced, could have foreseen."[96] But a deliberate decision for or against war had to be made, and Durham was not in a position to make it. "If we are to go on treating the peace between the two countries as a real one whilst Russia is covertly preparing for the struggle and has the power of choosing the moment to attack," a British officer warned Palmerston in 1838, "a single blow may level the British back once and forever—do for God's sake choose."[97] Palmerston chose not to go to war, and began to search for diplomatic alternatives. Nesselrode was pleased to supply them on certain conditions, above all that Russia and Britain meet as equals, not in a conference where their respective alignments would be measured against each other.

When Palmerston entertained the possibility of bipartisan cooperation, even before serious negotiations began, he caused an angry outburst in the ranks of his own party. For one thing, it was supposedly a matter of party principle to side with the wave of the future against the conservative order, with the liberal West against despotic Russia, and for another, there could be no security in cooperation with Russia. Urquhart called for national

95. H. L. Bulwer, *Life of Henry John Temple, Viscount Palmerston* (London, 1871–1874), vol. 3: 5 .
96. Durham to Palmerston (14 July 1836), *FO* 65/225.
97. Unidentified officer to Palmerston (27 October 1838), *FO* 65/248.

unity against Russia and against the new turn British foreign policy was taking, attacking Palmerston and Nesselrode for, of all things, secret collusion. In *An Appeal Against Faction* he said that Nesselrode's dispatch containing the theory of buffers demonstrated that "the Russian Minister was not addressing himself to the English Minister, but adjusting falsehoods concerted between them to blind the British nation."[98] Although Urquhart did not find the backing he hoped for, it was evident that Palmerston would have to rally support for an unpopular policy.

The process of sorting out alternatives was no less painful in Russia, and no less difficult to reconcile with "public opinion," or "national feeling." In addition to the heated personal differences, there were important administrative changes that awoke strong emotions. In the wake of the *Vixen* affair a number of men for whom an aggressive, imperialistic policy was a nationalistic policy were replaced by others more willing to accept the status quo. This took place at levels well above Simonich's head. In Nesselrode's area of administration, it was in November 1837 that Rodofinikin was replaced by Seniavin. The changes of highest-ranking personnel, however, took place in the military command in the Caucasus and at Sevastopol. In the spring, 1837, Nicholas appointed a special commission to propose alternatives to the military conquest of the Caucasus; ordered General Viliaminov to negotiate an armistice with Shamil; and visited the Crimea and the Caucasus, where he personally directed the changes in command.[99] "The Emperor's rapid visit has left deep traces, like the passage of a thunderbolt, and it is supposed that vast changes will take place in every branch of administration," wrote an Englishman who encountered the party.[1] "I have ordained peace," Nicholas told one of his officers, and long afterward the officer recalled that "the words of the Gosudar, 'I have ordained peace,' in theory

98. Urquhart, *An Appeal Against Faction . . . To Which is Added an Analysis of Count Nesselrode's Despatch of the 20th. Oct. 1838* (London, 1843), 42.

99. On the trip, cf. Curtiss, *The Russian Army,* 48–53; J. F. Baddeley, *The Russian Conquest of the Caucasus* (London, 1908), 311; Schiemann, *Geschichte Russlands,* vol. 3: 331n; E. I. Zarin, "Imperator Nikolai Pavovich v kreposti Anape 1837 g.," *Russkaia starina* (1884), vol. 43: 567–575.

1. R. Wilbraham, *Travels in the Trans-Caucasian Provinces of Russia . . . in the Autumn and Winter of 1837* (London, 1839), 254.

conclusively decided the question—while in reality insurmount-
able obstacles stood in the way of peace."[2] Disregarding what to
many of his staff were compelling realities, Nicholas went ahead
with preparations for a new policy. Most notably, he dismissed
General Rosen as Commander-in-Chief, replacing him with Golovin, and he disgraced N. N. Murav'ev by depriving him of his
rank and command of the Fifth Corps at Sevastopol and sending
him to a post in Siberia. Years later, after Murav'ev and others
who suffered at this time had been reinstated, the episode was
remembered as one of signal mistakes. Fighting in the Caucasus
dragged on as if Nicholas had never initiated moves for peace.
But far-reaching changes—the changes that paved the way to
formal agreement with Britain and were decried by Russians as
examples of abysmal folly—occurred elsewhere, as we have seen.

Considering the basic alternatives evident in the decisions
the Russian government made, the conclusion is inescapable that
Nesselrode exercised effective influence in favor of restraint. If
the *russkaia partiia* had prevailed, Russia would have accepted
the British challenge in the *Vixen* affair, and instead of quibbling
about rights, probably would have tried Bell and his crew and
imprisoned or shot them, giving Palmerston a clear choice between recognizing Russia's claims or issuing a declaration of
war. Menshikov would have had no worries about the straits,
because the government would have followed the dictates of
strategic realities—that the straits be opened, and that Russia
do all in her power to secure control of them. Simonich and
Witkiewicz would not have been recalled, the attack on Herat
would have been carried to its logical conclusion, the British
would not have been invited back to Teheran, and the alliance
of Russia, Persia, Kabul, and Gandahar would have remained
in force against the British invasion of Afghanistan. Perovskii
would not have encountered political obstacles to the conquest
of Khiva, and his expedition would have sallied forth to conquer,
not to secure the release of Russian prisoners and withdraw to

---

2. "Gosudar Nikolai Pavlovich. (Iz avtobiograficheskikh razskazov
   byvshago kavkazskago ofitsera)," *Russkii arkhiv* (1881), vol. 2:
   235. On the effort to end the war, cf. K. V. Sivkov, "O proektakh
   okonchaniia kavkazskoi voiny v seredine XIX v.," *Istoriia SSSR*
   (1958), vol. 2: 191–196.

Orenburg. In any Near Eastern crisis, Russia would have intervened suddenly and decisively, gaining strategic advantages. Russian interests in the Balkans, the Near East, and Asia would have been treated as if they were exclusive or perhaps to be shared with another power, such as France, willing to join an alliance against Britain and Austria. And it is quite probable that State Counsellor P. G. Divov would not have written in his diary for 1838: "The passing year witnessed an amazing series of events which did not shake the desire of the European cabinets to guarantee peace, although they held all the while the potential to ignite war in Europe, Asia and America."[3]

War would have been the logical outcome if Russian policy had been founded on the assumption that the interests of the two great powers were inimical, not identical, and if the Tsar had taken notice of the realities of international politics and had enacted the aggressive, imperialistic policy in keeping with national interest and with modern as well as traditional requirements for the maximization of the power of the state. War might well have been to Russia's advantage, if she controlled the straits, as both Russian and Western strategists knew. She would have been protected and unassailable, while the Black Sea Fleet could have sallied into the Mediterranean at will and forces could have been sent overland to disrupt British commerce in the Near East and Asia. Such were the speculations of nationalists who, long before the debacle at Sevastopol, cursed Nesselrode's alien German mind and cowardly cosmopolitan diplomacy.

In 1839 it remained to be seen whether the momentum imparted by the danger of war would carry through in a systematic effort, initiated by Brunnow's mission, to break down the bipolar configuration of power. In that year McNeill visited Petersburg and in an interview with Nesselrode remarked, by his own account, that "it was incredible to me that Simonich should have hazarded such a deviation from his duty without some prospect of support, and as that support could not be from the Emperor or H. E. [Nesselrode], I could only infer that there was some other influence, at variance with that of the Government, which was exercised with sinister intentions." He probably realized that

3. Divov, "1838 god," 635.

Simonich along with other Russians thought that Nicholas might
be persuaded, perhaps by a clash of Russian and British arms, to
abandon Nesselrode's policy and take a stand against Britain.
"We are speaking of things that are past," Nesselrode replied;
"let us look to the future."[4]

4. McNeill, *Memoir of the Right Hon. Sir John McNeill, G.C.B.* . . .
   (London, 1910), 239–240.

III. The Quest for Harmony

Status Quo as Modus Vivendi

RUSSIA'S OVERTURE to Britain in 1839 raised the possibility of bipartisan cooperation in various areas. At the end of August, Nesselrode told Clanricarde that since relations between the two countries had progressed to a stage of good understanding at which solid agreement seemed to be in the offing, Brunnow would be sent to London, as Clanricarde reported to Palmerston, "to offer the most unreserved explanations of the views, and policy of this country upon any point, upon which your Lordship might wish to have them, or which you might desire to discuss."[1] The resolution of the Eastern Question would be first on the agenda. But beyond the Near East, Brunnow would be prepared to discuss European affairs, undertake negotiations for freer trade and commerce in Asia, and respond fully on any issue Palmerston wished to raise. "You will invite the English Govern-

1. Clanricarde to Palmerston (27 August 1839), FO 65/253.

ment to discuss frankly what it thinks, what it wants, and what course it would like to take," Nesselrode instructed him.[2]

Brunnow was superbly qualified for the mission; in fact, his position and views gave the overture a portent it would not otherwise have had. He had attended the congresses of Laibach and Verona, had been Senior Adviser in the ministry since 1835, and more recently tutor to the Tsarevich Alexander in foreign affairs, and Privy Counsellor to the Tsar, and was serving temporarily as minister at Stuttgart. Most important, he was Nesselrode's protégé.[3] He was German, Protestant, Anglophile, a free trader, and a protagonist of the European system. He was a man of enlightened education and outlook. He held a degree in science from the University of Leipzig. His political philosophy revealed an affinity, as did Nesselrode's, for Montesquieu, Blackstone, Burke, and Gentz, and respect for ideals of equality before the law. He had made forays into journalism, had been co-editor of the *Odessa Messenger*, and before the end of his career was to publish a number of writings anonymously in the deliberate effort to counteract Russophobia. He was a talented diplomat. Guizot described him as "well-informed, clever, persevering without obstinacy, neither overly exacting nor impatient, an eloquent and lively talker, an experienced and ready repenter, and adroit in unravelling the views of others and enveloping his own in a dense mantle of concessions, reserves, and commentaries."[4] Nesselrode assured Clanricarde that "unless he were himself to proceed to London, it would be impossible for the Emperor to send thither any person more thoroughly acquainted with the foreign

2. Nesselrode to Brunnow (16 August 1839), in Martens, *Recueil*, vol. 12: 109.
3. One reason why the importance of the overture to Britain and the real origin of the movement to reopen the concert has escaped the attention of Western historians is that Brunnow has been regarded as a relatively minor figure, of no particular distinction. Cf. Temperley, *England and the Near East*, 111; Webster, *The Foreign Policy of Palmerston*, vol. 2: 647, 672n. Palmerston himself could hardly have committed a similar oversight since the embassy in Petersburg had informed him that Brunnow was Nesselrode's protégé, and in addition to the titles Brunnow bore for the negotiations (Minister Plenipotentiary, etc.) he was formally referred to as the Tsar's "Privy Counsellor." The fact that he was a candidate for the position of minister if Nesselrode's policy succeeded would have been an added inducement to negotiate, especially to the extent that Palmerston was aware of factional differences within the Russian government.
4. Guizot, *Mémoires*, vol. 4: 358–359.

affairs and policy of Russia than Baron Brünnow"; and Clanricarde reported that Brunnow had been "of the greatest use to Count Nesselrode, whose unreserved and entire confidence he has enjoyed for some years."[5] Now he would seek a relationship with Britain which might serve as the foundation of the policy he would follow as Nesselrode's successor.

Brunnow's guiding philosophy closely resembled Nesselrode's. His writings reveal a fondness for what he termed "the European family." He automatically viewed Russia in the context of European and world affairs, and reacted instinctively against the nationalistic drive for independence and autonomy. The interests of the whole represented a "higher order" of natural unity that was threatened by war and revolution together, and strengthened by a classic balance and the progressive development of free commerce. He shared with Nesselrode the conviction that Alexander I had ushered Russia into a new era, and boldly condemned the traditional tsarist foreign policy followed to the end of the reign of Catherine II as imperialistic and as having heightened discord and disunity. "In contemplating the execution of such aggrandizement, so detrimental to the enduring interests of European equilibrium," he said in 1838, "one finds it difficult today to comprehend how such a displacement of power could have occurred without bringing on a general war."[6] The eighteenth-century monarchs, Catherine included, undoubtedly contributed to the causes of the upheaval of 1789–1815. Common recognition that the status quo was vital to peace gave rise to the European system. "In our time" he said, "every change in the area of territorial possession becomes an object of solicitude common to all of the great powers."[7] But new problems arose after the revolutions of 1830, when "the Whig minister . . . believed that to remain in office he had no choice but to ally with the French Government."[8] In doing so he submitted to a "public

5. Clanricarde to Palmerston (27 August 1839), *FO* 65/253.
6. Brunnow, "Aperçu des transactions politiques," 197. For a nationalistic critique of Brunnow's views, cf. Tatishchev, *Imperator Nikolai I i inostrannye dvory*, 4–5, 168–170; *Vneshniaia politika*, 475–476, 544–552 *passim*.
7. Brunnow, "Aperçu," 217.
8. Brunnow, "Considérations générales sur les principes qui servent de base à notre politique 1838," in H. von Treitschke, *Deutsche Geschichte im Neunzehnten Jahrhundert* (Leipzig, 1927), vol. 5: 745.

opinion" that was opposed to the "true interests" of the community. Hence "the entire European political system was completely upset" and "Europe was divided into two camps."[9]

Rapprochement with Britain promised to mend this division and bring cooperation between the conservative and liberal states. With hopes for the renewal of a classic system, there were dreams of a future in which peace and harmony would prevail and Russia would take her place in a new world order, assuming "a course of development in accord with the position Providence assigned to her, between the Far East and Europe, in accord with her role as an intermediary between two worlds," as Brunnow later put it.[10] When Britain proved receptive to the overture, Nesselrode predicted that "Russophobia will expend itself like all of the other follies of the century, and the time will come when we will love as well as we now hate."[11]

The Overture to Britain

At his first meeting with Palmerston after arriving in London on September 15, Brunnow tabled Russia's offer to allow the Treaty of Unkiar Skelessi to expire in 1841 if Britain would agree to guarantee closure of the straits and "the existence and repose" of Turkey. "Do you wish to conserve the Ottoman Empire," he queried, "or do you not desire it?"[12] He told Palmerston that Britain had long misunderstood Russian policy, particularly the treaty, which Russia would be pleased to exchange for a concerted guarantee.[13]

The Russian gambit made brilliant use of the British belief that the Treaty of Unkiar Skelessi was intended to subvert the status quo. But there can be no doubt that the move was consistent not only with the original principles of the treaty but also with Nesselrode's intentions for it. In announcing the treaty in 1833 he had stated that Russia would "act in concert and in a spirit of perfect solidarity with anyone who is interested in establishing a new order of things destined to replace that existing

9. *Ibid.*
10. Brunnow, *La Guerre*, 85.
11. Nesselrode to Meyendorff (3 December 1839), *Lettres et papiers*, vol. 7: 296.
12. Brunnow (12 September 1839), in Goriainov, *Le Bosphore et les Dardanelles*, 67.
13. Martens, *Recueil*, vol. 12: 116.

today."[14] But Palmerston was welcome to claim that Russia was making a great sacrifice. Even if he announced that his anti-Russian policy had paid off and that he had brought Russia to heel, it would mean that there was no reason to continue such a policy. In actuality, British policy would swerve sharply from the old attitude while Russian policy would be confirmed in a larger arena. The false British interpretation of the treaty gave the proposal more weight, if it spawned an impression that Palmerston's policy had blunted the Russian sword in the Near East.[15]

Palmerston quickly grasped the usefulness of this opportunity. He raised no substantial objections to the basic outline of the treaty Brunnow proposed. Henceforward, the impediments to an early conclusion lay mainly in the large revision of British policy, especially in relations with France, not in the negotiations with Russia. The conflict between Turkey and Egypt had strained the Entente Cordiale past the breaking point, and were it not for the complex difficulties he faced in relations with France it is doubtful that he would have entertained the Russian overture at

14. Martens, *Die russische Politik*, 33. Cf. Martens, "Rossiia i Angliia," no. 2: 467.
15. This may be noted, for example, in Temperley's defense of Palmerston. Cf. "Prologue: The Sword and Shield of Constantinople," *England and the Near East*, 3–4. His interpretation hinges on the argument that Russia "abrogated the Treaty of Unikar Skelessi, so far at least as it gave her permission to enter the Bosphorous or implied any special relation with Turkey," *ibid.*, 112. But it did not grant Russia a right to enter the Bosphorus. This being understood, the "special relation" is not evidence of an aggressive policy. Every treaty implies a special relation between the signatories. There certainly existed the possibility of intervention to insure the Porte's capacity to keep the straits closed to foreign warships; but given the strategic importance of the straits to Russia, the treaty was in this respect merely an announcement of a fact of international affairs that would have existed without it. There was no Russian sword to turn aside. Nesselrode could well assert, as he did repeatedly afterward, that in principle the treaty was simply transferred to concerted European aegis by means of the conventions of 1840 and 1841. Furthermore, Palmerston agreed that the treaty should remain in effect to its date of expiration in 1841 side by side with the convention of 1840, which suggests that he knew there was little or no conflict and that his earlier statements against the treaty were more or less a charade. This was Brunnow's conclusion after the negotiations. He became convinced that a Russophobe mythology had been applied to the treaty in an effort to isolate Russia and align the Western powers against her. Cf. Brunnow, *La Guerre*, 37–39, 100, and *passim*.

all. Melbourne's government was weakened by the dénouement with France because it had gathered support from Francophiles and others who believed fervently in the liberal alliance against East European autocracy. A sudden confrontation with France, anticipated for example if Stopford tried to liberate the Turkish fleet, might well have terminated not only Liberal foreign policy but Melbourne's Cabinet as well. In a way, rapprochement with Russia was an ingenious disguise covering the deterioration of Palmerston's policy. As might be anticipated, then, his political maneuvers in dealing with Francophiles and Russophobes in the Cabinet and Parliament were far more eventful than the negotiations themselves. The only significant issue subject to bargaining at the outset was Brunnow's proposal that Russia be permitted to intervene singlehandedly if the other powers consented. Palmerston held that if the Russian fleet entered the Bosphorus, the British fleet should be allowed to enter the Dardanelles. But this was hardly an issue of contention, and Brunnow soon conceded to joint intervention—a "maritime picnic on the Sea of Marmara," as he phrased it.[16]

Completely satisfied with Palmerston's reception of the proposed treaty, Nesselrode looked forward to success. "In total," he said after a month had passed, "the information Brunnow has sent surpasses my expectations, but for the time being I miss the conclusions, the positive results."[17] He was confident that Palmerston would soon prevail over the opposition. Then the negotiations could be extended to include Austria and Prussia, and eventually France, thus producing "a result dignified by the mediation of the five powers and most solid for the future."[18]

Watching the British political scene closely, he recognized the need to be cautious, and gradually came to realize that Palmerston would require still more time to win the Cabinet over and prepare "public opinion" for the about-face. Finally he instructed Brunnow to take a recess and leave London. Palmerston worried that Nesselrode might not understand the long delay; Clanricarde

---

16. Brunnow to Nesselrode (8 October 1839), *FO* 65/256.
17. Nesselrode to Meyendorff (8 October 1839), *Lettres et papiers*, vol. 7: 289.
18. *Ibid.* Cf. Nesselrode to Nicholas I (4 September 1839), *Lettres et papiers*, vol. 11: 157–158.

approached Nesselrode on the subject, and happily reported: "I was surprised to find Count Nesselrode better informed, than I supposed he could be, of the opinions of the individual members of Her Majesty's Government. His Excellency seemed fully alive to the justness of the observations which I made to him upon the danger of awakening the jealousy of the Publick, or of the British Parliament, which an immediate assent to the Emperor's proposition might have occasioned."[19]

When Brunnow left London he went to see Metternich, who was still very much annoyed because his suggestion to hold a conference at Vienna had been put down, and was convalescing after illness and in an uncongenial frame of mind. He predicted that Brunnow would meet failure when he returned to London, but consented nevertheless to the basic form of the proposed treaty and agreed to send an Austrian delegate.

"Prince Metternich accepts all of our propositions," Nesselrode wrote to Meyendorff at Berlin. "If the devil doesn't scramble things up there is sure to be a transaction between Russia, England, and Austria, to which you certainly will not have any difficulty in gaining the accession of Prussia. . . . As for France, you sense before I what she thinks and what she will do. I always expect that she will not isolate herself."[20]

The Renewal of the European System

In December Brunnow again set out for London, accompanied this time by Dmitry Nesselrode, with instructions to secure a treaty signed by all five great powers if possible.[21] Since the basic form of the agreement—a treaty that would insure peace between the belligerents in the Near East and make closure of the straits part of the "public law of Europe"—had been settled, it was hoped that the other three representatives would join without delay. Nesselrode had moved ahead with the arrange-

19. Clanricarde to Palmerston (25 October 1839), *FO* 65/253.
20. Nesselrode to Meyendorff (27 November 1839), *Lettres et papiers*, vol. 7: 294–295.
21. Cf. copies of Nesselrode's instructions (5/17 December 1839 and 20 December 1839/1 January 1840), *FO* 65/207. Cf. discussion in Schiemann, *Geschichte Russlands*, vol. 3: 391–392; Martens, *Recueil*, vol. 12: 111; and Goriainov, *Le Bosphore et les Dardanelles*, 73–75.

ments for Austrian and Prussian participation, but on Palmerston's request left the question of France largely up to Britain.[22] His only stipulation was that if it should prove expedient to conclude a treaty of the four, it must be one that France might eventually find acceptable. Nesselrode had put Russia's hand on the table. Brunnow's assignment was to maintain a position that held no surprises. In fact, the main Russian effort was now directed toward supporting Palmerston, not negotiating with him. "Everything depends on Palmerston's resolve," said Nesselrode.[23]

There is little evidence that Nicholas I understood Palmerston's political situation at all. He expected Britain to abandon her alliance with France and accept the Russian offer without any fuss. He was greatly perturbed when Brunnow's first visit did not produce a treaty. "Brunnow is in London," he wrote to Paskevich in December, "and I hope soon to receive news of the signing of a treaty which has required trouble and time to conclude when nothing should have been easier."[24] His impatience was to become a problem for Nesselrode in the seven months it took for Palmerston to overcome the opposition.

Brunnow's first task in London was a minor one, but significant. He relieved Pozzo di Borgo of his duties as Ambassador, and himself took over—on a temporary basis, although it became more permanent later. Pozzo had been a capable diplomat, but he had channeled distrust of Britain into personal relations with Palmerston, and had been rewarded with hot-headed tirades against Russia which, although they revealed the unreasonable character of Palmerston's Russophobia, were best not recalled.

The first discussions of the proposed treaty took place at Palmerston's estate at Broadlands during the Christmas holiday. Austria's representative, Baron Philipp von Neumann, an old acquaintance of Nesselrode's, was present. Brunnow had met von Neumann at Calais on the way to Dover, and had briefed him on the text of the projected convention, which he and Nesselrode had

22. "Nous ne jouons qu'un rôle purement secondaire. Le débat n'est point entre la France et nous, mais entre l'Angleterre et la France." Nesselrode to Brunnow (1 February 1840), in Martens, *Recueil*, vol. 12: 124.

23. Nesselrode to Meyendorff (25 December 1839), *Lettres et papiers*, vol. 7: 297.

24. Nicholas I to Paskevich (14 December 1839), "Imperator Nikolai Pavlovich v ego pis'makh," 26.

composed in Petersburg.[25] It provided for closure of the straits
and a Near Eastern settlement in which Egyptian independence
would be recognized and Syria would be returned to Turkey. If
any significant difference arose after they reached London, it involved the speculation by von Neumann and Palmerston that too
much responsibility for closing the straits would be invested in
the great powers and too little in the Porte.[26] The same point was
raised later by Metternich, but it did not become an issue. There
were also conjectures as to the future status of the Black Sea. If
Palmerston needed inspiration, it was now clear that Russia intended to contain the Black Sea Fleet as long as the concert
existed. In short, the draft gave no cause for disagreement on the
substantial issues, and with minor alterations it was the text of
the convention. The wording was revised twice. First, Palmerston reworked it to make it more acceptable to the Cabinet. In
the process he consulted Sebastiani, and as a result received
Brunnow's admonition that France should not be allowed to
affect the wording of the text unless she joined the proceedings.
Then Brunnow and von Neumann polished this text. By the end
of January they had an entirely satisfactory document. The signing could take place whenever Palmerston was ready.

From the beginning of January, Nesselrode believed that as
long as Palmerston could stand up against the proponents of the
old Entente Cordiale in the Cabinet and prove that an accord between the three was in the offing, Prussia would soon send a delegate, and lastly, "France, which likes to join in all things, will not
want to remain alone against the four." "It is a role which does
not agree with her interests or her vanity," he said.[27] All signs
were favorable. Brunnow had done his job well, and Nesselrode
was "very content" with him.[28] The whole atmosphere of Anglo-
Russian relations was changing. At one point, Clanricarde reported Nesselrode "in high spirits" as a result of having read an
article in the *Morning Chronicle* in which the negotiations were

25. Cf. Martens, *Recueil*, vol. 12: 123.
26. Von Neumann's observations reflected Metternich's reluctance to in-
fringe on Turkish sovereignty. But Nesselrode wanted insurance that
the Porte would not have the right to control the straits.
27. Nesselrode to Meyendorff (6 January 1840), *Lettres et papiers*, vol.
8: 3.
28. Marie Nesselrode to Dmitry Nesselrode (18 January 1840), *Lettres
et papiers*, vol. 8: 5.

"so well expounded to the British Publick, he no longer entertained the least doubt that Russia and England would come to an agreement satisfactory to themselves and to Europe, and perhaps ultimately to France." Clanricarde had responded in an encouraging way, that he thought the Cabinet would eventually accept the proposal, although it might be objected to, as it apparently was by Palmerston himself, "as savoring too much . . . of 'Holy Alliance' principles."[29]

But delays followed delays. A representative for Prussia, Baron Henry von Bülow, soon joined the others, and it was evident that there would be a swift conclusion if Palmerston could untangle his own troubles. "Everything in London is at a standstill," Nesselrode wrote in April. "Palmerston racks his brain to invent new expedients. . . . Since half the Cabinet, Melbourne foremost, do not want to move without France, they will have to give in to Palmerston."[30] There was little to do but wait, and watch, and hope that Palmerston triumphed.

Time, however, was not necessarily on Nesselrode's side. The Tsar experienced fits of impatience, and in interviews with Clanricarde voiced an urge to ditch the whole project. He informed Clanricarde that there were people in Russia who opposed it because it deviated from the tenets of a sound policy. In May he warned Nesselrode that unless the affair were resolved within one month, he would take other measures to settle the Near Eastern situation. Palmerston could hardly strengthen his position any more. Metternich believed that an accommodation with France would be in the offing if it was possible for her to win small concessions—a possibility which, if admitted, would have gravely threatened Russian participation. Then war loomed on the horizon in the Near East once again, and Nicholas I began to redeploy troops as if preparing to descend on the straits.[31]

Palmerston put the question to a test in a cabinet meeting on July 5. He argued that agreement would be the best way to keep Russia from taking independent action, and that the sacrifice of the Treaty of Unkiar Skelessi would mean a Liberal victory.

29. Clanricarde to Palmerston (11 February 1840), FO 65/260.
30. Nesselrode to Meyendorff (13 April 1840), Lettres et papiers, vol. 8: 19–20.
31. Schiemann, Geschichte Russlands, vol. 3: 396.

But the Cabinet's decision confirmed what he already knew. The convention was rejected.

Afterward, he wrote out his resignation and handed it to Melbourne. But Melbourne, fearful that his Foreign Secretary's resignation might bring down his government, asked Palmerston to wait. The balance tipped in favor of the treaty in another meeting three days later. "Palmerston's threat to break up the Cabinet was no doubt the most important factor in forcing the decision," writes Webster.[32] British support for the treaty hinged on the weakness of the Liberal Party.

It took a single week for the representatives of the four great powers and Turkey to complete preparations to sign the convention, which was done on July 15, 1840.

The principal aim of the treaty, stated in the preamble, was to maintain "the integrity and independence of the Ottoman Empire as security for the peace of Europe." The Porte agreed "to admit no foreign ship of war into the Straits of the Bosphorus and the Dardanelles," except under the "contingency" of concerted intervention, which by article three was to be undertaken only "by mutual assent, for the purpose of placing the two Straits of the Bosphorus and the Dardanelles, as well as the Capital of the Ottoman Empire, in security against all aggression."[33] In short, it provided for the neutralization of the strategic pivot in relations between Russia and the Western powers. By articles one and two, Egypt was required to accept the provisions of a "Separate Act annexed to the Convention" which stated in detail the terms of a territorial and political settlement between Egypt and Turkey. Mohammed Ali was granted control over certain areas his armies had conquered, mainly the southern part of Syria, and hereditary rule of Egypt.[34] He was given ten days from the communication of these terms to accept them or face punitive action by the powers and new terms closer to the status quo ante. Relying too much on support from France, he refused and suffered quick and effective reverses at the hands of British armies.[35]

---

32. Webster, *The Foreign Policy of Palmerston*, vol. 2: 690.
　　29; in French and Russian, Martens, *Recueil*, vol. 12: 130–139.
33. Cf. text in French and English, *Parliamentary Papers* (1841), vol.
34. English text, *Parliamentary Papers*.
35. Cf. Temperley, *England and the Near East*, 117–163.

With the occupation of Near Eastern soil by British troops a need for further elucidation of the aims of the concert came to the fore. On September 17 an additional Protocol was signed by the four great powers and Turkey; it was remarkably similar to Nesselrode's buffer theory in conception, and comprised a general pledge to observe Turkish neutrality. It provided "That in the execution of the engagements resulting to the Contracting Powers from the above-mentioned Convention, those Powers will seek no augmentation of territory, no exclusive influence, no commercial advantage for their subjects, which those of every other nation may not equally obtain."[36]

"The convention is signed," Nesselrode told the Tsar, "I submit completely to the hope that Your Majesty will be pleased."[37] "Yes, I am entirely satisfied," Nicholas answered. "And to you, dear friend, the merit and the glory for having *well conceived* that which Brunnow has perfectly executed."[38]

But Nicholas did have strong reservations; he did not really believe that the status quo could be upheld. He leaned toward Orlov's opinion that a power-vacuum could not be maintained in the Near East. He replied to a subsequent memorandum by Nesselrode on the settlement, saying, "I will not now change my mind and eliminate the possibility of what may in the future prove to be a viable agreement, but. . . . *If Turkey dies,* what will take her place? One would hope it would be an *independent* Christian State, or one would hope for a partition *à l'amicable,* one would hope *excluding France.*"[39]

Nesselrode was more concerned about Turkey as a factor in relations with Britain. In his annual report for 1840 he emphasized that Russia had persuaded Britain to give up a "mistaken policy":

"Not desiring to vie with the English for maritime power, or to turn the Mediterranean into a Russian lake, or to break up the Ottoman Empire, or to overthrow British power in India—not

36. Additional Protocol, English text, *Parliamentary Papers.*
37. Nesselrode to Nicholas I (14 July 1840), *Lettres et papiers,* vol. 11: 170.
38. Nicholas I to Nesselrode, "Réponse" following *ibid.*
39. Note by Nicholas I in reply to memorandum by Nesselrode (9 August 1840), in G. H. Bolsover, "Nicholas I and the Partition of Turkey," *Slavonic and East European Review* (December 1948), vol. 27, no. 68: 123n.

demanding that England concede more than a just share of the commercial opportunities open to the two countries in Central Asia, without disadvantage for one or the other, we do not see where there would be an area of serious conflict as long as each one proves to be motivated by the same spirit of conciliation. In truth the causes of friction are no more than simple prejudices. The mistaken policy of England regarding Turkey has been the main source of these prejudices."[40]

Nicholas put aside his reservations when he received the British minister after the signing. Bloomfield found him "overjoyed" that whereas "England had formerly found great fault with his policy in the Levant," now "whatever he might be called on to do, would be done in the name of the four Powers, in the general Interest of the Alliance and with no selfish object."[41] Palmerston instructed Bloomfield to convey to him "how much pleased we are to be acting in concert with Russia in a matter of general European Interest,"[42] and how satisfied he was with the assistance Brunnow had given. Thus the Liberal foreign secretary exchanged congratulations with the Russian Tsar. "It is a great service that we have done for Europe," said Nesselrode.[43]

"The wine is poured and ready to drink," he said. He was ebullient. But work remained to be done. "That which France will pour for us will not be Lunel. But I hope that if we remain well-disposed it will change to *eau claire*. To this we must devote all of our diplomatic efforts."[44]

In the aftermath Palmerston continued to resist France, Metternich called for a new conference in Vienna, Nicholas celebrated French isolation, France was the scene of an outburst against the treaty, and Nesselrode worked steadily on the large project he had envisaged from the beginning—a full concert. While the events that led to this result may never be known in exact detail, there is much evidence that Nesselrode sustained his policy against considerable opposition. Most striking at first glance was

40. From Nesselrode's annual report for 1840, in Martens, *Recueil*, vol. 12: 160.
41. Bloomfield to Palmerston (8 August 1840), *FO* 356/29.
42. Palmerston to Bloomfield (29 July 1840), *FO* 356/29.
43. Nesselrode to Meyendorff (25 September 1840), *Lettres et papiers,* vol. 8: 40.
44. Nesselrode to Meyendorff (8 August 1840), *Lettres et papiers*, vol. 8: 35. Lunel is a dessert wine.

his determination to bring France into the agreement, when Nicholas was happy to see France isolated. There was a wide divergence between the two. Bloomfield and Clanricarde observed it, and according to Guizot, Barante found Nesselrode "disposed and even anxious, to testify his disapproval, or at least regret, about the position taken by the Emperor against King Louis Philippe."[45]

But Nicholas's attitude had not had any direct bearing on the exclusion of France from the treaty. Palmerston had been primarily responsible, and his hard-won victory over the Francophiles was in effect a defeat for Thiers, who had formed his second government in February and had sought concessions. "Thiers required this admonition," said Palmerston, "and the frantic Rage which pervades the whole of the Press and all the good citizens of Paris shews how much France needed such a lesson," namely that "Her word and her wishes are not to be Law for Europe."[46]

The "frantic Rage" in Paris made French accession seem highly improbable. Thiers found it necessary to ride out a wave of protest against the treaty, which was seen as a Russian ruse to divide and rule. He joined in the sword-rattling that continued for the rest of the year. It alarmed the Tsar, who took it seriously, but it had all of the earmarks of a political maneuver, and those who understood it as such were not frightened. "The news is always of war," Marie Nesselrode wrote to Dmitry; "Thiers could not find support without the war; if it were not there he would return to the opposition."[47] Nesselrode thought war was improbable. "If a continental war would fulfill the ambitious dreams of the French, a maritime war would be too destructive to all of their commercial and industrial interests to be entered lightly." France might seriously entertain a war with Russia, but not with Britain. Moreover, he thought that the crisis would have a beneficial effect. The four powers would "become more strong, more united" in opposing France, and the latter ultimately would "resign herself to what she cannot change."[48] He expected Thiers's public verbal

45. Guizot, *M. de Barante*, 140. Cf. Clanricarde to Palmerston (25 October 1839 and 5 November 1839), *FO* 65/253.
46. Palmerston to Bloomfield (14 August 1840), *FO* 356/29.
47. Marie Nesselrode to Dmitry Nesselrode (6 October 1840), *Lettres et papiers*, vol. 8: 47.
48. Nesselrode to Meyendorff (10 October 1840 and 8 August 1840), *Lettres et papiers*, vol. 8: 50, 37.

attacks to be followed by discreet diplomatic overtures initiated by Sainte Aulaire at Vienna. He apparently possessed accurate intelligence, because the first overture was in fact made by Sainte Aulaire. It soon was followed by others, not for accession but for separate guarantees to protect French interests, conveyed to Petersburg and London through the highest diplomatic channels, through Brussels and Berlin as well as Vienna. What was said in public and in the French chambers had little bearing on high politics. While giving vent to anti-Russian feeling, France was moving toward accord.

Nicholas and Nesselrode differed not only in their assessment of the danger, but in the course of action they advocated. When the first intimation that France was seeking a reconciliation reached the Tsar, he was not pleased. On a visit to Warsaw at the time, he received the news in a letter from Frederick Wilhelm IV suggesting a conference of the five. He immediately suspected that the idea stemmed from Metternich's "infernal mania to interfere with everything," and shot off a dispatch to Nesselrode in which he complained that he was not being kept well enough informed. As if surmising that Nesselrode might not take a firm stand against it, he advised him to reject the proposal "flatly and categorically" in any form.[49] Seeing Metternich as an appeaser who would receive his just desserts when he found himself at the mercy of France and had to appeal to Russia for help, Nicholas decided to offer his support to Britain and Prussia. He volunteered the Russian Baltic fleet to defend Britain against a French invasion, and although the offer was never seriously entertained in London, he came to believe that it was as good as a pact between gentlemen. "I have received excellent news from London," he said. "In case it should be impossible to avoid war, they will rely on our fleet for the defense of the coasts of England. . . . Thus this very fleet against which they have protested and which nearly became the cause of war between ourselves, this same fleet will be summoned to defend England if the need arises, since she is too weak to resist alone."[50] Nicholas was bemused with the irony of an imaginary war in which the Russian navy would save Britain, but it could hardly be said that he was engaged with the

---

49. Nicholas I to Nesselrode (18 August 1840), *Lettres et papiers*, vol. 11: 173–174.
50. Schiemann, "Russische-englische Beziehungen," 409.

military and diplomatic realities of the day. In comparison with the Tsar's dream, Nesselrode's conviction that the imposing strength of the British navy would keep France from risking war was more intelligent and well-informed.

The Tsar also was convinced that France was planning to attack Prussia with the aim of taking the left bank of the Rhine. He sent Paskevich to Berlin to offer an alliance and draw up plans for a combined Russian and Prussian military strategy. A few weeks later, Frederick Wilhelm once again transmitted French overtures, and Nicholas swiftly interpreted it as evidence of Prussia's fear of France. But he was becoming suspicious, and it was the beginning of a period in which his feelings toward Prussia cooled. Nesselrode, always conscious of his Rhenish background, reacted with strong words about the "sword of Damocles they keep suspended over the heads of the German princes," but again refused to believe that France was really inclined to go to war.[51]

Throughout this period, in fact, he only once showed genuine alarm, and the occasion did not involve France. It was when at Baron Ponsonby's instigation the Sultan proclaimed Mohammed Ali deposed from rule in Egypt. Nesselrode thought this could lead to new fighting in the Near East. He saw Bloomfield about it, expressed his opinion that the powers were not ready to meet a major crisis, and suggested that in the interest of peace and good relations between Russia and Britain, Ponsonby should be recalled. The request was not granted, although he soon received Palmerston's assurances that Ponsonby would work to prevent a conflict.[52]

The crisis over France, which Nesselrode privately treated as illusory, grew more intense in the Tsar's mind as the autumn progressed. At first, Nicholas thought he was confronted by a simple choice—concessions to France or war—and he clearly favored the latter. But it was not the most fortunate set of alterna-

51. Nesselrode to Meyendorff (24 October 1840), *Lettres et papiers,* vol. 8: 57. On Nicholas's attitude toward Prussia, cf. F. Ia. Mir'kovich, "Imperator Nikolai i korol Fridrikh-Vil'gel'm IV v 1840 g. Iz zapisok . . . ," *Russkaia starina* (1886), vol. 51: 305–334; V. R. Zotov, "Pri Nikolai I i Frederikhe Vil'gel'me IV," *Istoricheskii vestnik* (1894), vol. 56: 523–537.
52. On the exchange concerning Ponsonby, cf. Bloomfield to Palmerston (2 October, 10 October 1840, and 17 October 1840), *FO* 65/261. Ponsonby finally was instructed to encourage the Sultan to return hereditary rule to the Pasha.

tives, and before long he began to look for another way out, and was led to accept the solidarity of the four. "Having deeply pondered my attitude to Austria," he informed Nesselrode, "I have resolved, dear friend, to put an end to the doubts which have obsessed me regarding her intentions. I have put my thoughts down on paper in my own language, which perhaps is not diplomatic enough, but most certainly is that of a good and loyal soldier."[53] He wanted to appeal to Ferdinand for unity to meet the French menace.[54] It led as much to his own eventual acceptance of the decision of the four on France as to a united front.

The difficult part was preparing Nicholas to accept French accession when it came. Nesselrode quietly insisted that everyone, even France, shared a common interest in peace. He explained to Nicholas that while Thiers talked about a "march on the Rhine," Louis Philippe opposed it and tried "to find means of conserving peace."[55] "I do not change my views in any way whatever," replied Nicholas, "They are not the fruit of a vain fantasy."[56] Nesselrode explained that Austria and Prussia were together "searching among diplomatic expedients for means of preventing war," perhaps by a settlement with France,[57] and Nicholas responded, "I don't understand anything about Prince Metternich's new intentions. . . . As far as I am concerned, the *final word has been said* regarding France."[58] Nesselrode passed along a document Barante had given him and pointed out that it was "conceived in a moderate and conciliatory spirit" and showed that France was as much opposed to war as the other powers.[59] "I am not on any account going to accept the *principle instead of the deed*," said Nicholas.[60] But little by little he softened, and even though the

---

53. Nicholas I to Nesselrode, note in pencil (n.d.), *Lettres et papiers*, vol. 11: 181–182.
54. Rough draft of letter by Nicholas I to be sent to Ferdinand, *Lettres et papiers*, vol. 11: 182–183.
55. Nesselrode to Nicholas I (7 October 1840), *Lettres et papiers*, vol. 11: 186–187.
56. Nicholas I to Nesselrode, "Réponse" following *ibid.*, 187.
57. Nesselrode to Nicholas I (8 October 1840), *Lettres et papiers*, vol. 11: 188.
58. Nicholas I to Nesselrode, "Réponse" following *ibid.*, 189.
59. Nesselrode to Nicholas I (12 October 1840), *Lettres et papiers*, vol. 11: 192.
60. Nicholas I to Nesselrode, "Réponse" following *ibid.*, 193.

exact point at which he became amenable is unknown, it was undoubtedly a consequence of Nesselrode's steady influence.

With Nesselrode in charge of the ministry, Russia's relationship with France may have been considerably more flexible than
the Tsar's attitude suggested. Thiers was sagacious in public, even
Russophobic in his tone for a few months, but this actually
bothered Nesselrode little. He liked Thiers because he was usually
fair and conciliatory toward Russia, as was illustrated by a
discourse on the Eastern Question in the Chamber of Deputies.
"Your father is enchanted with Thiers's discourse," Marie Nesselrode wrote to Dmitry, "because it showed understanding and
did justice to the policy of the Russian Cabinet." [61]

Thiers and Guizot were accessible to Russian influence and
secret diplomacy. Both men frequented Russian circles in Paris,
including those of Princess Lieven and Marie Nesselrode's friends
the Duchesse de Dino and Madame Swetchine. Lieven was Guizot's mistress when Thiers appointed him Ambassador to Britain
in February 1840 to replace Sebastiani, and Thiers himself was
an intimate friend of Nesselrode's niece Maria Kalergis. There
were signs of unusual activity, and in the midst of it Paris received
a special visitor from Petersburg—Marie Nesselrode. Marie set
out in August 1840 and stopped in Baden, where she met Dmitry,
recently returned from London, and the Duchesse de Dino. "You
will have time to think the whole situation through," she wrote to
her husband from Baden, "to move ahead despite affairs that
grow more and more complicated." [62] Arriving in Paris, she took
a townhouse and stayed until March of 1841. She entertained
both Thiers and Guizot, the former so frequently at first that there
were rumors of a liason. She did not enter the French court or
go through any of the formalities of a state visit, which was thought
odd by some people, but was probably due to Nicholas's feelings
about Louis Philippe and his displeasure that she was there at
all. [63] Thiers resigned in October, and Marie welcomed Guizot's

61. Marie Nesselrode to Dmitry Nesselrode (18 January 1840), *Lettres
    et papiers*, vol. 8: 5.
62. Marie Nesselrode to Nesselrode (28 September 1840), *Lettres et
    papiers*, vol. 8: 46.
63. Cf. C. de Photiades, *La Symphonie en blanc majeur. Marie Kalergis,
    née C-tesse Nesselrode* (Paris, 1924), 52; V. du Bled, "Le Salon
    de madame Swetchine," *Cosmopolis* (1898), vol. 12: 421.

government as promising better relations between France and Russia. She returned to Petersburg only a few days before Nesselrode opened formal negotiations for French accession.

If it occurred to members of the British government, the idea that the danger of war was a political ruse did not impress them sufficiently to allay a gripping sense of alarm. "I presume we must consider whether Parliament should be called together or not," said Lord John Russell at a meeting of the Cabinet at the end of September, "because, as matters are now going on, it seems to me that we may at any moment find ourselves at war, and it is high time to consider the very serious state of affairs." [64] Palmerston came under heavy pressure to compromise, namely to undertake secret negotiations with France to repair the Entente Cordiale. This would have been done while maintaining outward support for Nesselrode's convention. Although Palmerston had won the day, he was still in the minority on France. Greville expressed the prevalent view that "Palmerston was very wrong not to endeavour to bring France into the Treaty and to offer the status quo, although it is very possible France would have refused it." The one argument in his favor was that which Greville attributed to Lord Minto, that anyone who had supported him on the convention would not be justified in opposing his stand in the contest with France. The decision against secret negotiations came at a meeting in which a proposal Metternich had made, that the four powers "consider the matter afresh in conjunction with France," was discussed. [65] This led to the subject of an individual British effort to reach agreement with France, and the Cabinet decided that Brunnow would be informed of any initiative Britain might take on her own.

Palmerston later spoke with Brunnow about the possibility of Britain holding separate discussions with France to try to ease tension, and Brunnow said that Russia would have no objection to such discussions as long as friendship with France was not seen as alignment against Russia. "The political error you committed in the past was that of being against Russia," he told Palmerston. The convention was intended to make relations between the

64. *The Greville Memoirs*, vol. 1: 320. Greville in no way attributed the exclusion of France to Russia.
65. *Ibid.*, 355, 325–326.

powers easier and enable them to follow real interests such as those which united Britain and France, he pointed out.[66]

Differences between Nesselrode and Nicholas on French accession reached their height in November and December in the culmination of the Tsar's efforts to form an alliance against France. After Paskevich's proposals to Prussia were rejected, the subject was sustained by a series of projects to include Austria and Britain, none of which were seriously entertained by the governments concerned. When the possibility of an offensive-defensive alliance was raised at one juncture, Nesselrode commented, "Has anyone ever heard of such nonsense?"[67] In December Brunnow was instructed to offer Britain a military alliance. He did not press very hard, however, and Palmerston politely turned it down, explaining that such an alliance did not seem necessary, that it would have an adverse effect on the balance of power, and that it would be objected to as against British principles and no doubt fail to pass Parliament. Undoubtedly the brainchild of "a good and loyal soldier," not of Nesselrode's sophisticated politics, it turned out to be an event of no consequence.[68]

Nesselrode remained optimistic throughout. "I have a presentiment," he said in mid-November, "that we will come out of this great crisis marvelously." And at the end of the month he predicted, "we will come out of this great crisis victoriously and without war."[69] Victory meant simply that the crisis would be intense enough to compel France to accede and the other powers to accept her. He may have been afraid that the concert would be lost if the crisis abated prematurely. For example, speaking of the King of Prussia, he said "I only hope that once the danger is

66. Brunnow (18 October 1840), in Martens, Recueil, vol. 12: 148–149.
67. Nesselrode to Meyendorff (24 October 1840), Lettres et papiers, vol. 8: 56. The proposal was then in the form drawn up by General Rauch.
68. The Russian bid for an alliance is sketched by F. S. Rodkey, "Anglo-Russian Negotiations 1840–41," American Historical Review (1931), vol. 36: 343–349. According to Rodkey, Clanricarde noticed a significant difference between the Tsar and Nesselrode. The former wanted a military alliance of a general nature, but Nesselrode "confined his proposals to the case of a French invasion of Germany"—which he did not expect. Ibid., 344–345.
69. Nesselrode to Meyendorff (6 November 1840 and 18 November 1840), Lettres et papiers, vol. 8: 66, 80.

less immediate, he will not fall back into the old languor." [70] The same might well have been said of the Tsar.

There is no outstanding event that accounts for the shift toward agreement in January and February of 1841. The unremitting complications and dangers attributable to the exclusion of France appear to have mellowed Nicholas enough to enable him to accept Nesselrode's point of view. By March, in any case, the Tsar was willing to admit France. Palmerston yielded at last to pressures in the Cabinet and to the general trend. What happened to Metternich is uncertain. In ill health, he lapsed into momentary silence, followed by a verbal attack on the new system. In February Nesselrode became confident that Metternich would not succeed in bringing about a conference in which France would negotiate "à la table ronde." Yet at that time he did not expect complete agreement from France right away, and was thinking about the expedient of France joining the other powers and Turkey in a declaration stating "that the Egyptian affair is ended, and that the straits remain closed to the warships of all nations." [71]

Metternich continued to resist the tactic of compelling France to sanction the system that Russia and Britain had arranged. Perhaps he even tried to drive the two powers apart in the expectation that France would support a conference at Vienna and restore his former influence.[72] But Nesselrode was more bemused than worried by this. "How many times did Metternich preach to us, admonishing us to move closer to England!" he exclaimed, "And now that we are on good terms with her, he fears that our relations are growing too intimate." [73] He opposed a new conference at which France would have full negotiating power for the most obvious reason: "The matter is quite simple," he

70. Nesselrode to Meyendorff (1 December 1840), *Lettres et papiers*, vol. 8: 81.
71. Nesselrode to Meyendorff (4 February 1841), *Lettres et papiers*, vol. 8: 118.
72. According to Martens, Nicholas himself "comprenait très-bien que tous ces conseils du prince provenaient de son resentiment de voir le rapprochement anglo-russe accompli. Metternich savait que ces deux puissances réunis pouvaient à elles seules trancher toutes les questions européennes. C'est pourquoi il désirait tant voir cette alliance brisée." *Recueil*, vol. 4: 497.
73. Nesselrode to Meyendorff (4 February 1841), *Lettres et papiers*, vol. 8: 117.

said, "France would want to isolate us in order to escape her own isolation."[74]

By now, Nesselrode's worries were the old ones, namely that something unforeseen would occur, perhaps a sudden outburst of "senseless passion" against Russia in the West which would "have enough force to align France and England" and divide Europe anew. "We are acting as if our forebodings will not come true," he said, "but while the reunion of the States is taking place, I will not sleep peacefully."[75]

Perhaps the most remarkable change occurred in France, where the sword-rattling gave way to thoughts of rapprochement with Russia. This took place in conjunction with an event which made it appear that Russia was taking the initiative to seek a convivial relationship. At the end of December Nesselrode instructed Count Peter Pahlen at Paris to bring up basic issues for discussion. The tone of his instructions was very conciliatory. The dispatch was either purloined or leaked; it was published, and publicly misinterpreted as an offer of an alliance. If it was intentional, the effect was precisely what Nesselrode desired, that is, it warmed French feeling to Russia. As a result, Palmerston sought reassurances in his own relations with Russia, and in an audience with the Tsar Clanricarde was told in no uncertain terms that Nesselrode's dispatch had been misunderstood.[76] Russia was not looking for an alliance with France. If it was planned, it was brilliant. "This national impetus toward an alliance with us," Marie Nesselrode wrote to her husband from Paris, "reassures me about our future relations with England."[77] Most important, it was now evident that whatever the Tsar's feelings, Russian policy was geared to Nesselrode's desire for a full "pentarchy."[78] "Do not believe the exaggerations of certain newspapers on the point," Princess Lieven confided in January 1841, "but believe what is

74. Nesselrode to Pahlen (6 March 1841), in Martens, *Recueil*, vol. 15: 183.
75. Nesselrode to Meyendorff (18 March 1841), *Lettres et papiers*, vol. 8: 132.
76. Clanricarde to Palmerston (18 January 1841), *FO* 65/272.
77. Marie Nesselrode to Nesselrode (11 December 1840), *Lettres et papiers*, vol. 8: 84.
78. The term, which had come into use during the congress era, appeared in the title of a book which Meyendorff subsidized in the same year as Russia's overture to Britain—[Goldman], *Europäische Pentarchie* (Leipzig, 1839).

true, that the tone of the last communication is quite proper, that Russia is sincerely anxious to see France return to the concert of Europe."[79]

A month later Guizot instructed Bourqueney at London to express his government's desire to join the other powers. Bourqueney proposed simultaneously to Brunnow and Palmerston that France would formally recognize the arrangement of 1840 in a new convention. In addition, he suggested two new guarantees: freedom of trade across the Suez isthmus, and the right to intervene in behalf of Syrian Christians. Brunnow and Palmerston rejected the guarantees, but Bourqueney did not withdraw the French offer. Then Brunnow and Palmerston each drew up a draft of a convention to be signed by the five powers and Turkey. They compared the two documents, which were basically identical, and composed a final text. The most important departure from the text of 1840 was that the principle of closure received more concentrated attention.

Brunnow had worked on a preliminary draft supplied by Nesselrode, and on March 1 he sent a copy showing the changes of wording he had worked out with Palmerston and Bourqueney back to Petersburg for approval. "There would be an undeniable advantage in bringing France to explicitly recognize the principle of closure of the straits," he said in an accompanying dispatch for the Tsar's attention. Nicholas consented.[80]

By this time, Nesselrode was taking every opportunity to encourage France to act in concert with the other powers. For example, in April when Guizot proposed general support for King Othon of Greece, Nesselrode told Brunnow: "If it has the effect of reuniting the unanimous suffrages of all the cabinets, we will extend our most loyal concurrence."[81]

Although several months were to elapse before the desired result, "the reunion of the states" in Nesselrode's words, was obtained in London, the path was very smooth. Nicholas was happy, convinced as he was that French accession would be a capitulation. To the end of June, Nesselrode continued to instruct Brun-

79. Princess Lieven to the duchesse de Talleyrand-Perigord (rcd. 6 January 1841), D. Talleyrand-Perigord, *Memoirs of the Duchesse de Dino* (London, 1909), vol. 3: 5.
80. Goriainov, *Le Bosphore et les Dardanelles*, 83.
81. Nesselrode to Meyendorff (24 March 1841), *Lettres et papiers*, vol. 8: 134.

now to support Palmerston in every way and encourage him to stand firm, while offering France the prospect of full membership in the concert. Finally he settled back to wait, and even took a vacation to tend his gardens at his summer home on the islands.

Everything turned out exactly as he expected. The date set for the signing, July 13 (the 15th had proved inconvenient), was intended to recall the date of the 1840 convention and emphasize continuity, belying a Western view that Russia's primary motive had been to isolate France. If Nesselrode's design was conservative, it had been carried out by extending a hand to a liberal minister who was inclined to examine Russian motives carefully. "At last, please accept my congratulations for having closed this affair with Palmerston," Brunnow wrote to Nesselrode.[82]

The preamble stated that it was the "unanimous determination" of the signatories that "their union and their agreement offer Europe the most certain pledge for the preservation of the general peace." The text consisted of four articles providing for closure, the Porte's right to grant passage to small ships engaged in diplomatic missions, the future accession of other states, and ratification.[83] It was potentially inclusive, and in effect it instituted a classic balance with respect to the Near East. It was well described by one of America's first scholars of international law, Henry Wheaton, as having secured the "status quo on which the peace of the Levant, and with it the peace of Europe depended."[84]

But it was unpopular from the beginning. Nationalistic Russians regarded it as a gross mistake. They would never accept Nesselrode's contention that Unkiar Skelessi had been continued in another form in the convention, because to them there was a world of difference between independent action and the commitment to act in concert. Now the Black Sea Fleet was bottled up by an obligation that the Western powers would enforce to Russia's disadvantage. As opposed to the alternative of eventual control of the straits for Russia, it constituted an immense setback, a limitation of strategic force in the one area in which the potential for the maximization of power in a contest with Brit-

82. Brunnow to Nesselrode (1 July 1841), in Martens, *Recueil*, vol. 12: 155.
83. Text in French and English, *Parliamentary Papers* (1842), vol. 45; in French and Russian, Martens, *Recueil*, vol. 12: 115–159.
84. H. Wheaton, *History of the Law of Nations in Europe and America* (New York, 1845), 572.

ain was such that Russia might have obtained a decisive advantage. This consideration helped to place the convention foremost among the engagements by which it was believed that Nesselrode had sacrificed Russian interests. Such a view was based on an assumption, prominent in the writings of the period, that Russia was involved in a protracted conflict with Britain, or the West in general, and that this was related directly to "the revolutionary division of Europe." Even the Tsar, having consented to the convention more or less as an expedient and without fully understanding the implications, continued his tendency, in Nesselrode's words, to see "the present relationship between the European powers as one coalition against the other."[85] Later they said Nicholas had been misled in his foreign policy and had followed a course inconsistent with his own deeper desires. Certainly he was ambivalent: Official Nationality rested on the belief that Russia could not be reconciled with her Western rivals. The initial Russian reaction was the antecedent of that amplified by the Crimean War, in which defeat was regarded as the consequence of folly. It was perfectly in line with the interpretation Tatishchev represented when he said that "the renewal of the 'European concert'" in 1841 was futile because it could not effect a "political union between Eastern and Western Europe."[86]

It proved no less difficult to reconcile the West with Russia. Despite the fact that the treaty was a "triumph" for Palmerston, as Webster has shown[87] (although the achievement was less the containment of Russia than cooperation with her), the change of attitude that accompanied it seemed incredible, and the myth of a Russian menace came back to haunt its makers. The *Times*, which had formerly printed anti-Russian articles at Palmerston's request, assailed him with the deduction that the agreement "implied the sudden oblivion of all those differences which have for so many years divided the cabinets of St. Petersburg and St. James." It contradicted "the whole *Tenour* of Russian policy and Russian history." What evidence did Palmerston have that Russia had changed so profoundly? "M. de Brunnow's arguments and M. de Nesselrode's assurances led Lord Palmerston to this

85. Nesselrode to Meyendorff (10 November 1841), *Lettres et papiers*, vol. 8: 147.
86. Tatishchev, *Vneshniaia politika*, 634.
87. Cf. Webster, *The Foreign Policy of Palmerston*.

conclusion," said the *Times*; "we know not whether they will have the same effect on the people of England."[88] Closure of the straits was interpreted as security for the Black Sea Fleet. Moderation was synonymous with an acceptance of weakness: Greville predicted the powers would soon discover "that the means will fall very short of accomplishing the end, and that peace will be preserved by their very impotence at great expense."[89] Whatever the force of Whig-Liberal pacificism and Tory patronage in relations with Russia, no trick would compel Victorian Britain to subordinate her interests to European equilibrium. Melbourne's government fell six weeks after the signing.

In France too, the salient attitude turned out to be against cooperation with Russia.[90] Guizot and his supporters countered the outburst against the treaty with the contention that "the status quo is not constituted against France," and that the government was "sincere and dedicated in pursuit of a policy of peace."[91] But the attackers, who ranged from monarchical imperialists to socialists, found the idea of identical French and Russian interests absurd, and blatantly so in the Near East, where Russian influence was antithetical to movements for national independence and to the rights of Western Christians. Louis Blanc epitomized the avant garde: "there was much grandeur" in the treaty, he said, and "testimony to the principle of community and reciprocity in human affairs." But it was "no less true that regarding French interests," which in his mind were those of the progress of civilization toward socialism, "it was a wrong and a misfortune."[92]

But the first threat of a return to bipolarity that Nesselrode had to deal with came not from the liberal powers, but from the conservative ones. Prussia, with little real interest in the Eastern Question and a mounting preoccupation with old claims against France in the Rhineland, and Austria, recoiling under Met-

88. The *Times* of London (1 May 1841).
89. *The Greville Memoirs*, vol. 1: 301.
90. The Russian origin of the convention was more generally known in France than in Britain.
91. *Lettre à Duvergier de Hauranne, sur la Convention du 13 Juillet et la Situation actuelle de la France* (Paris, 1841), 25. This lucid defense of the treaty was attributed to Bourqueney. For Guizot's comments, cf. his *Memoirs of Sir Robert Peel* (London, 1857), 152.
92. Blanc, *Révolution français*, vol. 5: 436; vol. 3: 218.

ternich's fresh personal antagonism to Palmerston and bitter dislike for Anglo-Russian partnership, waxed favorable to alignment against both members of the former Entente Cordiale. A conservative alliance was discussed at Vienna and Berlin soon after the treaty was signed, and in October it was proposed to Russia. Nicholas found the idea attractive. But Nesselrode advised him that it would be a "grave error" to exclude Britain, and, quietly turning his attention to other things, instructed Meyendorff in Berlin to stifle the project at its source. A conservative alliance would be incompatible with the European system: "First," he said of the proposal, "it draws too sharp a line of distinction between the three courts and England; and second, it makes the same mistake regarding France." The rapprochement with Britain, he explained, was intended to promote "a compact community," in which Austria, Prussia, and the German Confederation would be an integral part. The days of opposed alliances had come to an end.[93]

The renewal of the concert in 1841 is largely attributable to Russian initiatives and motives which would seem entirely improbable apart from Nesselrode's personal influence and philosophy. The specific arrangement intended to solve the Eastern Question, with heavy emphasis on closure of the straits and the status quo, bore the characteristics of the policy he had advocated for years and had tried to preserve in the Treaty of Unkiar Skelessi.[94] But more generally, it was an expression of ideals perhaps appropriately associated with the Holy Alliance. As Brunnow asserted, the overture to Britain in 1839 originated in fears of a titanic struggle "that would have destroyed the peace of the world,"[95] and certainly in a desire for peace and unity as much at odds with official nationalism as with the violent, divisive realities of Europe's modern transformation.

Toward a New Order

Bipartisanship allowed Russia to escape containment and isolation; it eliminated the potent influence of the Entente Cordiale, did away with the necessity to rely on Austria and Prussia,

93. Nesselrode to Meyendorff (10 November 1841), *Lettres et papiers*, vol. 8: 147–149.
94. Cf. Nesselrode's general report (1850), *SIRIO*, vol. 98: 287–298.
95. Brunnow, *La Guerre*, 35.

and thus resolved the problem of bipolarity. But an understanding of the rapprochement would be incomplete unless other motives are taken into account. The struggle against isolation and the independent "Russian" policy Nesselrode's opponents advocated was ultimately a contention for another philosophy of foreign relations. The objective was freer intercourse with the outside world—the key, in Brunnow's words, to "a new era of prosperity and wealth, of commercial and industrial development in accord with the needs of Europe and Asia."[96] In the broad perspective of the history of Russian foreign relations, the period of the rapprochement stands out as one of unusual diplomatic activity and involvement in foreign affairs too numerous to mention here. Of pointed interest are initiatives in behalf of freer trade and commerce. The beginning of an effort to create a new order, prematurely eclipsed by resurgent nationalism in the mid-1840s, emerges from the evidence.

The relaxation of tariffs and prohibitions from 1836 to 1838 naturally inspired rising expectations. "In 1839 Russia's foreign commercial relations entered a period of unprecedented expansion," stated a special supplement of the *Journal de St. Pétersbourg*.[97] This, it claimed, had been a source of large profits for Russian merchants. In a special supplement in 1843, "A Glance at the Exchange and Stores of St. Petersburg," the *Journal* compared the commercial scene in the Russian capital with that in London. Admiration for the British ran high at Russian expense. Commercial activity was much more lively in London; manufactured goods available in Petersburg were inferior, higher priced, and in limited supply. The Petersburg exchange was still relatively indolent. Since there was a demand for Russian goods abroad and for foreign goods in Russia, it was obvious that a basis for trade existed. What was wrong? Russia had "too few *capitalists*, who conduct trade according to their own ideas and their own plans, who import and export merchandise at their own pleasure and not at the command of directives, requisitions, and remote predictions." It recommended that individual initiative be stimulated by relaxing controls, promoting "free and open" competition, and purposefully educating Russian merchants about

96. Brunnow, *La Guerre*, 86.
97. "Mouvement du commerce extérieur de la Russie en 1841," *Journal de St. Pétersbourg* (17 October 1842), special supplement.

the practice and advantages of trade. It implied that the British model would be the superior one to follow.[98]

But the last of the Russian free traders certainly did not believe that a system of private enterprise would lead to a duplication of British industrialization. Russia's role in a new order would conform with the conditions of world economics. Her interdependent relationship with Britain would be primarily that of an agrarian country to an industrial one. Indigenous industries would grow rapidly, perhaps even with the support of foreign capital, if they were profitable, but by and large Russia would be dependent on Western manufacturers. This tendency to resist massive industrialization did not mean that they were less forward-looking or less appreciative of better manufacturers, more efficient transport, superior technology, and so forth, than their nationalistic opponents were. The spokesmen for the status quo included many individuals with extensive investments in advanced aspects of economic development, and avid interest in crucial areas of technological innovation such as the introduction of steam power. Perhaps most suggestive was the great importance they attached to transport. While Kankrin failed to see the usefulness of railroads at all, Nesselrode was fascinated by the possibilities they opened up. "Amen!" he said when the decision came to connect Petersburg and Moscow by rail, "I hope this will be for the very greatest good of Russia."[99] If they thought that "the geographical and climatical features of Russia will always prevent it being anything but a great village," as Cobden was told by one of Nesselrode's colleagues when he visited Russia, their physiocratic philosophy led them to reject the modern notion that an agrarian economy was primitive in comparison with an industrial one.[1] They emphasized the potential for trade with the industrial countries, and viewed "the globe" as "a highway for mercantile and industrial genius."[2] They empha-

---

98. "Coup d'oeil sur la Bourse et les magasins de St. Pétersbourg," *Journal de St. Pétersbourg* (22 April 1843), special supplement.

99. Nesselrode to Meyendorff (1 February 1842), *Lettres et papiers*, vol. 8: 164.

1. Cobden attributed the statement to Alexander Meyendorff, whom he described as "an active-minded and intelligent German possessing much statistical knowledge about Russian trade and manufactures." From Cobden's diary, in J. A. Hobson, *Richard Cobden, The Industrial Man* (London, 1919), 51–52.

2. Brunnow, *La Guerre*, 149.

sized Petersburg's role as the main gateway for maritime commerce with Western Europe and the Atlantic community, and recognized that Moscow was better suited to be the "center of national industry."[3] They were excited by the prospect that different types of production might complement each other, once commerce was physically possible. For the whole of her history Russia had been imprisoned by vast distances. In the late 1830s, projects that would have seemed impossible a decade earlier could be entertained. While the first rail line was completed and the Moscow-Petersburg line projected, plans were also entertained for railroads to Warsaw, Berlin, and Vienna, and eastward to Nizhni-Novgorod and Orenburg to connect with the Siberian and Oriental trade. There were other important advancements in transport between 1836 and 1843—the improvement of navigation on the Don, Dnieper, and Volga rivers, the opening of the Saimaa Canal system, and extensive improvements in the port facilities at Petersburg, Archangel, Odessa, and Astrakhan. The vision of the future that drew Nesselrode and his circle was one in which new avenues for commerce would link Russia with both the Orient and the Occident.

When Brunnow went to London in 1839 Nesselrode had instructed him to tell Palmerston that Russia was prepared to negotiate a treaty to guarantee the territorial status quo in Asia as well as the Near East. But Palmerston did not take up this aspect of the Russian overture, and there was no further progress toward a more comprehensive agreement on Asia during the negotiations for the convention of 1840. In December 1840 Nesselrode raised the subject once again; in a private interview with Clanricarde he urged that negotiations be opened for a treaty to fix the territorial limits of the Russian and British empires in Central Asia and secure free trade in the buffer zone.[4] He continued to pursue the subject although he received no encouragement from London, and later drew up specific suggestions concerning borders and diplomatic relations with the intermediate countries, which he sent to Palmerston.[5] In effect, he was inviting Britain to accept parity with Russia in the rights and privileges

3. "Notice sur l'état de la ville de Moscou en 1840," *Journal de St. Pétersbourg* (31 May 1842), special supplement.
4. Cf. Clanricarde to Palmerston (9 December 1840), *FO* 65/262.
5. Clanricarde to Palmerston (22 December 1840), *FO* 65/262.

she would enjoy in the very countries, including Khiva and Bokhara, that Perovskii and other Russians were so anxious to conquer. It was an offer to put an end to imperialism. Once again, Palmerston failed to respond. But Russian policy continued at least until 1843 to conform with the aims envisaged in Nesselrode's theory of buffers in 1838. There were numerous Russian efforts to fix territorial limits, stabilize political relations among the khanates, and open freer trade.

Persia was one of the countries in which marked changes in Russian policy were coordinated with the rapprochement.[6] Here, as we have seen, Russia threw away her advantage by failing to support the campaign against Herat, and by offering her good offices to invite the British back after McNeill had severed relations and departed. In the period 1839–1843 the Russian Central Asian Company, founded in 1834, increased its Persian operations. Trade routes, including navigation on the Caspian Sea, were secured, and there were expressions of optimism concerning Russia's ability to engage in peaceful competition with Britain.[7] The underlying thought was, in Nesselrode's words, that "our interests are naturally the same with respect to Persia."[8]

But Nesselrode soon faced obstacles. Diuhamel, instructed to encourage relations that would promote the renewal of British trade in Persia, but changeable from the time that he had replaced Simonich, decided that "the status quo, which European diplomacy upheld," would mean "an unendurable and artificial life leading to catastrophe" for Persia.[9] "I will always count on the reconciliation with England," Nesselrode admonished him. Russia was "determined to uphold the new system."[10] He instructed Brunnow to inform Diuhamel of events in London directly with-

---

6. Cf. Schiemann: "In Persia, Russian policy went hand in hand with the English," *Geschichte Russlands*, vol. 4: 28.
7. Cf. "O nekotorykh stat'iakh torgovli v Persii," *Zhurnal manufaktur i torgovli* (1843), vol. 3, no. 8: 283–296. Nesselrode did not think full-scale competition would be a factor, because he believed that the Russian and British economies were naturally suited to different kinds of production. He expected Russia to carve out a market in which she would offer rough textile products and rudimentary metal manufactures.
8. Nesselrode to Pozzo di Borgo (20 October/1 November 1838), *BMAddMSS* 36469.
9. Diuhamel, *Avtobiografiia . . .* , 122.
10. Nesselrode to Diuhamel (7 November 1839), in *ibid.*, 112.

out going through Petersburg. Brunnow wrote expressing his optimism, but Diuhamel struck a sour note in his replies. "You say, M. Baron, that as you endeavor to wipe out the old prejudice [Russophobia] in Europe, it will be up to me to establish amicable relations between Russia and England in Asia. With great pleasure I would devote myself to the attainment of these things, but it is scarcely possible to do so against the hostile tendencies of British politics in this part of the world." Realities did not conform with the new illusions. "Even if I were silent," he told Nesselrode, "events would bear me out and speak louder and more eloquently than I do."[11] Three months later Nesselrode dismissed him, and in July 1841 replaced him with A. I. Medem, who directed affairs in Teheran until another of Nesselrode's men, E. V. Putiatin, was appointed Ambassador in 1842. Putiatin and Medem together remained at Teheran until 1845, by which time Russia was returning to a contentious policy.

It was British intervention in Afghanistan that had alarmed Diuhamel most, and unknown to him, it also had disconcerted Nesselrode and Brunnow because it menaced the new system. Nesselrode's response was to invite joint Russo-British mediation of outstanding conflicts involving Persia, particularly the sporadic warfare between Persia and Turkey. He instructed Brunnow that it was "the earnest wish of the Imperial Cabinet to act in Concert" to settle conflicts in which Persia was involved.[12] Brunnow was to instruct the Russian ambassadors at Constantinople and Teheran to join their British counterparts in mediating a settlement if Britain consented. He told Aberdeen that "there is a great moral importance attached to this proposal," and Russia was anxious to prove her desire "not to act singlehanded, but openly and frankly in concert . . . in order to exert our common and united efforts."[13] But when the invasion of Afghanistan was discussed in Parliament in 1842–1843, Auckland defended the "bolder course," as he termed it, with the argument that it was necessary to protect British imperial interests from Russian aggression. This infuriated Brunnow. He considered asking to refute it before Parliament in person, but instead composed a

11. Brunnow to Diuhamel (12 November 1840) and Diuhamel to Nesselrode (April 1841), in *ibid.*, 119, 123.
12. Nesselrode to Brunnow (18 July 1842), *BMAddMSS* 43144.
13. Brunnow to Aberdeen (8 September 1842), *BMAddMSS* 43144.

rebuttal which he submitted to the British government. The only solid evidence Auckland had been able to cite concerned Simonich and Witkiewicz, who had not acted in accordance with Russian policy. They had been recalled and the alliance they negotiated with the Afghan tribes had been renounced. Auckland had decided to go through with his "bolder course" after he had been assured that Russia would not intervene. British interests would have been protected if the government had chosen to recognize the true nature of Russian policy, and had acted in concert to preserve the neutrality of Afghanistan so that Russia and Britain could enjoy access to the country on an equal basis.[14] What was not clearly seen in Britain, to Brunnow's annoyance, was the fact that Russia had foregone opportunities to turn the Afghan situation to her own advantage. For example, the tribes of Bokhara were Britain's enemies in the Afghan war, and this gave Russia an excellent chance to increase her influence in Bokhara.

There were two Russian missions to Bokhara after Witkiewicz's recall.[15] The first, led by E. P. Kovalevskii, was undertaken in the summer of 1839 in response to Palmerston's request to help secure the release of two British agents, Conolly and Stoddart, and to open negotiations for trade agreements. It was unsuccessful on both counts. The second mission, led by an officer named Butenev, also failed. The Khan promised to release the British agents but they were put to death before they could be delivered into Butenev's custody. Although the proposed treaty was not signed, Nesselrode's instructions are of interest for what they reveal about his motives. He did mention Russia's desire to strengthen her "political influence," and he instructed Butenev to ascertain "the best means . . . to develop Russian trade, the establishment of which in this part of Asia is one of the dearest objects of the solicitude of our government."[16] Butenev was to propose a treaty that would protect the free transit of merchants and eliminate arbitrary taxes and penalties. If possible Bokhara should agree to fix an upper limit to duties on imports at no more

14. Brunnow, memorandum marked "private and confidential" (February 1843), *BMAddMSS* 43144.

15. Cf. N. Zalesov, "Ocherk diplomaticheskikh snoshenii Rossii s Bukaroiu s 1836 po 1843 god.," *Voennyi sbornik* (1862), no. 9: 3–46.

16. *Ibid.*, 14–16.

than 5 percent ad valorem for all classes of goods, and in return Russia would guarantee reciprocal rights of trade and transit.

At the same time, Russia was more successful in her efforts to open freer trade with Khiva, and here again there was evidence of a desire to cooperate with Britain. The grievance that had served as the pretext for Perovskii's expedition was eliminated a few months after his return to Orenburg when the Khivan Khan decided to release all of the several thousand Russians in his slave emporium. In August 1840 a British officer, Richmond Shakespear, came into Orenburg with a group of Russian prisoners from Khiva. Shakespear announced to Perovskii that he was an "accredited representative" of the British government, and had been charged to act "in a benevolent sense" as mediator between Russia and Khiva.[17] Perovskii could not believe him, and the papers he produced to support his story were duly forwarded to Nesselrode. Soon after Shakespear emerged from the steppe, additional groups of prisoners began to arrive, a Russian emissary was sent to Khiva, and in November 1840 Russia and Khiva resumed diplomatic relations which had been broken at the time of Perovskii's march. On November 16, 1840 Palmerston alluded to Shakespear's mission in a dispatch to Bloomfield: "Her Majesty's Government have no desire to put forward the part which the British influence had in bringing about the pacific arrangement between Russia and Khiva. . . . On the contrary, the effect produced is the more likely to be lasting the less British Interference shall appear in the eyes of the Public in Russia to have been exerted in this matter."[18] Russian nationalists were angered by every hint of British activity in Khiva. In any case, the return of the Russian slaves dissolved a point of friction between Nesselrode and Perovskii and eliminated the main obstacle to an agreement with Khiva.

Two Russian missions, the first in 1841 by Captain D. I.

17. N. A. Khalfin, "Britanskaia ekspansiia v Srednei Azii," 111. Shakespear, in contrast with other British operatives in Asia, was sympathetic to Russia. He believed that her interests in the region were real and that her grievance against the Khivan slave-market was justified. He later wrote: "I humbly hope . . . that the British name will be blessed with the proud distinction of having put an end to this inhuman traffic." R. Shakespear, "A Personal Narrative of a Journey from Heraut to Orenburg," *Blackwood's Edinburgh Magazine* (1842), vol. 51: 717.

18. Palmerston to Bloomfield (16 November 1840), *FO* 65/259.

Nikiforov and the second in 1842 by Colonel N. Danilevskii, were sent to Khiva to negotiate a treaty to settle the status of nomadic tribes along the borders of Orenburg, and to secure freer trade.[19] Nesselrode wanted Russian merchants to have the right to travel freely and to sell their goods in all of the markets of the khanate without fearing arbitrary seizure. Unburdensome customs duties on exports and imports should be agreed upon, ideally as a single duty of not more than 5 percent ad valorem on goods crossing the border to be sold in either Russia or Khiva. Russian representatives should be permitted to take part in deciding the value of goods for the purpose of levying duties. Khiva should cooperate in ending depredations on caravans. Transit commerce to other regions of Asia, and vice versa to Russia, should be protected and free from prohibitive restrictions. He instructed Danilevskii to advise the Khan to adhere to a policy of strict neutrality. In order to commemorate the solemnity of the Russian admonitions and to encourage the Khan to enter a treaty, Danilevskii delivered a declaration of Russian friendship and separate letters of greeting by Perovskii and Nesselrode.

In the treaty signed by the two countries on January 10, 1843, Khiva pledged to remain neutral and to prohibit the sale and ownership of Russian slaves. Four of the nine articles treated commercial relations. Khiva agreed to uphold the freedom of Russian merchants to move about and sell their wares without being subject to arbitrary restrictions and penalties, especially the confiscation of their property. An upper limit of 5 percent ad valorem was accepted. Duty-free transit commerce between Russia and other parts of Asia was permitted, and the Khan promised to help protect caravans. In a separate declaration Russia granted reciprocal rights of trade and transit commerce to Khivan merchants in Russia. None of the provisions of this treaty were prejudicial or exclusive with regard to Britain or other countries

19. Cf. N. Zalesov, "Popsol'stvo v Khivu kapitana Nikiforova v 1841 g.," *Voennyi sbornik* (1861), no. 11: 41–92; and "Posol'stvo v Khivu podpolkovnika Danilevskago v 1842 godu," *Voennyi sbornik* (1866), no. 5: 41–75. No reliable account in such detail exists in English. Other noteworthy sources are I. N. Zakharin, "Posol'stvo v Khivu v 1842 godu (Po razykazam i zapiskam ochevidtsa)," *Istoricheskii vestnik* (1894), vol. 56: 523–537; N. Modestov, ed., "K istorii osvobozhdeniia russkikh plennykh iz Khivu," *Russkii arkhiv* (1914), vol. 3: 96–119; (1915), vol. 1: 31–48, vol. 2: 276–301.

trading in Khiva.[20] As in the case of the overtures to Bokhara, Nesselrode was personally responsible for the flow of instructions from Petersburg, and his actions were consistent with those for Persia and other regions of Asia.[21]

The evidence suggests that Nesselrode's theory of buffers was adhered to in principle as a guideline for Russian policy. But the evidence is limited, and promising avenues for study remain unexplored. Additional research on Russian commercial activities in Asia and on the history of the Russian Central Asian Company may reveal more about the philosophy behind Russian efforts to promote foreign trade and the nature of the contention between Nesselrode and the nationalists on this subject. It was also during this period that Russia made vigorous efforts to develop trade with China, accompanied by the typical concern for improved transportation. Nesselrode was active on committees to examine China policy, and given the dream that Russia would become a highway for the Oriental trade with Europe, his attitude toward China takes on new interest. There may be further evidence of the conflict between his philosophy and the nationalistic, state-oriented economics associated with the movement for the conquest of Central Asia that resumed in the mid-1840s and was later a vital aspect of Gorchakov's policy of *recueillement*.

The Russian pursuit of a new order was more obvious in Europe. Although the Russian tariff revisions of 1836–1838 had been enacted with Britain foremost in mind, and Nesselrode had taken initiatives beginning in 1837 to try to start negotiations with Britain for a treaty on trade and navigation, Russia's first treaty under her modified trade policy was not with Britain but with the Kingdom of Sweden and Norway, ruled by Karl XIV Johan (Bernadotte). Russia's Baltic trade was growing, and promised to increase rapidly if restrictions were eased and old tensions put aside. And perhaps even more important, the Kattegat and the Skagerrak were Petersburg's maritime gateway from the Baltic to Western Europe and the high seas. Although in the late 1830s Britain became fearful that Russia's interest in Sweden and Norway was part of a design for conquest, this

20. Zalesov, "Posol'stvo v Khivu podpolkovnika Danilevskago," 50–51.
21. Cf. lists of documents by and to Nesselrode in the appendices of Zalesov, *ibid.*, 55–57; "Posol'stvo v Khivu kapitana Nikiforova," 81–92; and "Ocherk diplomaticheskikh snoshenii Rossii s Bukharoiu," 33–46.

feeling was not shared by Karl Johan, who was receptive to Nesselrode's overtures. Karl Johan, concerned about what his biographer Höjer terms the "protracted danger of war" between Russia and Britain, had decided to guide Sweden and Norway along a neutral course.[22] Beyond the peril of taking sides and being vulnerable to reprisals by one or the other, Karl Johan believed that he could help keep peace by becoming an influential neutral member of the European concert. Through Nesselrode's efforts on the Russian side a "treaty of trade, navigation, and friendship" with Sweden and Norway was signed on May 8, 1838. It provided for reciprocity in the treatment of ships and cargoes according to most favored nation standards. The text consisted of ten articles setting guidelines for regulations and duties in all of the ports of Russia, Finland, Sweden, and Norway. Reciprocity also was instituted with regard to merchandise of one party carried in the ships of the other. Restrictions on the local trade between Finland and Sweden and Norway were eased.[23]

Russian relations with Sweden received additional emphasis in June 1838 when Nicholas paid a surprise visit to Stockholm after a journey to Warsaw and Berlin. A trip to Stockholm had been arranged for the Grand Duke Mikhail, and the Swedish court had no forewarning that Nicholas intended to come. "Sire, you were expecting the son, but here stands the father before you," said Nicholas on being presented to the Swedish King.[24] Nicholas was treated to a fine series of parades and military maneuvers. The citizens of Stockholm demonstrated against him on one occasion, and this was played up in Britain as a sensational event, but by and large Nicholas was well pleased with his stay.[25]

Austria was the next country to receive Russian overtures, in November 1838, for a treaty on the navigation of the Danube. Russian customs and quarantine regulations had been impeding the flow of commerce on the river. Earlier in the year Nesselrode

22. Cf. T. Höjer, *Karl XIV Johan* (Stockholm, 1960), vol. 2: 254–259.
23. "Traité de commerce, de navigation et d'amitié" (8 May 1838), in G. F. Martens, *Nouveau Recueil*, vol. 23 (15): 580–591.
24. V. I. Fel'kner, "Poezdka Imperatora Nikolaia Pavlovicha v Stokol'm v 1838 g. Vospominaniia . . . ," *Russkaia starina* (1875), vol. 12: 165.
25. Cf. Nicholas I to Paskevich (6 March 1843), "Imperator Nikolai Pavlovich v ego pis'makh," 30.

had proposed to the Tsar that Russia give proof of her desire to respect the principle of free navigation on the Danube that had been agreed upon at the Congress of Vienna, telling him that this would help improve relations with the West. Nicholas consented, and Nesselrode himself conducted the negotiations with the Austrian Ambassador.[26]

Owing to the Near Eastern crisis and uncertainties arising from Metternich's attitude toward Russia, the "convention for the free navigation of the Danube" was not signed until a year and a half after the initial overture, on July 25, 1840. The preamble stated that Russia and Austria were "animated by the desire to facilitate, to expand, and to augment better and better commercial relations." Their trade relations would be advanced "by promoting the greatest possible development of navigation on the Danube." "To apply the same principle to this river that the Congress of Vienna established for free navigation of rivers that border or cross different countries," Russia and Austria "resolved, in common accord, to regulate all things related to the object of their reciprocal interest."[27]

By July 1840 Russia had made overtures to Prussia for a reduction of customs restrictions. Nicholas sent Kankrin to Berlin to conduct talks on trade policy with Count Albert von Alvensleben, but the first round of talks did not go well. Alvensleben showed little interest and Kankrin was ill. Without having achieved his aims, Kankrin, exhausted and on the verge of submitting his resignation, returned to Petersburg. Nesselrode instructed Meyendorff to do what he could to further the negotiations, and he met with some success. In the summer of 1842, two years after the first Russian overture to Prussia, agreement was reached to lower duties. Nicholas signed two decrees, dated July 21 and September 9, granting Prussia freer trade in Poland.[28] "It appears that in Prussia they are beginning to have a better understanding of things," Nesselrode wrote to Meyendorff, "and I hope that a new and better era in our relations with Prussia will be dated from this time."[29]

26. Cf. Martens, *Recueil*, vol. 4: 486–487.
27. Cf. *ibid.*, 487–493.
28. *Ibid.*, 544.
29. Nesselrode to Meyendorff (6 December 1842), *Lettres et papiers*, vol. 8: 186–187.

But Britain was the main object of Russian solicitude, and Nesselrode was highly encouraged when Peel's ministry took office in 1841. He appreciated Peel's conciliatory attitude to Russia, and his free-trade philosophy.[30] And Aberdeen seemed a good choice as Foreign Secretary. "I tell you," Brunnow wrote of Aberdeen, "that outside of my work with yourself I have never met anyone more easy to do business with (or anyone who provides more of a contrast with Palmerston). He is astonishingly like you. What he says is solid, true, and carries the seal of integrity."[31] The only disappointment was that Aberdeen did not send a new ambassador to Petersburg, where Lord Stuart (Charles de Rothsay), whom Palmerston had appointed to replace Clanricarde in 1840, was not a promising candidate to carry on the momentum of détente. In fact, he was senile. "Lord Stuart is no better than a walking corpse," Nesselrode quipped.[32] But Stuart's duties fell on Bloomfield's shoulders, and the latter, who had been Secretary since 1839, enjoyed good rapport with Nesselrode. "Count Nesselrode has invariably shown me much kindness, and latterly in the delicate position in which I am placed by Lord Stuart's unfortunate and hapless condition, he has given me greater proofs of consideration than I had any right to expect," he reported.[33]

Russia's new trade policy and overtures to Britain in 1837 did not quickly bring the response Nesselrode was hoping for. If they had, the trend toward free trade might have been fortified against the disasters that followed. Despite the crises of the late 1830s, trade with Britain improved, and in 1840 Palmerston showed a passing interest in negotiating a treaty on trade and navigation. Conditions became less favorable to a treaty in 1841 when the Russian government announced that it was raising tariffs as a temporary, emergency measure to increase revenues and meet a severe economic crisis. The tariff of 1841 was asso-

30. "I had a letter from Nesselrode," Peel wrote in 1844. "Foolish people complain of my having said civil things about Russia and the Emperor. What I said has done very great public good." G. Peel, ed., *The Private Letters of Sir Robert Peel* (London, 1920), 252.
31. Brunnow to Nesselrode (9 September 1841), in Martens, *Recueil*, vol. 12: 204.
32. Nesselrode to Meyendorff (19 March 1842), *Lettres et papiers*, vol. 8: 171.
33. Bloomfield to Aberdeen (26 September 1843), BMAddMSS 43144.

ciated with Kankrin, and, ironically, it was the rising volume of
trade between 1837 and 1841 that made the new tariff seem
worthwhile as a revenue measure. Bloomfield thought the new
tariff was very discouraging and not likely to be rescinded in the
near future.[34]

After the second straits convention, the first treaty Russia
entered with Britain was called an agreement for "order and
safety on the high seas." This was the "treaty for the suppression
of the slave trade" signed in London on December 20, 1841.[35]
Nesselrode was in favor of making the abolition of the slave trade
part of general European law, and no doubt also realized that it
was one of Peel's pet projects and would be a monument to cooperation with Britain. Hopes that it would be enacted by a full
concert were dashed when France signed but refused to ratify.
Peel's temper flared because he thought France had been swayed
by her relations with the United States. But Nesselrode, always
solicitous toward the United States, thought that it merely illustrated "the fickleness and frivolity of the French."[36]

Despite many small advances, however, the most important
step toward a strengthening of the rapprochement and the European system after the straits convention, the treaty on trade and
navigation with Britain of 1843, was stillborn. After he came to
office, Peel instructed the Board of Trade to draw up terms for
a commercial agreement with Russia. The proposed treaty contained an astonishing design. It called for reciprocity of trade and
navigation on the basis of tariffs and regulations applied to domestic commerce in each country; in other words, it was a plan
for free trade between Russia and Britain, and if the treaty could
be brought into full effect, it would lead to the creation of an
economic community. All countries having reciprocal most favored nation agreements with Russia and Britain would be compelled to embrace free trade or bring their own treaties into question. And, in turn, other countries having such agreements with
these countries would be similarly affected.

Many mysteries surround the opening of negotiations for the
treaty at the end of 1841. We know little about Nesselrode's

34. Bloomfield to Palmerston (31 July 1841), *FO* 356/29.
35. Text, Martens, *Recueil*, vol. 12: 170–196.
36. Nesselrode to Meyendorff (7 March 1842), *Lettres et papiers*, vol.
    8: 167.

specific moves. Peel was certainly sincere, and expected Russia to be receptive. Nesselrode had previously made repeated soundings on the subject. But as far as we know there was nothing in Nesselrode's or Brunnow's communications to suggest that Russia was ready to do anything so revolutionary as abolish her tariffs, even in a bilateral relationship. Why did Peel think Russia would be receptive? It is possible that Nesselrode and his colleagues, may have taken liberties and initiated the process of negotiation with the expectation that the Tsar could be persuaded to sanction the treaty over the objections of Kankrin and the nationalists if the British government joined them in strongly urging him to do so. The argument that it would increase trade and alleviate Russia's economic problems could be brought to bear.

In some ways, Nesselrode and Peel faced similar obstacles. On the question of free trade with Russia, Peel came up against the Liberals, who were generally nationalistic, protectionistic, and imperialistic. He even found himself at odds with Aberdeen, who did not share his zeal for free trade. Nesselrode was opposed by Kankrin and the nationalists. From the first draft to the completed convention over a year later, "Kankrin refused to alter the Russian tariff to make it equitable," according to Martens.[37] Kankrin argued that such a treaty would give Britain a franchise in Russia's domestic markets. Of course Nesselrode agreed with him, and only differed as to whether this was a good thing. But in the end Britain received no such franchise, and it was doubtful that Russia would have gained access for her products under the Navigation Acts. Reciprocity proved unattainable, in essence because in both countries the regulation of foreign trade was conducted by domestic legislative processes, not by diplomacy.

The "convention on commerce and navigation" signed by Russia and Britain on January 11, 1843, provided that Russia and Britain were "desirous of extending, increasing, and consolidating the commercial relations between their respective dominions and possessions, and of thereby procuring all possible facilities and encouragements for those of their subjects who partake in those relations"; they were "persuaded that nothing can more contribute to the accomplishment of their mutual wishes in this respect, than the reciprocal abolition of the differential and countervailing duties which are at present exacted and levied on

37. Martens, *Recueil*, vol. 12: 209.

the vessels or produce of either of the two States in the ports of the other."[38] Article four stated that, "All productions of the soil, industry, and art of the dominions and possessions of His Majesty the Emperor of all the Russias . . . and also all the productions of the soil, industry, and art of the United Kingdom . . . shall enjoy reciprocally, in all respects, the same privileges and immunities, and may be imported and exported exactly in the same manner, in vessels of the one as in vessels of the other High Contracting Party."[39] On the Russian side, reciprocity could not be effected as intended by this article if Kankrin's tariffs remained in force.

The treaty did advance freedom of commerce. Reciprocity in levying warehouse charges and in freedom to reexport goods without duties other than those paid by the nationals of each country was granted by article seven. Article two provided that Russian vessels in British waters, and British ships in Russian waters, "shall be subject to no other or higher duties or charges, of whatsoever nature they may be, than those which are now, or shall hereafter be imposed on national vessels." Reciprocal rights of free navigation meant, for example, that British vessels must be "admitted with their cargoes into the ports of the Russian Empire, without paying any other duties whatsoever than those payable by Russian vessels." Other articles provided that the ships of either country were to enjoy the right to seek refuge or repair in the ports of the other without being subject to any restrictions or charges not applied to the ships of the host country. On the other hand, the coasting trade was excluded from the action of this treaty.[40] (One may imagine the feelings of Menshikov, Lazarev, and other Russian naval officers who, having witnessed the obnoxious agreement with Britain and the Western powers to close the straits to Russian warships, now were instructed that British ships had the right to sail in and out of Russian ports with the freedom of Russian ships!)

The Russian government legislated several changes of commercial procedure after the conclusion of the treaty. On January 20, 1843, Nicholas signed an *ukaz* extending new privileges to

38. Text, Martens, *Recueil*, vol. 12: 210–223; *Parliamentary Papers*, vol. 61. Cf. *Journal de St. Pétersbourg* (6 April 1843) and *Zhurnal manufaktur i torgovli* (1843), vol. 2, no. 4: 1–18.
39. Text, *ibid.*
40. *Ibid.*

foreign merchants and vessels. By this *ukaz* bonding ports were established at Kronstadt and Archangel (bonding ports were already in operation at Petersburg and Riga). Most important, goods bonded at these four ports could be reexported free of customs charges. Kankrin gave orders to relax fines levied for errors in bills of lading, and procedures were laid down so that masters of foreign vessels could take a larger share of responsibility for clearing their own cargoes. At the same time foreign merchants were granted the privilege of duty-free trade with one another and with Russian merchants belonging to the first and second guilds within designated areas. These changes affected not only the British but all foreign merchants, with the result that the wharves and exchanges within the designated areas became free international market places.[41]

"These facilities and relaxations in the regulations of the foreign trade in Russia have been the spontaneous and happy consequence of this valuable treaty of commerce," said Russian consular instructions issued in Britain. The benefits of the treaty were described: "This treaty fully evinces the amicable feelings existing between the two Countries, it marks strongly the wise and friendly views of Russia on the important point of an extended Commercial intercourse with the British Empire."[42]

It was clearly seen that free trade meant Russian dependence on British manufactures. Peel had discussed Russian economic policy with Brunnow, and had expressed the view that Kankrin's policy should be abandoned. Nature had endowed Russia with an essentially agrarian economy which would best be developed to its full without industrial preoccupations necessitating endless protection. He implied that there would be no need to promote impossible aims if dependence on British manufactures was accepted. Brunnow forwarded these observations to Nesselrode before the end of January 1843, and according to Martens they "excited such a lively interest on the part of the Vice-Chancellor" that he passed them along to Kankrin.[43] Kankrin did not share his enthusiasm in the least. He replied with a memorandum in

41. Cf. "Circular issued by the Russian Consulate General in London to the Russian Consuls in England on the Ratification of the Treaty of Commerce," (n.d. February 1843), *BMAddMSS* 43144; and *Journal de St. Pétersbourg* (28 January 1843).
42. "Circular," *ibid.*
43. Martens, *Recueil*, vol. 12: 210.

which he attacked free trade with the obvious argument that Russia must be independent and that it was precisely the backwardness of her industries that made barriers to Western manufactures essential.

Kankrin had never been quick to recognize the possibility of Russian industrialization, but his position was the logical antecedent of those who did. The overriding concern was less for private interests and industrial capitalism, than for economic independence, expressed, for example, in the strong desire not to encourage further foreign influence and investment at Russian expense. There were certainly many officials who believed that the Russian economy was essentially agrarian, and this was to a certain extent true of Kankrin himself, but the "Slavophiles" and the "Westernizers" in the government had one large thing in common: they were nationalists. They wanted no part of "cosmopolitical economy" with Russian dependence on Britain. Power went with autonomy. As the architect of Russia's first great industrialization drive, Minister of Finance Sergei Witte, observed: "The experience of all peoples clearly shows that only the economically independent countries are fully able to assert their political power."[44] For those who were keenly sensitive to the British challenge, Nesselrode's complacent Anglophilism and insistence on the status quo and the quest for free trade merely gave Britain added advantages.

"The English now triumph in Asia," Paskevich wrote to Chernyshev at the end of 1843, noting that they were opening China "to their commerce and industry," and that they had "reestablished the honor of British arms in India" and were "consolidating their dominion over these vast possessions."[45] The years 1843–1844 witnessed the quiet resumption of the policies that eventually led to the conquest of the Caucasus, Khiva, and other Asian territories, while the old proponents of these policies, such as Perovskii and Murav'ev, returned to key roles in central planning. The era of the buffer theory was over.

But Nesselrode's exertions in behalf of freer trade did not end in 1843. He turned next to Prussia and Austria, and his

---

44. T. H. Von Laue, *Sergei Witte and the Industrialization of Russia* (New York, 1963), 2.
45. Paskevich to Chernyshev (28 November 1843), *SIRIO*, vol. 122: 494–495.

actions, no less futile, suggest that he had hoped for a pattern of accessions from which an economic community would emerge.

He believed that Prussia and Austria would sign treaties with Britain designed "to make unequal rights disappear," and that Russia, by the agreements he intended to conclude with them, would join a community embracing "all of their possessions."[46] It would include Poland, Finland, India, and the rest of the British Empire, Austria-Hungary, and the states of the Zollverein. Soon after the treaty with Britain, he drafted a new proposal for the reduction of duties on imports from Prussia—"the solution," he said, "on which I pin all of my hopes."[47] Unfortunately his hopes were not shared by Kankrin or Nicholas I.[48] "Given this situation," he wrote to Meyendorff concerning Kankrin's opposition in particular, "we are not going to have an easy time."[49] If they made headway with Prussia, Kankrin would still block formal agreement because "to extend tariff reductions to the Zollverein without also according them to England truly would be impossible" given the precedent set by the treaty of 1843. It was the overall idea that Kankrin resisted. "All I want is for him to take the rates to be accorded to Prussia and extend them to the whole world," Nesselrode confided to Meyendorff. "But he argues against me that this would be detrimental to our manufactures and cause too great a loss of revenues from customs duties."[50]

When the project fell through, Nesselrode turned to Austria. Tengoborskii was sent to Vienna, where prospects were enhanced by the successful conclusion of the Danube convention and a pioneering international postal convention in February 1843. But again obstacles cropped up on the Russian side. When he left Petersburg, Tengoborskii was not accredited to conclude a treaty, only to conduct talks on trade, navigation on the Danube, smuggling, and other related matters, and when he had won Austria

46. Nesselrode to Meyendorff (14 January 1843), *Lettres et papiers*, vol. 8: 196.
47. Nesselrode to Meyendorff (30 December 1843). *Lettres et papiers*, vol. 8: 191.
48. "Mais je dois vous prévenir que ni l'Empereur ni Cancrine n'entendent encore de cette oreille," *ibid.*
49. Nesselrode to Meyendorff (30 March 1843), *Lettres et papiers*, vol. 8: 204.
50. *Ibid.*, 204–205.

over to a fairly comprehensive agreement, permission to sign it did not come through from Petersburg. He himself returned to plead the case, but the Tsar made few concessions, and when he later managed to conclude the limited, inconsequential treaty of July 20, 1845, he complained to his Austrian colleagues about Russia's "system of "prohibitions"—her "wall of China." "It is this which makes any commercial negotiation between us very difficult, not to say impossible," he said.[51]

Although Kankrin's ministry came to an end in 1844, there was little hope for a relaxation of the trade policy that had impaired Nesselrode's diplomacy. The resurgence of economic nationalism was evident in the recommendations submitted by the committee on trade of 1844. Whereas Nesselrode had participated in the meetings of the Vasil'chikov committee to examine alternatives to Kankrin's policy in 1840–1842, he was not included on the committee of 1844, which was dominated by his old opponents—Orlov, Menshikov, and L. A. Perovskii. It proposed measures favorable to exports, especially of grain from the southern provinces, and severe restrictions on the import of manufactures. As reported to Aberdeen, it signified a reaction against the flow of British and other Western manufactures into Russia while exports declined, and, added to the effects of this imbalance, a drain of capital from foreign investments in Russia, "in many instances by Englishmen in manufacturing establishments."[52] Of course Nesselrode had seen the necessity for equilibrium, as a precondition for freer commerce, but what the Orlov committee wanted was a favorable balance without dependence on Western manufactures. This was not necessarily a defense of private capital in Russia. The real thrust of their argument was carried by their principal concerns as ministers—state security, state finance, military power, domestic order. The relationship with Britain that Nesselrode advocated was one they felt their country could ill afford.

Dramatic events now betrayed Nesselrode's reversals to the Western powers and undercut his policy further. Nicholas I, undoubtedly under the influence of nationalistic advisers, but also giving in to longstanding personal inclinations, decided that the status quo could not be upheld and that Turkey should be divided

51. Martens, *Recueil*, vol. 4: 546.
52. Buchanan to Aberdeen (26 November 1844), *FO* 65/301.

among the great powers, mainly between Russia and Austria on the European side of the straits. Russia would obtain a cordon to the Bosphorus and a common border with Greece—a partial fulfillment of Pan-Slav ambitions, although Constantinople might be a neutral city governed by all of the interested powers. Here was the ghost of the plan Nesselrode had put down in the 1820s. Nicholas himself discussed the possibility with the Austrian minister in Petersburg before the end of 1843. But Metternich was not receptive. In February 1844, Orlov, now clearly the Tsar's chief confidant and companion, and soon to take charge of the Third Division—the inner rampart of national security—was sent to Vienna to overcome the resistance. But Metternich stood firm.[53]

This granted Nesselrode a reprieve, a chance to rally if he could. He felt it was most important for Russia to strengthen her ties with Britain and suggested that Nicholas should visit London. Beyond the negative British reaction to the proposals to Austria, there were signs that Britain was pulling away from Russia and, after Queen Victoria's visit with Louis Philippe at Eu, returning to an alliance with France. The Tsar remained undecided for some time, and before he made up his mind the British became aware that he might go to Sevastopol instead, to be on hand for a new offensive in the Caucasus. "Count Nesselrode is most anxious that the Emperor should go to England, and will do all he can to promote the journey," Bloomfield reported to Aberdeen.[54]

Nicholas finally decided to follow Nesselrode's advice—to a certain extent. He would make the pilgrimage to London. He wished to impress the British with his integrity and forthright honesty and sound them out on the subject of a partition. Orlov would accompany him as his aide.

Nicholas and Orlov spent one week in England, beginning on Saturday June 1, 1844. Their activities were mainly social, designed to leave a favorable impression not only with the Queen and members of the government, but with the public as well. It turned out to be one of the more spectacular of history's ineffectual gestures. On Sunday, after an Orthodox service, Nicholas was received by Queen Victoria in the great hall at Buckingham Palace. The whirl of appearances and formalities began on Monday with a tour of London, and for the rest of the week, "wherever

53. Cf. G. H. Bolsover, "Nicholas I and the Partition of Turkey."
54. Bloomfield to Aberdeen (2 April 1844), *BMAddMSS* 43144.

he moved he was followed by a host of the fair and fashionable. The showy equippages of the nobility were in perpetual motion. . . . The streets were a levy *en masse.* . . . And Buckingham Palace, with its guards, cavalcades, musterings of the multitude, and thundering of brass bands, seemed to be the focus of a national revolution"[55] There was a train ride to Windsor, two appearances at Ascot, a military parade, and finally on Saturday a déjeuner in a salon decorated as a Turkish tent, an appearance at the opera with the Queen, and the royal leave-taking. On Sunday Nicholas departed aboard the steamer *Black Eagle,* to the roar of cannon from the batteries along the Thames.

There was little time for serious diplomacy. Nicholas and Orlov visited briefly with Peel on Monday afternoon, and that evening held the first of several superficial discussions of the Eastern Question with Peel, Aberdeen, and Wellington. Nicholas was candid. "In Russia there are two views of Turkey," he said. "Turkey must fall to pieces. . . . Nesselrode denies this, but I for my part am fully convinced of it. We cannot preserve her existence no matter how hard we try."[56] His motives were transparent. He spoke ill of France and maligned Louis Philippe, probing for sympathy. Russia was determined to have her share of the pieces when Turkey crumbled, and Britain would be more likely to condone a partition, "à l'amicable," if she were at loggerheads with France.

Nesselrode had rescued Nicholas from gross blunders on other occasions, but this time it would be more difficult. He went to England himself in August, and remained there until October. In discussions with Peel and Aberdeen he wisely took the position that he had come merely to clarify the Tsar's attitude: whatever happened, and whatever the differences between himself and Nicholas I, Russia would respect Turkish independence and strive to uphold the status quo as long as possible; she would not act without consulting Britain first. He also warned Peel that there was, as Peel related it afterward, "a powerful party in Russia" which preferred "a French alliance" and held that "Russia and England must ultimately, and at no remote period, come into

55. "The Week of an Emperor," *Blackwood's Edinburgh Magazine* (1844), vol. 56: 127.
56. Tatishchev, *Vneshniaia politika*, 588.

hostile contact."⁵⁷ "The general feeling of the Great Russian Party on foreign policy is not friendly to England," Bloomfield reported to Aberdeen during Nesselrode's visit. Were it not for "the Emperor's personal feelings toward the Queen and Her Majesty's Government, and the known sentiments of the Russian Minister of Foreign Affairs, we might be expected to see a change in the intimate relations which are established."⁵⁸

But the change was already taking place. It was obvious that the Tsar no longer shared his minister's views. Nesselrode stood alone. If the British government gave credence to the Tsar's statements regarding Turkey and his thinly disguised desire to drive a wedge between Britain and France, then they had to discount Nesselrode's words that "on the vital point regarding the integrity of the Ottoman Empire, the Russian Court is in accord with the courts of London and the Tuileries."⁵⁹ They could not accept Nesselrode's obvious wish to promote good relations between the liberal powers as official policy, although they may have preferred to. The French government, too, was more favorable to Nesselrode's policy than to any Russian alliance that Orlov and the nationalists might promote. "Nesselrode has made a very good impression in England," Barante commented. "Our policy and, moreover, our political ministrations would proceed piteously without him."⁶⁰

England gave Nesselrode no cause for disappointment. The Englishmen he met, above all Peel, measured up to his expectations. The country pleased and fascinated him. He rode the railroads hither and thither, to Brighton where he stayed awhile, and north into the country, expressing a desire to see Scotland, although the extent of his journey remains unknown. He visited the Botanical Gardens and made the acquaintance of English horticulturalists. He attended the opera and other musical events.

57. C. S. Parker, ed., *Sir Robert Peel from his Private Papers* (London, 1899), vol. 3: 261–262.
58. Bloomfield to Aberdeen (21 September 1844), in V. J. Puryear, *England, Russia, and the Straits Question, 1844–1856* (Berkeley, 1931), Appendix C: 436.
59. Nesselrode (n.d. July 1844), in M. Cyprien-Robert, "Du rôle de la diplomatie européene dans la question des frontièrs turko-grecques," *Revue des deux mondes* (1845), vol. 10: 804.
60. Barante, *Souvenirs*, vol. 7: 122.

It seems that he made himself comfortable, and felt at home. In fact, the length of his visit is difficult to explain, unless it was prolonged by simple enjoyment, since Brunnow, at the embassy, took care of diplomatic affairs, and there were no negotiations —(his talks with Peel and various members of his Cabinet were strictly informal).

When at last Nesselrode returned to Petersburg, he learned that things had not run smoothly in his absence. Bloomfield was agitated by an impression that Russia wished to foment war between Britain and France, and Nesselrode immediately did what Nicholas and Orlov had neglected to do in his absence—he reassured the British minister that this was untrue.

Change was now very much in the wind. In October, Louis Philippe paid a visit to England and was fêted in grand style, even grander than for the Tsar of All the Russias. As an article in the *Revue des deux mondes* stated afterward, "all reserve disappeared and the Entente Cordiale made its entry into the world with clamor and ceremony."[61] The liberal powers were again allies. Without Austrian support, Russia was isolated on the issues that mattered. A delicate, perhaps illusory balance was giving way to bipolarity. It was not the Ottoman Empire, but the European system that was crumbling.

Nesselrode tried to counteract the dénouement with a promise, having no force whatsoever as a treaty, to consult Britain before Russia made any move in the Near East. This promise was contained in what was later known as the "Nesselrode Memorandum," outlined in consultation with Peel and Aberdeen, which he sent to Aberdeen as "the most certain guide for the course we would follow in common accord." Bipartisan cooperation was vital: "Independent action by the two powers could only result in misfortune," he said, whereas "in concert . . . it is to be hoped that the peace of Europe will be maintained even in the midst of trying conditions."[62] Aberdeen acknowledged that he was in agreement with the points made in the memorandum and expressed cordial appreciation of Nesselrode's exertions. "Your

61. M. P. Duvergier de Hauranne, "Des rapports actuels de la France avec l'Angleterre et du rétablissement d'alliance," *Revue des deux mondes* (1845), vol. 10: 1039.
62. From the copy of the memorandum in Brunnow to Aberdeen (26 November 1844), *BMAddMSS* 43144. For an English translation, cf. Puryear, *England, Russia and the Straits Question*, Appendix E.

visit to this country gave me the most sincere pleasure," he wrote, "and was attended with no other cause of regret, than that after so long a separation, I should not have been able to enjoy more of your society." [63]

But the rapprochement was over, and Nesselrode's earlier statement that the two powers shared great commercial interests and foremost leadership of the community would have had a hollow echo. If independent action had not been a real possibility, there would have been no reason to compose the "Nesselrode Memorandum," and no reason for Nesselrode to fear that the treaty of 1841 and the European concert would be swept aside by a crisis. While there was peace, there was hope; but Nesselrode realized that although his policy had enabled Russia to avoid war, it had not succeeded in its larger goals.

63. Aberdeen to Nesselrode (21 January 1845), *BMAddMSS* 43144.

Bibliography

Archives

Archival documentation is given in the footnotes. The most valuable collections for the subject proved to be those of the Foreign Office archives at the Public Record Office, and the private papers of various statesmen held at the British Museum. The numerous documents by Nesselrode, Brunnow, and Pozzo di Borgo in the British archives comprise the most important collections of Russian documents for the rapprochement available. While other major archival collections were consulted in the course of research, even those at Paris and Vienna proved to be sparse and peripheral in comparison with those at London. Since research focused on Russian diplomacy, specifically Nesselrode's role in relations with Britain, it was necessary to rely on published documents from Russian archives. This was a rewarding course, because many sources had not been fully utilized before. But the promise of the Soviet holdings remains to be explored.

Published Sources

The following selection of published documents and monographs is offered as a guide to materials generally available. References to specific documents and to monographs of limited relevance not listed below are presented in the footnotes. The reader is cautioned that objectivity was not necessarily a criterion in the selection of historical works, and that many are introduced because they represent different interpretations and the strong positions which formerly fed debate not only among historians but policy-makers as well.

Anonymous works are listed first.

Documents and Monographs Written Before 1857

Avènement de l'empereur Alexandre II. Le Passé. L'Avenir. Le Czar Nicolas, sa vie et sa mort, par un diplomate (Brussels, 1855).

Blackwood's Edinburgh Magazine. "Commercial Policy—Russia" (1843), vol. 53: 807–826.

Foreign Quarterly Review. "Russian Actual Policy: Persia, Hindostan, and Central Asia" (1839), vol. 23: 161–212.

Illustrated London News. "Count Charles Robert Nesselrode," (24 August 1844), 117–118.

Nouveau suppléments au Recueil, G. F. Martens, ed. "Mèmoire sur les moyens . . . pour rompre l'alliance entre la France et l'Angleterre, presénté au cabinet de St. Pétersbourg" (n.d. April 1834), vol. 27 (3): 743–750.

Parliamentary Papers. "Quantities and value of principal articles imported into and exported from" Russia (1840), vol. 55; (1841), vol. 56.

Quarterly Review. "Foreign Policy" (1840), vol. 67: 253–302. "Reconstruction of the Federative Policy of Europe," (1828), vol. 38: 172–192.

La Russie et l'équilibre européen (2nd ed., Paris, 1854).

Zhurnal manufaktur i torgovli. "O nekotorykh stat'iakh torgovli v Persii" (1843), vol. 3, no. 8: 283–296.

Ancillon, J. P. F. *Du Juste milieu, ou du rapprochement des extrêmes dans les opinions* (Brussels, 1837), 2 vols.

———. *Tableau des révolutions du système politique de l'Europe depuis la fin du quinzième siècle* (revised edition, Paris, 1823), 4 vols. The first edition was published in Berlin, 1803–1805.

Anguetil, T. *Réponse d'un soldat à un diplomate, sur la question d'Orient* (Brussels, 1854). An answer to E. P. Brunnow, *La Guerre d'Orient, ses causes et ses conséquences* (Brussels, n.d.).

Arnoul, H. *Réponse à un député sur le voyage de S.M. l'empereur Nicolas* (Paris, 1844).

Aubernon, N. J. *Considérations historiques et politiques sur la Russie, l'Autriche et la Prusse, et sur les rapports de ces trois puissances avec la France et les autres États de l'Europe* (Paris, 1827).

Barante, Brugière de, A. G. P., Baron. *Notes sur la Russie 1835–1840, par M. le baron de Barante* (Paris, 1875).

———. C. de Barante, ed. *Souvenirs du baron de Barante, de l'Académie française 1782–1866* (Paris, 1890–1901), 8 vols.

Barrault, E. *Guerre ou paix en Orient* (Paris, 1836).

Bell, J. S. *Journal of a Residence in Circassia, during the years 1837, 1838, and 1839* (London, 1840), 2 vols.

Beznosikov, K. S. "Russkii chelovek," *Russkii arkhiv* (1884), vol. 2: 464–477.

Brunnow, E. P. (F.I.) "Aperçu des transactions politiques du Cabinet de Russie," (1838), *SIRIO*, vol. 31: 197–416.

———. "Considérations générales qui servent de base à notre politique 1838," in H. von Treitschke, *Deutsche Geschichte im Neunzehnten Jahrhundert* (Leipzig, 1927), vol. 5: 745–746.

———. *Projet de code civil pour la Bessarabie, 1824–1825* (St. Petersburg, 1914).

———. *La Guerre d'Orient, ses causes et ses conséquences* (Brussels, n.d.). The date of publication was 1854.

Bushuev, S. K., ed. "Anglo-russkii intsident so shkunoi 'Viksen' (1836–1837 gg.)," *Krasnyi arkhiv* (1940), vol. 102: 189–238.

Carné, L. de. "De l'Équilibre européen," *Revue des deux mondes* (1840), vol. 24: 476–480.

Chernyshev, A. I. "Vsepoddanneishii doklad grafa Chernysheva—imperatora Nikolaia I," *SIRIO* (St. Petersburg, 1867–1917), vol. 122: 304–307. In the same volume, "Istoricheskoe obozrenie voennosykhoputnago upravleniia s 1825 po 1850 god.," vol. 98: 299–477.

Cobden, R. *Russia, By a Manchester Manufacturer* (London, 1836).

Custine, A. L. L., Marquis de. *La Russie en 1839* (2nd ed., revised, Paris, 1843), 4 vols.

Cyprien-Robert, M. "Du Rôle de la diplomatie européene dans la question des frontières turko-grecques," *Revue des deux mondes* (1845), vol. 10: 790–809.

Dal, V. I. "Pis'ma k druziam iz pokhoda v Khivu," *Russkii arkhiv* (1867), vol. 1: 402–431, 606–639.

———. "Noveishiia izvestiia o Khive," *Syn Otechestva* (1839), vol. 12, e: 11–18.

Delcro-Dorcel, J. *Question d'Orient: Notice sur M. le comte de Nesselrode* (Paris, 1854).

Diuhamel, A. O. "Avtobiografiia Aleksandra Osipovicha Diuhamelia," *Russkii arkhiv* (1885), vol. 1: 179–217, 489–525; vol. 2: 82–126, 222–256, 371–427. Also published as *Avtobiografiia Aleksandra Osipovicha Diuhamelia* (Moscow, 1885).

Divov, P. G. "1838 god v Petersburge. (Po dnevniku P.G. Divova)," *Russkaia starina* (1902), vol. 111: 635–650.

Duvergier de Hauranne, M. P. de. *De la Convention de 13 juillet et de la situation actuelle de la France* (Paris, 1841).

———. "Des Rapports actuels de la France avec l'Angleterre et du rétablissement d'alliance," *Revue des deux mondes* (1845), vol. 10: 1037–1080.

Ficquelmont, K. L. *Lord Palmerston, l'Angleterre et le continent* (Paris, 1852), 2 vols.

———. *Pensées et réflections morales et politiques* (Paris, 1859).

————. *La Politique de la Russie et les principautés danubiennes* (Paris, 1854).

Flandin, J. B. *Aux armes! Guerre aux Puissances signataires du traité du 15 juillet dernier ou mémoire adressé au roi et aux ministres* (Paris, 1840).

Fonton, F. de. *La Russie dans l'Asie Mineure ou campagnes du meréchal Paskevitch en 1828 et 1829* (Paris, 1840). Fonton served as a diplomat under Nesselrode. He has been suggested as a possible author of *Entretiens politiques sur la France et la Russie* (1842). See M. Cadot, "Qui est l'auteur . . . ?" *Revue d'histoire moderne et contemporaine* (January–March, 1961), vol. 8: 61–65.

Fournier, M. *Russie, Allemagne et France. Révélations sur la politique russe, d'après les notes d'un vieux diplomate* (Paris, 1844).

Galkin, M., ed. "K istorii osvobozhdeniia russkikh plennykh iz Khivu (Iz arkhiva Orenburgskoi uchenoi arkhivnoi komissii)," *Russkii arkhiv* (1914), vol. 3: 95–117.

Ganesco, G. *Diplomatie et nationalité* (Paris, 1856).

Gentz, F. von. *Fragmente aus der neusten Geschichte des politischen Gleichgewichts in Europa* (St. Petersburg, 1806).

————. *Mémoires et lettres inédites du chevalier de Gentz* (Stuttgart, 1841).

————. *On the State of Europe Before and After the French Revolution, Being an Answer to the Work entitled "De l'état de la France à la fin de l'an VII" by Citizen Hauterive, 4th edition* (London, 1803). The first edition, *Von dem politischen Zustande von Europa vor und nach der französischen Revolution*, was published in Berlin, 1801.

————. *Zur Geschichte der orientalischer Frage. Briefe aus dem Nachlasse F. Von Gentz, 1823–1829* (Vienna, 1877).

Goldman, *Europäische Pentarchie* (Leipzig, 1839).

Golovin, I. G. *Discours sur Pierre le Grand prononcé à l'Athénée, le 20 mai 1844* (Paris, 1844).

————. *La Russie sous Nicolas I* (Paris, 1845). Edition cited herein: *Russia Under the Autocrat Nicholas the First* (London, 1846; reprint, New York, 1970).

Golovkin, F. G. "Iz vospominanii grafa F. G. Golovkina; Nessel'rode," *Russkaia starina* (1907), vol. 130: 107–111.

Gorchakov, A. M. "Kniaz Aleksandr Mikhailovich Gorchakov v ego razskazakh iz proshlago," *Russkaia starina* (1883), vol. 40: 159–180.

Grech, N. I., *La Vérité sur le différend Turco-Russe* (Brussels, 1853).

Greville, C. F. *The Greville Memoirs* (London, 1885), 3 vols.

Grigorev, V. V. "Razbor sochineniia: Ocherki torgovli Rossii s Srednei Azei," in P. Nebol'sina, ed., *Otchety o XXV prisuzhdenii Demidovskikh nagrad* (St. Petersburg, 1856).

Guizot, F. "M. Guizot . . . au duc de Broglie . . . (Sur la notification à lui faite du traité du 15 juillet 1840)," in C. de Martens, *Le Guide diplomatique* (Leipzig, 1866), vol. 3: 218–225.

―――. *Mémoires pour servir à l'histoire de mon temps* (Paris, 1872), vol. 6.

Hagemeister, J. A., *Essai sur les ressources territoriales et commerciales de l'Asie occidentale* (n.p., 1839).

―――. *Der Europäische Handel in der Turkei und Persien* (Riga and Leipzig, 1839).

Haxthausen, A., *Studien über die innern Zustände, das Volksleben und insbesondere die ländlichen Einrichtungen Russlands* (Berlin, 1847–1852), 3 vols. An English translation is *The Russian Empire. Its People, Institutions, and Resources* (London, 1856).

Henningson, C. F., *Eastern Europe and the Emperor Nicholas* (London, 1846).

Janowski, J. H., *La politique oriento-méridionale du cabinet de Pétersbourg considérée dans son rapport avec la cause polonais* (Paris, 1836).

Jelavich, B., ed. *Russia and Greece During the Regency of King Othon 1832–1835* (Thessalonika, 1962). Includes more than twenty documents by Nesselrode.

Jouannin, J. M., *Statu quo d'Orient, revue des événements qui se sont passes en Turquie pendant l'année 1838* (Paris, 1839). Jouannin states that his purpose is "to prove that the status quo, if perpetuated, could only insure the final triumph of Russia," *ibid.*, 36.

Jouffroy. *Question d'Orient, par un cosmopolite* (Brussels, 1853).

Kankrin, E. F.; A. Keyserling, ed. *Aus den Reisetagebüchern des Grafen Georg Kankrin, ehemaligen kaiserlich russischen Finanzministers, aus den Jahren 1840–1845* (Braunschweig, 1865), 2 vols.

Khomiakov, A. S. "Zametka . . . ob Anglii i ob Angliiskom vospitanii," *Russkii arkhiv* (1881), vol. 2: 38–40.

Kohl, J. G. *Russia and the Russians in 1842* (Philadelphia, 1843). Of interest for its attempt to deal with the role of the Germans.

Kosyrev, E. N. "Pokhod v Khivu v 1839 godu (Iz zapisok uchastnika)," *Istoricheskii vestnik* (1898), vol. 73: 538–545.

Kraemer, M. *De l'intérêt du Cabinet de Vienne et de Berlin dans la question d'Orient* (Paris, 1840).

Krasinski, V. *Panslavism and Germanism* (London, 1848).

Lefrançois, A. J. *De l'alliance franco-russe, considérée comme resultat des affaires d'Orient* (Nantes, 1841).

Lemoinne, J. "Les Anglais et les Russes dans le Caboul," *Revue des deux mondes* (1842), vol. 46: 1003–1034.

Loève-Veimars, F. A. "Des rapports de la France avec les grands et les petits états de l'Europe. I. De la Russie," *Revue des deux mondes* (1837), vol. 11: 185–236.

McNeill, J. *Progress and Present Position of Russia in the East* (London, 1836).

Marchant-Duroc, A. *Véritable but du voyage de l'Empereur de Russie à Londres* (Bordeaux, 1844).

Martens, F. F., ed. *Recueil des Traités et conventions*, etc. (St. Petersburg, 1894–1909), 15 vols.

Martens, G. F., ed. *Nouveau Recueil des principaux Traités*, etc. (Göttingen, 1817–1842), 17 vols., and *Nouveaux suppléments au Recueil* (Göttingen, 1839–1842), 3 vols.

Meyendorff, P. K. von; O. Hötzsch, ed. *Peter von Meyendorff: ein russischer Diplomat an den Höfen von Berlin und Wien* (Berlin, 1923), 3 vols.

Miliutin, D. A., ed. *Opisanie voennykh deistvii 1839 goda v severnom Dagestane* (St. Petersburg, 1850).

Mirkovich, F. Ia., ed., "Imperator Nikolai i Korol Fridrikh—Vil'gelm IV v 1840 g. Iz zapisok," *Russkaia starina* (1886), vol. 51: 305–334.

Modestov, N., ed., "K istorii osvobozhdeniia russkikh plennykh," *Russkii arkhiv* (1914), vol. 3: 96–119; (1915), vol. 1: 31–48, vol. 2: 276–301.

Nesselrode, K. R.; A. D. Nesselrode, ed. *Lettres et papiers du chancelier comte de Nesselrode, 1760–1856* (Paris, 1904–1912), 11 vols. A compilation of the important documents held in the family Archive de Nesselrode, *MAE*. The notes exchanged with Nicholas I, vol. 11, and the correspondence with Meyendorff, vol. 8, hold special interest for the period of the rapprochement. The "Autobiographie," vol. 2, was published also in *Russkii vestnik* (1865), vol. 66: 519–568; and in *Russkii arkhiv* (1905), vol. 43: 491–534; it appeared in a German translation, *Selbstbiographie* (Berlin, 1866). Nesselrode's general report on the twenty-fifth anniversary of the reign in 1850, in vol. 10 of the *Lettres et papiers*, is found also in *SIRIO*, vol. 98: 287–298; and H. von Treitschke, *Deutsche Geschichte im Neunzehnten Jahrhundert* (Leipzig, 1927), vol. 5: 740–744.

———. Documents related to a wide range of events during Nesselrode's ministry are found in several main collections and in other publications. Cf. Martens, *Recueil*, 15 vols.; G. F. Martens, *Nouveau Recueil*, 17 vols., and *Nouveaux suppléments au Recueil*, 3 vols.; von Hötzsch, ed., *Peter von Meyendorff*, 3 vols.; Pozzo di Borgo, *Correspondance diplomatique*, 2 vols. Unfortunately no collection of Nesselrode's correspondence with Brunnow has come to light, and for this most important line of communication we must rely on the dispatches in British archives, which comprise a small portion of the total, and on fragments reproduced by Tatishchev, Goriainov, Martens, and others, and in the selections treating specific aspects of the Eastern Question given below. Documents by Nesselrode also are scattered through the published papers of foreign statesmen such as Palmerston, Metternich, and Guizot, less frequently in those of Russians in other branches of government, such as Paskevich, and in the Russian periodical series. Noteworthy in the last category are: "Zashchita politiki Rossii i polozheniia priniatago eiu v Evrope" (the original unsigned but attributed to Nesselrode by the editor), *Russkaia starina* (1873), vol. 8: 800–805; and D. K. Nesselrode, "Graf Kapodistriia i graf K. V. Nessel'rode 1820–1821 gg.," *Russkaia starina* (1884), vol. 41: 219–223.

―――. Documents related to the Eastern Question in the most prominent collections for the period 1826–1856 comprise overwhelming evidence of Nesselrode's leading role as proponent of a policy which was highly conciliatory and "European." Martens, *Recueil*, vol. 12; Wellington, *Despatches, Correspondence and Memoranda*, vol. 3; B. Jelavich, ed., *Russia and Greece During the Regency of King Othon*; Murav'ev, *Russkie na Bosfore*, appendices; Mosely, *Russian Diplomacy*, appendices; Bushuev, ed., "Anglo-Russkii intsident;" *Parliamentary Papers: Correspondence Relative to the Affairs of the Levant* (for 1839–1844); Goriainov, "O tainom soglashenii po delam Vostoka;" Puryear, *England, Russia, and the Straits*, appendices; N. Kapterev, *Pravoslavnyi palestinskii sbornik* (St. Petersburg, 1898), vol. 15: 678–681; Zainchkovskii, *Vostochnaia voina*, appendices; "K istorii Parizhskago mira 1856 g.," *Krasnyi arkhiv* (1936), vol. 75: 10–61.

―――. The *Journal de St. Pétersbourg*. As Nesselrode's responsibility and a forum for public diplomacy, an important source. Noteworthy in relation to diplomacy are the explanation of the *Vixen's* capture (31 December 1836); the announcement of the treaty on trade and navigation with Britain (28 January 1843 and 6 April 1843); and the explanation of Russia's attitude to Europe in 1848 (19 March 1848). Of special interest for the views presented are: "Notice sur l'état de la ville de Moscou en 1840" (31 May 1842), special supplement; "Mouvement du commerce extérieur de la Russie en 1841" (17 October 1842), special supplement; and "Coup d'oeil sur la Bourse et les magasins de St. Pétersbourg" (22 April 1843), special supplement.

Parker, C. S., ed. *Sir Robert Peel from his Private Papers* (London, 1899), 3 vols.

Pelchinskii, V. S. *La Russie en 1844 . . . par un homme d'état russe* (Paris and Leipzig, 1845).

Perovskii, V. A. "K bumagam grafa V.A. Perovskago ego prikaz pred vystupleniem v Khivinskii pokhod i zametki na ego pis'ma," M. N. Galkin-Vraskii, ed., *Russkii arkhiv* (1879), vol. 3: 242–243.

Pogodin, M. P. *Istoriko-politicheskie pis'ma i zapiski v gody Krymskoi voiny* (Moscow, 1874), especially "O russkoi politike na budushchee vremia," 231–244.

Polenov, V. A. "Obozrenie prezhniago i nyneshniago sostoianiia Ministerstva Inostrannykh del," (1837), *SIRIO* (St. Petersburg, 1867–1917), vol. 31: 163–195.

Pozzo di Borgo, C. *Correspondance diplomatique du comte Pozzo di Borgo, ambassadeur de Russie en France et du comte de Nesselrode* (Paris, 1890), 2 vols.

Quinet, E. *1815 et 1840* (Paris, 1840).

Reid, S. J. *Life and Letters of the First Earl of Durham, 1792–1840* (London, New York and Bombay, 1906), 2 vols.

Richemont, *De la question d'Orient et du traité de Londres du 15 juillet 1840* (Paris, 1840).

Schilder, N. K., ed. "Adrianopol'skii mir 1829 goda. Iz perepiski grafa Dibicha," *Drevniaia i novaia Rossiia* (1879), vol. 15, no. 3: 533–585; (1880), vol. 16, no. 3: 477–485.

Seymour, H. D., *The Black Sea and the Sea of Azof* (London, 1855).

Shakespear, Sir R. "A Personal Narrative of a Journey from Heraut to Orenburg," *Blackwood's Edinburg Magazine* (1842), vol. 51: 691–720.

Simonich, I. O. *Vospominaniia polnomochnogo ministra 1832–1838 gg.* (Moscow, 1967).

Strachan, P. L. *On the Oriental Question and the Balance of Power* (Paris, 1841).

Tengoborskii, L. *Encore quelques mots sur la question d'Orient* (Brussels, 1854).

————. *Études sur les forces productives de Russie* (Paris, 1852–1854), 4 vols. An English edition is *Commentaries on the Productive Forces of Russia* (London, 1855–1856), 2 vols.

————. *Des finances et du crédit de l'Autriche, de sa dette, de ses ressources financières et de son système d'imposition: avec quelques rapprochement entre ce pays, la Prusse et la France* (Paris, 1843), 2 vols.

———. *De la politique anglo-française dans la question d'Orient* (Brussels, 1854).

Thiers, A. "Discours sur la question d'Orient" (25 & 27 November 1840), *Discours parlementaires de M. Thiers* (Paris, 1879–1889), vol. 5: 149–297.

Thomas, A. "Négociations de l'Angleterre et de la Russie au sujet de la Perse et de l'Afghanistan," *Revue des deux mondes* (1845), vol. 57: 773–828.

Tolstoi, Ia. N. *Lettre d'un Russe à un journaliste français sur les diatribes de la presse anti-russe* (Paris, 1844). Tolstoi was a proponent of Russian alignment with France. He was stationed in Paris by S. S. Uvarov for the Ministry of Education.

Tyutchev, F. I. "Graf K. V. Nessel'rode" (1850), *Polnoe sobranie stikhotvorenii* (Leningrad, 1939), 93.

———. "Na novy 1855 god," *Russkii arkhiv* (1867), 1638.

———. "Rossiia i Germaniia" (1844), *Russkii arkhiv* (1873), vol. 2: 1994–2042.

Urquhart, D. *An Appeal Against Faction . . . To which is Added an Analysis of Count Nesselrode's Despatch of the 20th. Oct. 1838* (London, 1843).

———. *Diplomatic Transactions in Central Asia from 1834 to 1839* (London, 1841).

———. ed., *The Portfolio. State Papers Illustrative of the History of Our Times* (London, 1836), 2 vols.

Vaillant, J. A. *Réponse à la lettre de M. de Nesselrode, en date du 12 juin 1854* (Paris, 1855).

Vigel, F. F. *La Russie envahie par les allemands* (Paris and Leipzig, 1844).

———. "Moskva i Petersburg," *Russkii arkhiv* (1893), vol. 2: 566–584.

Wellington, Duke of. *Despatches, Correspondence, and Memoranda* (London, 1868), vol. 3.

Wiesner, A. *Russisch-politische Arithmetik* (n.p., 1844).

Wilbraham, R. *Travels in the Trans-Caucasian Provinces of Russia . . . in the Autumn and Winter of 1837* (London, 1839).

Zakharin, I. N. (pseud. "Iakunin"). "Posol'stvo v Khivu v 1842 godu (Po razyskazam i zapiskam ochevidtsa)," *Istoricheskii vestnik* (1894), vol. 56: 523–537.

Zhukovskii, V. A. "Russkaia i Angliiskaia politika. Pis'mo V.A. Zhukovskago k kniaziu Varshavskomu, grafu I. F. Paskevichu-Erivanskomu," *Russkii arkhiv* (1878), vol. 2: 426–436.

Sources Written After 1856

Istoricheskii vestnik. "Arkhiv grafa Nessel'rode ot 1819 do 1839 g."
(1909), vol. 117: 707–713; "1840–1846 g." (1910), vol. 120:
1068–1081. "Fel'dmarshal Paskevich i diplomatiia v 1827–1829
godakh" (1892), vol. 4: 494–518, especially "Original'nost
Nessel'rodovskoi diplomatii," 507–510. "Vostochnaia politika
Imperatora Nikolaia I-go" (1891), vol. 46: 346–385.

Kolokol. "Russkie nemtsy i nemetskie russkie" (15 October 1859),
no. 54.

Ocherk istorii Ministerstva Inostrannykh del, 1802–1902 (St. Petersburg, 1902). The official history.

Russkii arkhiv. "Imperator Nikolai Pavlovich v Vene v 1835 godu"
(1882), vol. 1: 198–205. "Neskol'ko slov po povodu zapiski
gr. Nessel'roda" (1872), vol. 1: 343–350.

Russkii biograficheskii slovar. "Brunnow, Filipp Ivanovich," vol. 3:
371–384.

Russkii vestnik. "Rossiia i Avstriia v vostochnom voprose" (1878),
vol. 85: 122–149 (review of Martens, *Recueil*, vol. 5). "Rossiia
i Evropa na vostoke pred adrianopol'skim mirom" (1877), vol.
79: 105–148.

Abaza, V. A. "Vzgliad na revoliutsionnoe dvizhenie v Evrope s 1815
po. 1848 g.," *Russkii arkhiv* (1887), vol. 2: 82–109.

Baddeley, J. F. *The Russian Conquest of the Caucasus* (London,
1908).

Balfour, Lady F. *The Life of George, Fourth Earl of Aberdeen*
(London, 1922), 2 vols.

Bapst, E. *L'Empereur Nicolas I et la deuxième république française*
(Paris, 1898).

———. *Les origines de la guerre de Crimée* (Paris, 1912).

Bell, H. C. F. *Lord Palmerston* (London, 1936), 2 vols.

Bernhardi, T. *Geschichte Russlands und der europäischen Politik
in den Jahren 1814–1831* (Leipzig, 1863–1877), 3 vols.

Bertier de Sauvigny, G. de. *Metternich et son tèmps* (Paris, 1959).

———. "Sainte-Alliance et Alliance dans les conceptions de Metternich," *Revue historique* (April–June, 1960), 249–274.

Berzhe, A. P. "Aleksandr Sergeevich Griboedov. Deiatel'nost ego
kak diplomata 1827–1829," *Russkaia starina* (1874), vol. 11:
516–534.

———. "Samson-khan Makintsev i russkie begletsy v Persii, 1806–
1853 gg.," *Russkaia starina* (1876), vol. 15: 770–804.

Blackwell, W. L. *The Beginnings of Russian Industrialization, 1800–
1860* (Princeton, 1968).

Bled, V. du. "Le salon de madame Swetchine," *Cosmopolis* (1898), vol. 12: 406–424.

Bloomfield, Baroness G., *Reminiscences of Court and Diplomatic Life* (London, 1883).

Bolsover, G. H., "Aspects of Russian Foreign Policy, 1815–1914," R. Pares and A. J. P. Taylor, eds., *Essays Presented to Sir Louis Namier* (London, 1956), 320–356.

————. "David Urquhart and the Eastern Question, 1833–37; A Study in Publicity and Diplomacy," *The Journal of Modern History* (December 1936), vol. 8, no. 4: 444–467.

————. "Lord Ponsonby and the Eastern Question, 1833–1839," *Slavonic and East European Review* (July, 1934), vol. 13, no. 37: 98–118.

————. "Nicholas I and the Partition of Turkey," *Slavonic and East European Review* (December, 1948), vol. 27, no. 68: 115–145.

Boudou, A., S.J. *Le Saint-Siège et la Russie: Leurs relations diplomatiques au XIX siècle. 1814–1847* (Paris, 1922).

Bourquin, M. *Histoire de la Sainte Alliance* (Geneva, 1954).

Bulwer, H. L., *Life of Henry John Temple, Viscount Palmerston* (London, 1871–1874), 3 vols.

Bushuev, S. K., *Iz istorii vneshnepoliticheskikh otnoshenii v period prisoedineniia Kavkaza k Rossii* (Moscow, 1955).

Charlels-Roux, F., *Thiers et Méhémet-Ali: la grande crise orientale et européene de 1840–1841* (Paris, 1951).

Crawley, C. W. "Anglo-Russian Relations, 1815–1840," *Cambridge Historical Journal* (1929), vol. 3: 47–73.

Curtiss, J. S. *The Russian Army Under Nicholas I, 1825–1855* (Durham, 1965).

————. "Russian Diplomacy in the mid-19th century," *South Atlantic Quarterly* (Summer 1973), no. 72: 396–405.

Danevskii, V. P. *La Russie et l'Angleterre dans l'Asia centrale. Observations critique sur "La Russie et l'Angleterre dans l'Asia centrale," par F. Martens* (London, 1881).

Debidour, A. *Histoire diplomatique de l'Europe depuis l'ouverture du Congrès de Vienne jusqu'a a la clôture du Congrès de Berlin (1814–1878)* (Paris, 1891), 2 vols.

Eckhardt, J. *Aus der Petersburger Gesellschaft* (Leipzig, 1880).

Fadeev, A. V. *Doreformennaia Rossiia (1800–1861 gg.)* (Moscow, 1960).

Felkner, V. I. "Poezdka imperatora Nikolaia Pavlovicha v Stokgol'm v 1838 g.," *Russkaia starina* (1875), vol. 12: 160–173.

Filippov, M. M., "Rossiia i nemetskiia derzhavy v 1840–1860 godakh," *Istoricheskii vestnik* (1890), vol. 39: 374–405.

Firsov, N. N., "Otnosheniia Rossii i Anglii v tsarstvovanie imperatora Aleksandra I," *Drevniaia i novaia Rossiia* (1878), vol. 1, no. 3: 242–266.

Girardin, S.-M. "La Question d'Orient en 1840 et en 1862. Le Traité du 15 juillet 1840 et les *Mémoires* de M. Guizot," *Revue des deux mondes* (1862), vol. 41: 271–292.

Gash, N. *Sir Robert Peel: The Life of Sir Robert Peel after 1830* (London, 1972).

Gleason, J. H., *The Genesis of Russophobia in Great Britain* (Cambridge, Mass., 1950). Concentrates on the 1830s.

Golosov, D., and G. L. Ivanin. "Pokhod v Khivu 1839 godu. otriada russkikh voisk, pod nachal'stvom general-adiutanta Perovskago," *Voennyi sbornik* (1863), vol. 1: 3–72; vol. 2: 309–358; vol. 3: 3–71.

Gooch, G. P. "The Eastern Crisis of 1840," *Cambridge Historical Journal* (1923–1925), vol. 1: 170–177.

Goriainov, S. M. *Le Bosphore et les Dardanelles* (Paris, 1910).

————. "O tainom soglashenii po delam Vostoka, sostoiavshemsia v 1844 g. mezhdu Nikolaem I i velikobritanskim pravitel'stvom," *Izvestiia Ministerstva Inostrannykh del* (1912), vol. 3: 201–233.

Grabar, V. E. *Materialy k istorii literatury mezhdunarodnogo prava v Rossii, 1647–1917* (Moscow, 1958).

Graham, G. S. *Great Britain in the Indian Ocean. A Study of Maritime Enterprise 1810–1850* (Oxford, 1967).

————. *Peculiar Interlude. The Expansion of England in a Period of Peace 1815–1850* (Sydney, 1959).

————. *The Politics of Naval Supremacy: Studies in British Maritime Ascendancy* (Cambridge, 1965).

Grimm, A. T. von. *Alexandra Feodorowna, Kaiserin von Russlands* (Leipzig, 1866), 2 vols.

Grimsted, P. K. *The Foreign Ministers of Alexander I: Political Attitudes and the Conduct of Russian Diplomacy, 1801–1825* (Berkeley and Los Angeles, 1969).

Grunwald, C. de, *La Vie de Nicolas I* (Paris, 1946).

————. *Metternich* (London, 1953).

————. "Nesselrode et le 'gendarme de l'Europe,' " in *Trois siècles de diplomatie russe* (Paris, 1945), 173–197.

Grzhegorzhevskii, I. "Ocherk voennykh deistvii i sobytii na Kavkaze, 1835–1838 gg.," *Russkaia starina* (1876), vol. 15: 144–162.

Guichen, E. de. *La crise d'Orient de 1839 à 1841 et l'Europe* (Paris, 1921).

Guizot, F. "Le Roi Louis-Philippe et l'Empereur Nicolas," *Revue des deux mondes* (1861), vol. 31: 5–47.

————. *M. de Barante, a Memoir Biographical and Autobiographical* (London, 1867).

Gulick, E. V. *Europe's Classical Balance of Power* (Ithaca, 1955).

Hammen, O. J. "Free Europe versus Russia, 1830–1854," *Slavic Review* (1952), vol. 11, no. 1: 27–41.

Handelsman, M. *Czartoryski, Nicolas Ier et la Question du Proche Orient* (Paris, 1934).

Hasenclever, A. *Die Orientalische Frage in den Jahren 1838–41* (Leipzig, 1914).

Hurewitz, J. C. "Ottoman diplomacy and the European state system," *Middle East Journal* (Spring 1961), 141–152.

Hyde, H. M. *Princess Lieven* (London, 1938).

Ivanin, M. *Opisanie zimniago pokhoda v Khivu v 1839–1840 g.* (St. Petersburg, 1874).

Ivanov, N. P. *Khivinskaia ekspeditsiia 1839–1840 g.* (St. Petersburg, 1873).

Jelavich, B. *Russia and the Greek Revolution of 1843* (Munich, 1966).

Jomini, A. H. *Etude diplomatique sur la guerre de Crimée* (St. Petersburg, 1874), 2 vols. A Russian version with minor changes is "Rossiia i Evropa v epokhu Krymskoi voiny," *Vestnik Evropy* (1886), vol. 117: 657–724; vol. 18: 176–242, 655–734; vol. 19: 253–311, 543–595; vol. 120: 204–260, 658–714; vol. 121: 179–235, 550–619.

————. "Rol i znachenie Rossii v Evrope pered Krymskoi voinoi," *Nabliudatel* (December 1885), vol. 12: 77–112.

Kerner, R. J. "Russia's New Policy in the Near East after the Peace of Adrianople; Including the Text of the Protocol of 16 September, 1829," *Cambridge Historical Journal* (1937), vol. 5: 286–290.

Khalfin, N. A. "Britanskaia ekspansiia v Srednei Azii v 30–40–kh godakh XIX v. i missiia Richmonda Shekspira," *Istoriia SSSR* (1958), vol. 2: 103–112.

Kochubinskii, A. A. "Nashi dve politiki v slavianskom voprose," *Istoricheskii vestnik* (1881), vol. 5: 201–232, 455–486.

Korsh, V. "Diplomatiia i voina v vostochnom voprose," *Vestnik Evropy* (1879), vol. 75: 632–689.

————. "Rossiia i Angliia v srednei azii," *Vestnik Evropy* (1879), vol. 79: 732–753.

Kozhevnikov, F. I. *Russkoe gosudarstvo i mezhdunarodnoe pravo (do XX veka)* (Moscow, 1947).

Lamarche, H. *L'Europe et la Russie. Remarques sur le siège de Sebastopol et sur le Paix de Paris* (Paris, 1857).

Langer, W. L. *Political and Social Upheaval, 1832–1852* (New York, 1969).

Leffmann, B. *Gentz und Nesselrode. Ein Beitrag zur diplomatischen Geschichte des Jahres 1813* (Bonn, 1911).

Lobanov-Rostovsky, A. *Russia and Asia* (New York, 1933).

———. *Russia and Europe, 1825–1878* (Ann Arbor, 1954).

Lodyzhenskii, K. *Istorii russkago tamozhennago tarifa* (St. Petersburg, 1886).

Maggiolo, A. *Pozzo di Borgo, 1764–1842. Corse, France et Russie* (Paris, 1890).

Mann, G. *Secretary of Europe. The Life of Friedrich Gentz* (New Haven, 1946).

Marriott, J. A. R., *The Eastern Question* (4th ed., Oxford, 1940).

Martens, C. de. *Le Guide diplomatique. Précis des droits et des fonctions des agents diplomatiques et consulaires* (5th ed., Leipzig, 1866).

Martens, F. F. *Die russische Politik in der orientalischen Frage* (St. Petersburg, 1877). Published also as "Etude historique sur la politique Russe dans la question d'Orient," *Revue de droit international et de législation comparée* (1877), vol. 9: 49–77.

———. "Imperator Nikolai I i Koroleva Viktoriia. Istoricheskii ocherk," *Vestnik Evropy* (1896), vol. 182: 74–130.

———. *La Paix et la guerre* (St. Petersburg, 1892).

———. *La Russie et l'Angleterre au début de leurs relations réciproques* (Paris, 1891).

———. "La Russie et la France pendant la restauration," *Revue d'histoire diplomatique* (Paris, 1908), vol. 22: 161–248. Includes quotations from documents by Nesselrode not available elsewhere.

———. ed., *Recueil des Traités et conventions*, etc. (St. Petersburg, 1894–1909), 15 vols. (commentary by Martens).

———. "Rossiia i Angliia v tsarstvovanie Imperatora Nikolaia I," *Vestnik Evropy* (1898), vol. 189: 5–31; vol. 189, no. 2: 465–502.

———. *Russland und England in Central-Asien* (St. Petersburg, 1880).

———. *Sovremennoe mezhdunarodnoe pravo tsivilizovannykh narodov* (St. Petersburg, 1898, 1900), 4 vols. in 2.

Martin, K. B. *The Triumph of Lord Palmerston: A Study of Public Opinion in England Before the Crimean War* (London, 1963).

Mosely, P. E. *Russian Diplomacy and the Opening of the Eastern Question in 1838 and 1839* (Cambridge, Mass., 1934).

Murav'ev, N. N. *Russkie na Bosfore v 1833 godu* (Moscow, 1869).

Nesselrode, A. D. de. *L'Âme russe* (Paris, 1913).

Nikitin, S. A. "Russkaia politika na Balkanakh i nachalo Vostochnoi Voiny," *Voprosy istorii* (1946), no. 4: 3–29.

Nolte, F. *L'Europe militaire et diplomatique au XIX siècle (1815–1884)* (Paris, 1884), 4 vols.

Norris, J. A. *The First Afghan War, 1838–1842* (New York, 1967).

Petropulos, J. A., *Politics and Statecraft in the Kingdom of Greece, 1833–1843* (Princeton, 1968).

Photiades, C. de. *La Symphonie en blanc majeur. Marie Kalergis, née C-tesse Nesselrode* (Paris, 1924).

Pintner, W. M. *Russian Economic Policy Under Nicholas I* (Ithaca, 1967).

Pirenne, J. H. *La Sainte Alliance (1815–1848)* (Neuchatel, 1946–1949), 2 vols.

Pisarev, D. I. "Metternikh," *Sochineniia D.I. Pisareva: Pol'noe sobranie v shesti tomakh* (St. Petersburg, 1894–1913), vol. 1: 562–635.

Pol'etika, V. A. "Po povodu 'Ekonomicheskikh Provalov.' Pis'mo V.A. Pol'etika k V.A. Kokorevu," *Russkii arkhiv* (1887), vol. 8: 535–540.

Polferov, Ia. Ia. " 'Predatel' iz vremen grafa Perovskago," *Istoricheskii vestnik* (1905), vol. 100: 496–503.

Polievktov, M. A. "Nessel'rode, Karl Vasil'evich," *Russkii biograficheskii slovar*, vol. "N".

———. *Nikolai I, biografiia i obzor tsarstvovaniia* (Moscow, 1918).

Pouthas, C.-H. "La politique de Thiers pendant la crise orientale de 1840," *Revue historique* (1938), no. 182: 72–96.

Puryear, V. J. *England, Russia, and the Straits Question, 1844–1856* (Berkeley, 1931).

———. *International Economics and Diplomacy in the Near East: A Study of British Commercial Policy in the Levant 1834–1853* (Berkeley, 1935).

———. "Note on the British Fleet Episodes at the Dardanelles in 1849 and 1853," *France and the Levant* (Berkeley and Los Angeles, 1941), appendix.

Putiatin, N. V. "Adrianopl v 1829 godu," *Russkii arkhiv* (1878), vol. 2: 215–222.

Raeff, M. *Michael Speransky: Statesman of Imperial Russia 1772–1839* (The Hague, 1957).

———. "Les Slaves, les Allemands et les 'Lumières'," *Revue canadienne d'études slaves* (1967), vol. 1, no. 4: 521–551.

Riasanovsky, N. V. *Nicholas I and Official Nationality in Russia 1825–1855* (Berkeley and Los Angeles, 1959).

———. "Russia and Asia—Two Nineteenth-Century Views," *California Slavic Studies* (1960), vol. 1: 170–181.

———. *Russia and the West in the Teaching of the Slavophiles: A Study in Romantic Ideology* (Cambridge, Mass., 1952).

Rieben, H. *Prinzipiengrundlage und Diplomatie in Metternichs Europapolitik 1815–1848* (Aarau, 1942).

Rodkey, F. S. "Anglo-Russian Negotiations 1840–1841," *American Historical Review* (1931), vol. 36: 343–349.

———. *The Turko-Egyptian Question in the Relations of England, France and Russia 1832–1841* (Urbana, 1924).

Rohden, R. *Die klassische Diplomatie von Kaunitz bis Metternich* (Leipzig, 1939).

Schenk, H. G. *The Aftermath of the Napoleonic Wars: The Concert of Europe—An Experiment* (London, 1947).

Schiemann, T. *Geschichte Russlands unter Kaiser Nikolaus I* (Berlin, 1904–1914), 4 vols.

———. "Lettres et papiers du Chancelier Comte de Nesselrode 1760–1850" (review article), *Zeitschrift für osteuropäische Geschichte* (1911), vol. 1: 253–254.

———. "Russische-englische Beziehungen unter Kaiser Nikolaus I," *Zeitschrift für osteuropäische Geschichte* (1913), vol. 3: 485–498.

Schilder, N. K. *Imperator Aleksandr Pervyi, ego zhizn i tsarstvovanie* (St. Petersburg, 1904), 4 vols.

———. *Imperator Nikolai Pervyi, ego zhizn i tsarstvovanie* (St. Petersburg, 1903), 2 vols.

———. "Imperator Nikolai I i Vostochnyi vopros (1826–1830)," *Russkaia starina* (1900), vol. 10: 31–52, vol. 11: 237–255, vol. 12: 493–508; (1901), vol. 1: 27–46, vol. 2: 263–281, vol. 3: 497–516, vol. 4: 5–32.

———. "Nemets i frantsuz v zapiskakh svoikh o Rossii v 1839 g.," *Russkaia starina* (1886), vol. 51: 21–54.

———. "Rossiia v ee otnosheniiakh k Evrope v tsarstvovanie Imperatora Aleksandra I-go 1806–1815," *Russkaia starina* (1888), vol. 57: 269–320; (1889), vol. 61: 1–52; (1890), vol. 65: 143–221.

Schroeder, P. W. *Austria, Great Britain, and the Crimean War: The Destruction of the European Concert* (Ithaca and London, 1972).

Shumigorskii, E. S. "Odin iz revnostneishikh nasaditelei nemetskago zasil'ia v Rossii: Graf Karl Vasil'evich Nessel'rode," *Russkaia starina* (1915), vol. 161: 160–165.

Slonimskii, L. Z., "Nasha mezhdunarodnaia politika v nedalekom proshlom," *Vestnik Evropy* (1888), vol. 134: 320–353.

Solov'ev, S. M., "Epokha kongressov. IV," *Vestnik Evropy* (1867), vol. 4: 276–324.

————. *Imperator Aleksandr Pervyi: Politika. Diplomatiia.* (St. Petersburg, 1877).

————. "Potstso di Borgo i Frantsiia: Nachalo vtoroi chetverti XIX–go veka," *Vestnik Evropy* (1879), vol. 76: 5–81, vol. 77: 252–273.

————. "Rossiia, Avstriia i Angliia vo vremia dvizhenii 1848–1849 gg.," *Russkaia starina* (1877), vol. 20, 407–426.

————. "Vostochnyi vopros v 1827, 1828 i 1829 godakh," *Drevniaia i novaia Rossiia* (1877), no. 10: 105–119.

————. "Vostochnyi vopros 50 let nazad," *Drevniaia i novaia Rossiia* (1876), no. 2: 129–141.

Srbik, H. von. *Metternich, der Staatsmaan und der Mensch* (Munich, 1925), 2 vols.

Swain, J. E. *The Struggle for Control of the Mediterranean prior to 1848: A Study of Anglo-French Relations* (Philadelphia, 1933).

Tageev, B. "Perovskii, graf Vasilii Alekseevich," *Russkii biograficheskii slovar*, vol. 5: 530–540.

Tarle, E. V., *Krymskaia voina* (Moscow, 1950), 2 vols.

Tatishchev, S. S., *Diplomaticheskiia besedy o vneshnei politike Rossii. 1890* (St. Petersburg, 1898).

————. *Imperator Nikolai I i inostrannye dvory* (St. Petersburg, 1889).

————. *Iz proshlogo russkoi diplomatii. Istoricheskie issledovaniia i politicheskie stati* (St. Petersburg, 1890).

————. "Russkaia diplomatiia staraia i novaia," *Russkii vestnik* (1887), vol. 187: 276–339, 706–792.

————. *Vneshniaia politika Imperatora Nikolaia Pervago: vvedenie v istoriiu vneshnikh snoshenii Rossii v epokhu Sevastopol'skoi voiny* (St. Petersburg, 1887).

de Taube, M. "Études sur le développement historique du droit international dans l'Europe Orientale," *Academie de Droit International, Recueil des cours* (1926), vol. 1 (11 of the collection), 341–533, especially the conclusion: "La Russie nouvelle au sein de la communauté internationale européene (XVIII–XIX siècles)."

————. *La politique austro-russe dans la première moitié du XIX siècle et les origines du conflit actuel* (St. Petersburg, 1914, and Moscow, 1915).

Temperley, H. W. V. *England and the Near East. The Crimea* (London, 1936).

————. *The Foreign Policy of Canning, 1822–1827. England, the Neo-Holy Alliance and the New World* (London, 1925).

Terent'ev, M. A. *Rossiia i Angliia v bor'be za rynki* (St. Petersburg, 1876).

———. *Rossiia i Angliia v srednei Azii* (St. Petersburg, 1875).

Veniukov, M. I. "Mezhdunarodnye voprosy v azii," *Russkii vestnik* (1877), vol. 129: 473–503.

———. "Postupatel'noe dvizhenie Rossii v srednei Azii," *Sbornik gosudarstvennykh znanii* (1877), vol. 3: 58–106.

Vulf, P. "Angliiskaia shkuna *Wixen*—voennyi priz, vziatyi brigom 'Aiaks' u beregov Kavkaza v 1836 godu," *Morskoi sbornik* (1886), April: 91–106.

Walker, C. E., *The Role of Karl Nesselrode in the Formulation and Implementation of Russian Foreign Policy, 1850–1856*. Doctoral dissertation, West Virginia University, 1973.

Webster, C. K. *The Foreign Policy of Palmerston, 1830–1841. Britain, the Liberal Movement, and the Eastern Question* (London, 1951), 2 vols.

———. *Palmerston, Metternich, and the European System 1830–1841* (London, 1934).

———. "Urquhart, Ponsonby, and Palmerston," *English Historical Review* (1947), vol. 62: 327–351.

Zaionchkovsky, A. M., *Vostochnaia voina 1853–1856 gg. v sviazi s sovremennoi ei politicheskoi obstanovkoi* (St. Petersburg, 1908), 2 vols. in 4.

Zakharin, I. N. (pseud. "Iakunin"). "Druzhba Zhukovskago s Perovskim, 1820–1852 gg.," *Vestnik Evropy* (1901), vol. 208: 524–552.

———. *Graf V. A. Perovskii i ego zimnii pokhod v Khivu* (St. Petersburg, 1901).

Zalesov, N. "Ocherk diplomaticheskikh snoshenii Rossii s Bukharoiu s 1836 po 1843 god.," *Voennyi sbornik* (1862), no. 9: 3–46.

———. "Posol'stvo v Khivu kapitana Nikiforova v 1841 g.," *Voennyi sbornik* (1861), no. 11: 41–92.

———. "Posol'stvo v Khivu podpolkovnika Danilevskago v 1842 godu," *Voennyi sbornik* (1866), no. 5: 41–75.

Zhigarev, S. A. *Russkaia politika v vostochnom voprose* (Moscow, 1896).

Index